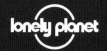

Travel

P H O T O G R A P H Y

A GUIDE TO TAKING BETTER PICTURES

Richard I'Anson

LONELY PLANET OFFICES

Australia
Head Office
Locked Bag 1, Footscray, Victoria 3011
☎ 03 8379 8000, fax 03 8379 8111
talk2us@lonelyplanet.com.au

USA
150 Linden St, Oakland, CA 94607
☎ 510 893 8555, toll free 800 275 8555
fax 510 893 8572, info@lonelyplanet.com

UK
72–82 Rosebery Ave,
Clerkenwell, London EC1R 4RW
☎ 020 7841 9000, fax 020 7841 9001
go@lonelyplanet.co.uk

France
1 rue du Dahomey, 75011 Paris
☎ 01 55 25 33 00, fax 01 55 25 33 01
bip@lonelyplanet.fr, www.lonelyplanet.fr

Travel Photography: A Guide to Taking Better Pictures
2nd edition October 2004
ISBN 1 74104 184 8

Published by Lonely Planet Publications Pty Ltd
ABN 36 005 607 983

text © Richard I'Anson 2004
photographs © Richard I'Anson 2004

Cover photograph: Taj Mahal, Agra, India

Printed through Colorcraft Ltd, Hong Kong
Printed in China

CONTENTS

THE AUTHOR

Richard I'Anson is a Melbourne-based landscape, travel, editorial and stock photographer. He travels regularly in Australia and overseas, photographing people and places for clients, books and his stock collection.

Richard received his first camera as a gift from his parents when he was 16, and hasn't stopped taking photographs since. After studying photography, film and TV for two years at Rusden State College, he worked in a camera store and minilab before going freelance in 1982. His work has been widely published in books, magazines, brochures and calendars, and has been exhibited in both solo and group exhibitions. He also produces limited-edition prints for corporate and domestic use. In 1998 he published his first book, *Chasing Rickshaws,* a collaboration with Lonely Planet founder Tony Wheeler. In 2004 he published *Rice Trails: A Journey through the Ricelands of Asia and Australia,* another collaboration with Tony Wheeler.

To establish himself in this niche area of photography, Richard travelled for almost three years in Asia between 1986 and 1990. He has won several Australian Institute of Professional Photography awards and in 1996 achieved the level of Master of Photography.

Lonely Planet has been using Richard's photographs for 14 years and his work has been featured in over 300 editions of Lonely Planet titles. He has also helped to establish the company's image library, Lonely Planet Images. Much of his work can be viewed at www.lonelyplanetimages.com and www.richardianson.com.

From the Author

I feel extremely privileged to see the world through the eyes of a photographer. I love taking photographs and I love travelling. I can talk about both for hours, but to put down on paper what I'd been doing instinctively for 20 years for the first edition of this book was indeed a daunting proposition. I still remember that the pain in the neck from hours at the keyboard was even greater than the pain in the shoulders I'm accustomed to from lugging camera gear around. By the end of it I was well and truly ready to focus on infinity again.

This second edition presented a new challenge in the form of digital photography. My work continues to be shot on film, but I've travelled with several digital cameras over the last four years in order to try and keep up-to-date with the rapidly changing developments in digital capture.

Many people have helped me along the way. Thanks to my clients, in particular Nick Kostos and Sue Badyari from World Expeditions, who put their faith in me to disappear for weeks at a time and come back with the images they need. Continuing thanks to Eddie Schreiber and Neil Davenport at Schreiber Photographics; Wade Hatton at Olympus; and Peter Cocklin at Kodak Australia for support and encouragement over the years. For the digital section I received invaluable help from Penny Leith at Kodak Australia and Rick Slowgrove and Scott Jackson at Canon Australia. Rik Evans from Camera Action Camera House in Melbourne gave his time generously to answer a serious number of questions on all aspects of digital photography. Thanks also to Margaret Brown, Technical Editor at *PhotoReview Australia* magazine, for help fine-tuning the Digital Photography chapter.

At Lonely Planet, Roz Hopkins, Janet Austin, Brendan Dempsey, Jane Pennells, Karina Dea, Bridget Blair, Martine Lleonart and Tony Wheeler all made significant contributions as I once again grappled with the transition from photographer to author.

Thanks to the team at Lonely Planet Images for sharing in the experience as the book developed. Special thanks to Ryan Evans and Gerard Walker for their pre-press expertise in making the images look just right on the printed page.

At home my thanks, as always, goes to Iris, Alice and Sarah whose support, interest and understanding are so generously given and are greatly appreciated.

THIS BOOK

From the Publisher

This book was produced in Lonely Planet's Melbourne Office. It was commissioned by Janet Austin and project managed by Bridget Blair. Brendan Dempsey was responsible for design and layout, and Martine Lleonart and Brigitte Barta edited. James Hardy designed the cover and Ryan Evans, Gerard Walker and Claire Gibson arranged pre-press preparation of the photographs. Laetitia Clapton, Roz Hopkins and Karina Dea contributed to the development of this book. Thanks to Margaret Brown of *PhotoReview Australia* magazine for proofing the technical information in the Digital Photography section.

Using this Book

Travel Photography aims to increase the percentage of good photographs you take. It's not designed to make you a professional travel photographer, but to give you the information you need to make the most of the picture-taking situations that come your way. It aims to help you create photographic opportunities and to make your travel experience more photo friendly.

This book covers a range of film and digital photographic equipment, from compact point-and-shoot cameras to state-of-the art SLRs. Whatever equipment you have, the principles and advice given will apply. Also, note that prices are given in US dollars throughout the book.

Although this book is about travel photography, many of the ideas and techniques discussed are applicable to photography in general. It could also be said that all photography (outside the studio) is travel photography. One person's back yard is another's dream destination. Even if you don't have immediate plans to leave your own back yard, you can put into practice much of what's discussed here at home, next time you photograph your family, your pets, or go on a day trip. In fact, I highly recommend that you do just that. Study the resulting photographs, and then go back out and take some more. You'll learn a lot from your own successes and failures and reap the rewards in better photographs on your next trip.

The Author's Approach

The way I go about taking travel photographs has developed over the years and is in a constant state of review. I aim to capture the reality of a place (as I see it) through strong individual images that build on each other to create a comprehensive coverage of a destination or topic, so that viewers get a sense of what it's like to be there. My own interpretation, my style, is expressed through choice of camera format, lens, film type and speed, exposure, what I choose to photograph, viewpoint, composition, the light I photograph in and, finally, the images I choose to show.

My equipment changed little over the first 15 years of my career. Olympus OM4Ti 35mm SLR cameras and Zuiko prime lenses served me well. Many of the images in this book were taken with this equipment. However, with the announcement by Olympus that they were no longer making the camera and lenses I was using, I needed to switch brands. It had been niggling at me for some time that I was missing out on technology that could help my photography, such as auto-focus and image-stabiliser lenses and advanced metering systems. Additionally, I was finally convinced that a couple of high quality zooms rather than five prime lenses would make my life easier – I seemed to be always changing lenses. I prefer to use available light (daylight or incandescent) no matter how low. I always use fine grain films.

In Australia (where I live), I photograph landscapes and cityscapes with:

▸ a Mamiya 7ii 6 x 7cm rangefinder camera (always mounted on a tripod)

▸ a 50mm f4.5 and 150mm f4.5 lenses

▸ a Gitzo G1228 carbon-fibre tripod with Fobar Superball head

▸ a Lowe Pro soft-sided bag which holds all of the above gear.

Overseas my standard outfit consists of:

▸ two Canon EOS 1v SLR camera bodies, one with Power Drive Booster E1

▸ two Canon EF zoom lenses: a 24-70mm f2.8 L USM and a 70-200 f2.8 L USM image stabiliser

▸ a Canon 300mm f2.8 L USM lens

▸ a Canon 1.4x teleconverter

▸ a Hassleblad X-Pan 35mm panoramic camera with 45mm f4 lens (I don't use it a lot, but it's an excellent back up camera and easy to carry if the big 35mm gear isn't required)

▸ a Gitzo G1228 carbon-fibre tripod with Fobar Superball head (I photograph landscapes and cityscapes on the tripod; everything else is hand-held)

▸ a Canon 420EX flash unit

▸ a Lowepro Street and Field Reporter 400 AW soft shoulder bag, which holds everything except the tripod and 300mm lens

▸ a Lowepro Street and Field Rover Light backpack when trekking, which makes carrying the tripod easy.

I use circular polarising filters and have stopped carrying any other filters. I use Kodak Ektachrome E100VS as my standard film. For extra speed I switch to Kodak Ektachrome E200, which I rate at 800 ISO. I've also replaced my film compact camera for capturing pictures of family and friends with a Kodak DX6440 4 MP digital compact camera.

Digital images in this book were taken on a Kodak DX6440 4 MP standard compact camera; a Kodak DX6490 4 MP advanced compact camera; and a Canon EOS 10D 6.3 MP professional SLR camera.

Photo Captions

The photographs and captions in this book are provided to help you learn about taking photos under a variety of circumstances. They include the following information:

▸ camera, lens and film or file size (however, some films given are not available anymore or known by a different name in a different country)

▸ shutter speed and aperture

▸ tripod, filters and flash, if used.

FOREWORD

Once upon a time I took all of Lonely Planet's photographs.

But then, once upon a time, another publisher said, 'the images in Lonely Planet books look as if they were taken by the author using an Instamatic borrowed from his mother'.

Things have changed. These days the photographic standards of our books are so high that I'm really pleased when one of my shots is good enough to make the grade or, as still happens occasionally, make the front cover. That certainly doesn't make me one of Lonely Planet's ace photographers – I'm not going to quit my day job – but when the sun's shining the right way, the subject cooperates and I've managed to wind the film on, I can produce results that look pretty good. Luck plays a bigger part in it than it would for one of our Nikon aces, but as I said, I'm not quitting my day job.

Travelling with Richard I'Anson to work on our photographic projects – *Chasing Rickshaws* and *Rice Trails* both combined Richard's images with my words – has certainly taught me a lot about travel photography, although I have to admit I find I take far fewer pictures when Richard is around than I would normally. Either I think, 'what I'm doing is redundant, Richard will have taken it anyway', or I think, 'is this a stupid idea, would Richard think I've got the picture framed wrong, the settings haywire, the light coming the wrong way?'

Sometimes working with Richard is simply solid confirmation that all those standard travel photographer clichés really are true. 'The light is best at dawn', we're told over and over again. It's obviously not just a throw-away platitude because I've had more than my fair share of waking to pre-dawn gloom and yawning in another sunrise when I've travelled with Richard. I've also been pleased to find somebody else who moves as fast as me – Richard always seems to be sprinting from one photo opportunity to another and the fact that he generally lists to one side, heeled over by the weight of camera equipment hanging from one shoulder, never seems to slow him down.

No matter how good your equipment and how skilled the practitioner, successful travel photography can come down to sheer luck. Or sheer perseverance. Our visits to Nepal have brought clear reminders of lady luck's importance, but also of how important it can be to simply tough it out in search of the perfect photo. On one trip our search for rice terraces with snow-capped mountains in the background had been thwarted day after day by non-stop rain (in what should have been the post-monsoon dry season). Finally, the sun broke through just hours before our departure. We diverted our airport-bound taxi to the edge of the Kathmandu Valley and sprinted up a hill to find, on the other side, the perfect view – rice fields being harvested, picturesque houses in the foreground, soaring Himalayan peaks as a backdrop. And a river separating us from the picture. We tore off our shoes, rolled up our trousers, waded across the river, got the photographs, interrogated the farmers, and still made it to the airport in time for our flight – a little damp, rather muddy, but with the images we needed.

On another Nepal visit I staggered to the top of Kala Pattar, the Everest viewpoint which actually overlooks the base camp. Richard was already there, wedged against a rock, hanging on in a wind which felt fierce enough to strip the Gore-Tex off your back and the camera out of your hand. I soon decided to head back down to my tent, leaving Richard to look for that perfect sunset shot of the world's highest peak. Perseverance won out; he got it.

On a recent photographic expedition with Richard, our three-week trek up to the Everest Base Camp brought with it a new dimension to travel photography: the shift to the digital world. Richard hasn't made the shift completely – although my money's betting that he'll make the change sooner than he expects – but like many serious photographers he definitely has a foot in both camps. On our Everest trek his sideways lean was even more noticeable than usual since the camera bag now contained a digital camera as well as his film equipment.

The increasing importance of digital photography and the many interesting and exciting new challenges it brings to travel photography play a key part in this new edition of *Travel Photography*. At the end of the day, however, equipment and expertise are only part of the photographic story. It's travel which takes us out there and puts those amazing images, whether they're people, places, nature or scenery, in front of our cameras.

TONY WHEELER
FOUNDER, LONELY PLANET

INTRODUCTION

The idea for this book began on a bus in Nepal. I was on my way to Dhunche, the starting point of the Langtang trek. On hearing that I was a photographer, one of the three travellers (squashed into a seat made for two) in front of me asked if I could fix her camera. I could hear the desperation in her voice – she had come a long way to go trekking and now thought she had no way of recording this great event. I'm not a camera technician, but I do know that batteries can be given an extra lease of life with a quick clean. I found myself cleaning many more batteries and answering lots of questions about picture-taking on my travels, so I decided that once home I would try to pass on some of the experience I've gained.

Most people come back from a holiday with one or two photographs they consider above average, even great, but have no idea how they achieved such heights. Modern automatic cameras have eased the burden of having to understand what's going on when you press the shutter. However, this often means the process and the variable elements that go into creating a successful image remain a mystery and cannot be repeated.

Camera manufacturers repeatedly make claims along the lines that all you have to do (after buying their camera) is point it at something, and stunning, professional images will be yours. Consequently, cameras are blamed when photos don't turn out and credited when they do. Cameras don't take pictures, people do.

Understanding the elements that go into creating good photographs means that you can learn to repeat them, and take control of the picture-taking process. Every decision you make, including choice of film or digital capture; camera, lens and film; the combination of film speed, shutter speed and aperture; whether you use a tripod or not; the position from where you take the photo; and the time of day is a creative decision. It's certainly easier to let the camera make some of those decisions for you. However, if you want to elevate your images from simple record shots of your travels to the next level of quality and individuality, then you need to take control of all the elements that go into creating photographs.

Whatever your approach to travel photography, be prepared to cover an expansive range of subjects, including people, landscapes, cities, markets, festivals and wildlife. Some people specialise in one or two subjects, but travel photographers need to be confident photographing the full range of subjects that are encountered on the road. Additionally, the successful travel photographer requires several contrary skill sets:

▸ the ability to plan every detail but be totally flexible in order to respond quickly to new and/or unforeseen events

▸ the energy to walk for hours on end and the patience to wait around for just as long (sometimes days) for the right light or the right subject, or both

▸ strong social skills to make quick connections with people, as well as the ability to be comfortable with your own company for long stretches of time

▸ finally, technical and creative abilities need to be complemented with at least some understanding of business and marketing – you can have the greatest pictures in the world, but they'll remain unseen unless some business skills are applied.

You need to develop an eye for all sorts of images: from tiny details to sweeping panoramas, from carefully composed portraits to action shots of people and wildlife. The travel photographer has to be comfortable in crowded market places and empty deserts, high in the mountains and in dimly lit caves. Pictures have to be produced in conditions as varied as snow and below-zero temperatures, torrential rain, gale force winds, high humidity and the glare of the midday sun.

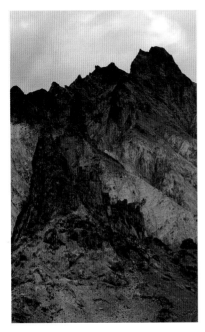 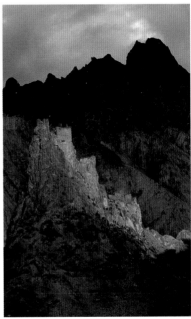

Hankar Fort ruins, Marka Valley, Ladakh, India

Whenever I'm standing around wondering if the wait is going to be worth it I call on past experiences to keep me going. At first light, after a short walk from camp, I was disappointed to see the eastern horizon engulfed in heavy cloud and the planned shot slipping away. One hour later, for less than a minute, the ruins lit up as hoped for. Patience regularly reveals itself as an absolute prerequisite for travel photography.

▲ 35mm SLR, 24-70mm lens, 1/30 f11, Ektachrome E100VS, tripod, 6.25am

▲ 35mm SLR, 24-70mm lens, 1/125 f16, Ektachrome E100VS, tripod, 7.25am

The continuing challenge is to take consistently good photographs in very inconsistent conditions.

Travel photography is also about equipment, films and pixels, exposures and composition, weather and light – but most of all it's about being there, and your personal response to the places and events you have the good fortune to visit.

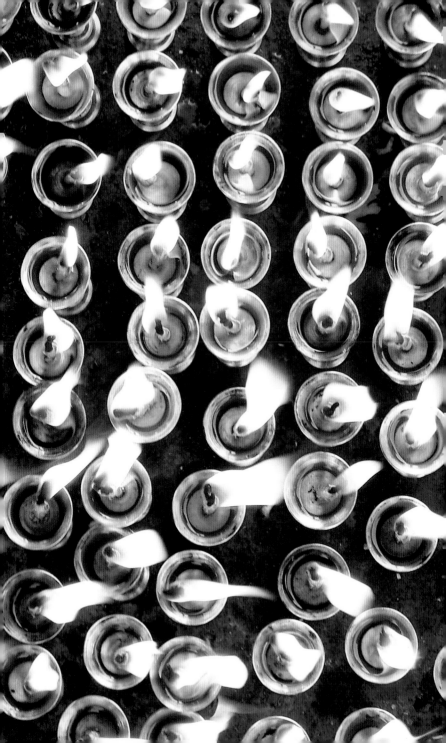

A SHORT HISTORY OF TRAVEL PHOTOGRAPHY

The connection between photography and travel runs deep. The oldest surviving image produced by a camera was made around 1826 when Joseph Nicephore Niepce photographed a street scene at Saint Loup de Varennes, in France. Arguably, this is also the oldest surviving travel photo. The photograph, taken in daylight, required an eight-hour exposure.

In Paris in 1839, Louis Jacques Mande Daguerre introduced the photographic process now known as the daguerreotype. The process was complicated, requiring lots of equipment and handling of chemicals, but was embraced quickly. Each daguerreotype was unique and recorded scenes with excellent detail. It also allowed people to travel with cameras. The first owners photographed their local area: Notre Dame cathedral, the River Seine and the Pont Neuf; subjects that are considered a 'must take' by today's tourists. The appeal of photography was as obvious to travellers in the middle of the nineteenth century as it is today. Daguerre himself suggested that his camera could easily be taken along on a journey. He was right, but it wasn't quite that simple. The travelling photographer also had to carry a portable darkroom tent and enough chemicals to stock a small laboratory.

Around the same time, William Henry Fox Talbot, Daguerre's English contemporary, invented the calotype (better known today as a negative). This made multiple copies of an image possible, but without the detail achieved in a daguerreotype. Talbot too imagined the appeal his invention would have to travellers:

> ...the traveller in foreign lands, who like most of his breed, cannot draw, would benefit immensely from the discovery of such a material. All he has to do is to set up a number of small cameras in different locations and a host of interesting impressions are his, which he did not have to draw or write down.
>
> *Masters of Early Travel Photography,*
> R Fabian & H Adam, 1983

In 1851, Frederick Scott Archer invented the wet collodion plate, which became the standard photographic process until 1880. This new process, which reduced exposure times to a mere two seconds, matched the detail possible with a daguerreotype and the calotype's ability to be reproduced, and overcame the long exposure times required by both. It didn't, however, ease the burden for the travel photographer. Each glass plate had to be prepared in the field and processed immediately while still damp. A standard outfit in the 1850s included a camera (on the large size), tripod, glass plates and plate holders; a tent-like portable darkroom; chemicals for coating, sensitising, developing and fixing the plates; and dishes, tanks and water containers. Even so, photographers carted their equipment around the world. The Great Wall, feluccas on the Nile, temples on the Ganges at Varanasi, high passes in the Himalaya and the Grand Canyon had all been photographed in great detail by 1860.

Butter lamps at Swayambhunath Temple, Kathmandu Valley, Nepal
◀ Advanced compact digital, 6.3-63.2mm lens at 21mm, 1/60 f3.2, 80 ISO, 1728 x 2304 4 MP JPEG

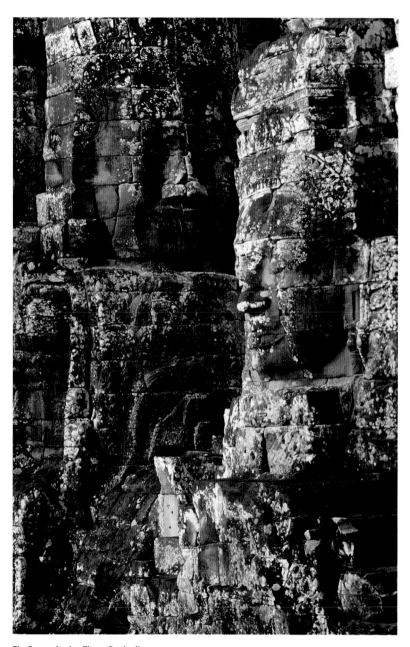

The Bayon, Angkor Thom, Cambodia
▲ 35mm SLR, 100mm lens, 1/15 f11, Ektachrome E100VS, tripod

Many of the travel photographs taken in the mid-1800s were recorded during scientific and exploratory trips, but they also served to create public interest in distant lands. Although cumbersome in the field, the collodion process produced good-quality images that were easily reproduced. As tourism increased, so did the demand for pictures as souvenirs, and photographers began shooting for commercial reasons. According to Fabian and Adam, the first postcard was introduced by the Austrian postal service in 1869. In 1910, France printed 123 million postcards and the world's mail systems processed around 7 billion in the same year.

The bulk, weight and messiness of the photographic process restricted the gathering of images in the early years to a small group of people who were part adventurer, part scientist, part camera technician and part artist. But by the end of the nineteenth century tourists could take their own pictures. In 1888, George Eastman, the founder of Kodak, invented a camera using a roll of film. He launched the first point-and-shoot with the now famous slogan: 'You press the button, we do the rest'. The camera came loaded with a 100-exposure film and a memorandum book that had to be filled in to keep count of the photos. When the film was finished the camera was posted back to the factory. The camera was returned with the prints and loaded with a fresh roll of film. In the first year Eastman sold 13,000 cameras. They proved instantly popular with tourists; one testimonial stated:

It is the greatest boon on earth to the travelling man, like myself, to be able to bring home, at so small an outlay of time and money, a complete photographic memorandum of his travels.

The Birth of Photography: The Story of the Formative Years 1800-1900,
B Coe, 1977

Further refinements saw the introduction of the Kodak Brownie camera in 1900, which made the photographic process accessible to millions of people around the world. Photography had become a mass medium and tourists were travelling with small, easy-to-use cameras. According to some, by the start of the twentieth century, the world had been photographed to death.

Of course, the world wasn't photographed to death a hundred years ago, and it still hasn't been. It's true there aren't many places left that haven't been photographed and we all know what the world's most famous destinations look like even if we haven't been there ourselves. The content of our pictures rarely surprises the travel-savvy society we live in, yet images are published every year that cast a new light on old subjects and push our visual awareness into new territory. And so what if everyone you know has photographed the Taj Mahal and the Eiffel Tower? There's nothing quite like the thrill of seeing places yourself and making your own version of the classic shot.

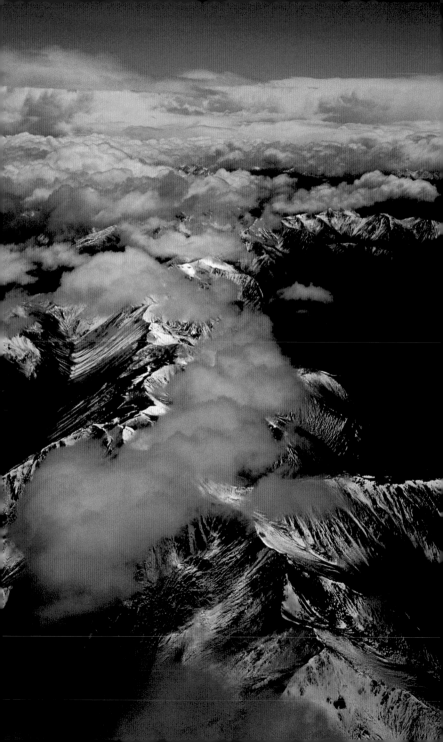

PART ONE:

There are many things to consider before you hit the road that will have an impact on the pictures you take, and the enjoyment you experience taking them. Selection of camera, lenses and film are the most obvious, but there are lots of other pieces of equipment and photographic accessories that can help you return home with the photos you want.

F I R S T   T H I N G S   F I R S T

Aerial of Southern Alps, South Island, New Zealand
◄ 35mm SLR, 50mm lens, 1/250 f5.6, Ektachrome E100VS

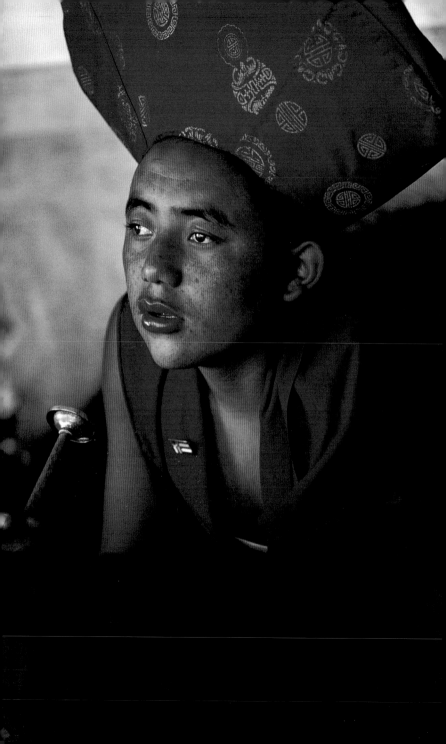

EQUIPMENT

What equipment to take is not an easy decision, especially if you're starting from scratch. There's a huge selection of cameras, lenses and accessories to choose from. You can narrow the selection down by identifying your goals, the kind of pictures you want to take, and how you intend to show them. If all you require is a record of your trip in the form of colour prints for an album, a fully automatic compact film or digital camera will probably do the job. If you have ambitions to make large prints to hang on the wall, spend as much on lenses as you can afford. If you're trekking in Nepal and want to photograph the first rays of sun on the snowy peaks of the Himalaya, you'll need a tripod to do it well.

Until you've made several trips and are confident anticipating your needs, what you actually take will have to be a compromise between what you think you need, what you can afford, and how much weight you're prepared to carry. Finding the balance is the trick. Aim to keep things simple, accessible and manageable. If your equipment is a burden you won't enjoy taking pictures. You don't need tons of expensive gear to take great photos; you just need to know how to get the best out of the equipment you have and to use it within its limitations.

FILM CAMERAS

There's a staggering range of cameras available in various formats and types in all price brackets, and new models are released regularly. Consult a buyer's guide published by a photographic magazine or Internet newsletter for a thorough overview of what's available at the time you're ready to buy. (See p36 for information on buying a film camera and p75 for digital camera purchasing.) All camera formats and types have their strengths and weakness, but most travellers have to settle on just one to do everything for them. Outlined below are the film camera formats and types that are of most interest to travellers.

Camera Formats

Camera formats are based on the size of the film frame.

Advanced Photo System (APS) The smallest and newest format, launched in 1996. APS has a film frame size of 17mm x 30mm.

35mm The most popular format and the film size upon which the majority of camera systems are based. Produces 24mm x 36mm negatives and slides.

Medium Formats There are a range of medium-format cameras that use roll film known as 120. The most popular formats are 6cm x 4.5cm (known as 645), 6cm x 6cm (2¼ inches square) and 6cm x 7cm. Depending on the camera, you get a different number of frames per roll, ranging from 10 to 15. Medium format cameras offer a considerably larger negative or transparency than 35mm – an important consideration if very large prints are required.

Panoramic Available in 35mm and medium format. A true panoramic camera has a format ratio of at least 1:3 (ie, the film is three times as wide as it is high). Two 35mm frames side by side would be panoramic. In medium format a 6cm x 12cm panoramic camera gives six frames per roll. A 6cm x 17cm panoramic camera produces only four frames per roll, which are almost three times as wide as they are high. Many compact and single lens reflex (SLR) cameras now offer the possibility of 'panoramic' (or long and thin) pictures as a feature. The image is actually exactly the same as the standard image, but the top and bottom of the frame are masked and cut off, giving the impression of a panoramic image. You can do exactly the same thing by cropping any negative or slide.

Novice monk at Lamayuru Gompa festival, Lakdakh, India
◄ 35mm SLR, 70-200mm lens, 1/100 f3.5, Ektachrome E100VS, image stabiliser

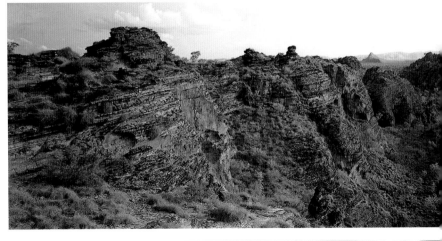

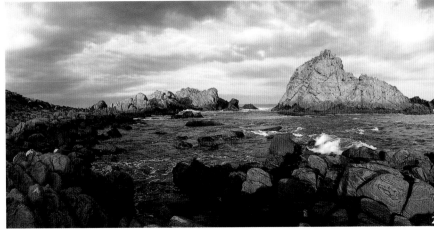

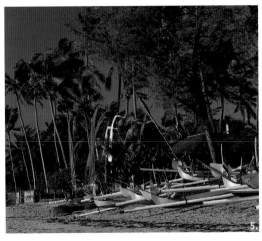

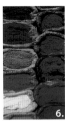

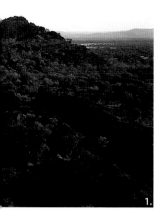

CAMERA FORMATS

These photos illustrate the different camera formats reproduced at actual size:

1. **Mirima National Park, Australia**
   Linhof Technorama 6 x 17cm Format

2. **Cape Naturaliste, Australia**
   Noblex 6 x 12cm Format

3. **Bumburet, Pakistan**
   Olympus OM4Ti, 35mm SLR Format

4. **Tikse, Ladakh, India**
   Hasselblad X-Pan, 35mm Panoramic Format

5. **Sanur, Bali, Indonesia**
   Pentax 6 x 7cm Format

6. **Kathmandu, Nepal**
   Olympus i ZOOM 75 APS Format

7. **Tirta Ganga, Bali, Indonesia**
   Bronica SQ 6 x 6cm Format

8. **Hunter Valley, Australia**
   Bronica ETRs 6 x 4.5cm Format

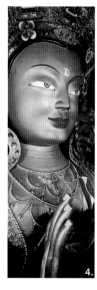

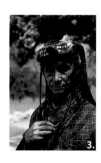

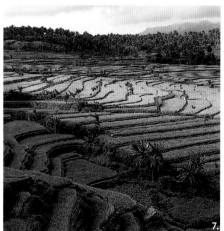

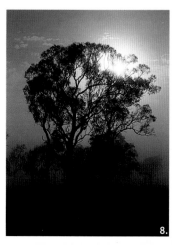

CAMERA TYPES

Advanced Photo System Cameras (APS)

Although they are compact and incorporate the latest technologies, APS cameras have lost popularity due to the proliferation of compact digital cameras.

One of the key features of APS is that information about each picture is recorded onto magnetic data stripes on the film when it's taken. The data informs the printing machine about the conditions under which the photograph was taken, such as if the flash fired and what zoom setting was used, in theory eliminating bad prints. APS cameras are available in compact and SLR models. Film cartridges contain 15, 25 and 40 exposure lengths and colour negative film is readily available in 100, 200 and 400 ISO.

ADVANTAGES

▸ cameras are 10-15% smaller than comparable 35mm models
▸ choice of three picture frame sizes, which are selected at the time of exposure and can be changed from frame to frame: classic (10cm x 15cm; 4in x 6in prints), horizontal (10cm x 18cm; 4in x 7in prints) and panoramic (10cm x 30cm; 4in x 12in prints)
▸ easy to use; most models fully automatic with built-in flash and zoom lenses
▸ film comes in a cartridge and provides foolproof film loading
▸ processed film is returned in the cartridge so is never handled, protecting it from fingerprints and scratches

DISADVANTAGES

▸ advanced features are reflected in higher prices
▸ film and processing costs are higher than for 35mm
▸ film needs to be processed with special equipment, which may not be widely available in all countries
▸ range of colour slide and B&W film very limited
▸ range of SLR models available is limited

Compact 35mm Cameras

Compact 35mm, or point-and-shoot, cameras are ideal for taking photos with a minimum of fuss. Perfect if you want to travel light and only require colour prints of your travels.

ADVANTAGES

▸ doesn't require accessories
▸ easy to use; most models fully automatic with built-in flash and zoom lenses
▸ good option as second camera for SLR users
▸ models available to suit all budgets
▸ small, light and easily carried in a pocket or small bag
▸ wide range of films to choose from
▸ viewing of the subject is uninterrupted by the shutter because it is seen through a viewfinder, not the lens

DISADVANTAGES

▸ cheaper models have low-quality lenses
▸ limited automatic override features
▸ not suitable for colour slide film
▸ you can't change lenses
▸ accurate framing is limited, and it's possible to photograph your fingers or thumbs without realising, because subjects are seen through a viewfinder, not the lens

35mm Rangefinders

These cameras sit between compacts and SLRs in terms of size and features but are considerably more expensive than compacts. Rangefinder refers to the focussing system, which splits or doubles the image on the focussing point. Correct focus is achieved by superimposing the double image. Manual and auto-focus rangefinders are available.

ADVANTAGES

- accepts interchangeable lenses
- compact and well built
- high-quality lenses
- suitable for colour slide film
- very quiet operation
- viewing of the subject is uninterrupted by the shutter because it is seen through a viewfinder, not the lens

DISADVANTAGES

- expensive
- limited features for the price compared to SLRs
- limited range of lenses
- accurate framing is limited, and it's possible to photograph your fingers or thumbs without realising, because subjects are seen through a viewfinder, not the lens

35mm Single Lens Reflex (SLR) Cameras

There's no doubt that the ideal camera for serious travel photography is a 35mm SLR, preferably one that allows you to manually override all of the automatic features. This will let you take complete control of the technical side of photography if you choose. SLR cameras are available in APS, 35mm and medium formats.

ADVANTAGES

- automatic SLRs are easy to use, even for those who are technically challenged
- interchangeable lenses and accessories to suit every application
- manual SLRs (or auto models with manual override) are great for gaining an understanding of the technical aspects of photography and the ideal tool for creative photography
- models available to suit all budgets
- most new models have sophisticated light meters, auto-focus and built-in flash units as standard features, as well as a host of other automatic features that make these as easy to use as the point-and-shoot cameras
- accurate framing is possible because subject is viewed through the lens
- wide range of films to select from

DISADVANTAGES

- heavier and bulkier than compact cameras
- the starting price of a basic model SLR is more expensive than a compact
- viewing of the subject is interrupted by the shutter because it is seen through the lens, not a viewfinder

LENSES FOR SLR CAMERAS

The ability to interchange lenses is one of the most persuasive reasons for buying an SLR. It increases your creative options and ability to solve photographic problems. Don't compromise on lens quality. If you're on a tight budget, go for a camera with fewer features and buy the best lenses you can afford. Lens quality determines image sharpness, colour and the light-gathering capacity of the lens, which can determine how you shoot in various lighting conditions.

Lens Lingo

All lenses have a designated focal length and maximum aperture, which are used to describe the lens. The focal length is the distance from the centre of the lens when it's focussed at infinity to the focal plane, the flat surface on which a sharp image of the subject is formed. Film is stretched across the focal plane. A normal, general-purpose camera lens is designed to have a focal length approximately equal to the diagonal of the negative or image area. With 35mm film the image area is 24mm x 36mm and the diagonal measures 45mm. Consequently, a 50mm lens is regarded as standard for 35mm cameras and covers about the same field of view as the human eye looking straight ahead. Wide-angle lenses provide a wider field of view and closer focussing than a standard lens. Telephoto lenses have a narrower field of view and a greater minimum focussing distance than standard lenses.

The maximum aperture describes the widest opening available on the lens and is described as an f-number (see p89). The wider the maximum aperture the greater the light-gathering power of the lens. Lenses with wide maximum apertures (f1.2, f1.4, f1.8, f2, f2.8) are also considered fast. The lower the maximum aperture the slower the lens because its light gathering ability is less. A lens with a focal length of 100mm and a maximum aperture of f2, is called a 100mm f2 lens. The wider the maximum aperture the bigger and heavier the lens is (and the more it costs).

Zoom lenses have variable focal lengths. At one end the lens may have a focal length of 28mm and at the other a focal length of 90mm. At its widest position (28mm) the lens is at its maximum light gathering capabilities, say, f2.8, but this changes as it zooms in to its longest position (90mm) to, say, f4.5. This lens would be referred to as a 28–90mm f2.8–4.5 zoom. On very pricey professional zooms the maximum aperture does not change as the focal length varies.

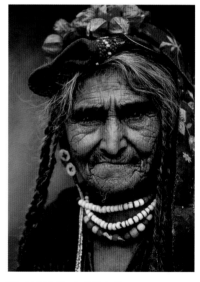

Woman from Dha, Ladakh, India

Image stabiliser lenses are incredible. How did I ever get by without them? In the low light of early evening, in a densely treed part of the village, the technology made this shot possible.

▲ 35mm SLR, 70-200mm lens, 1/60 f2.8, Ektachrome E100VS, image stabiliser

Another feature available on some lenses is image stabilisation (IS). This technology counteracts camera shake and allows the lens to be hand-held at shutter speeds two or three steps slower than is required for non-IS lenses (see p96). For example, with a 200mm lens IS technology allows hand-held photography at 1/60 second or even 1/30 second, rather than the recommended 1/250 second for non-IS lenses. This means images can be taken in lower light without a tripod or the need to switch to a faster ISO film or setting.

Lenses can be grouped by focal length into seven main categories: superwide, wide, standard, telephoto, super telephoto, zoom and special-purpose lenses (which includes macro, shift, mirror and fisheye lenses). Every lens or lens group has certain subject matter that it's particularly suited to (this is noted later). In reality, you can photograph any subject with any lens as long as you can get close enough or far enough away.

Super Wide-Angle Lenses

Super wide-angle lenses include 17mm, 21mm and 24mm focal lengths. With their very wide angle of view, these lenses lend themselves to landscape, interiors and working in confined spaces. The 17mm and 21mm are a bit too wide for general photography. Unless they're used well, it's easy to include unwanted elements in the composition and for subjects to appear too small. The 24mm produces images that have a distinctly wide-angle perspective, but can be used in many situations. Particularly suited to taking environmental portraits, they allow you to get close to your subject to create a sense of involvement in the picture while including the location as well.

Wide-Angle Lenses

Photographers often use 28mm and 35mm wide-angle lenses as a standard lens. They produce pictures with a natural perspective, but take in a considerably wider angle of view than standard lenses. Fixed focal length compact cameras commonly use a 35mm lens, as it's considered suitable for a wide range of subject matter.

Standard Lenses

Standard lenses have focal lengths of 50mm or 55mm, which have an angle of view that is close to what the eye sees. Before zoom lenses became the norm, SLRs were commonly sold with a 50mm f1.8 lens. Standard lenses still have an important place in the market because they're compact, light and the fastest lenses available, making them ideal for low-light photography.

Telephoto Lenses

Telephotos range from 65mm to 250mm. Their most common characteristics are increased magnification of the subject and a foreshortening of perspective. Medium telephotos range from 85mm to 105mm and make excellent portrait lenses. They give a pleasing perspective to the face and let you fill the frame with a head-and-shoulder composition without being in the face of your subject. The long telephotos, from 135mm to 250mm, are ideal for picking faces out of a crowd and showing details on buildings and in landscapes. They also allow the frame to be filled when moving closer is not possible, such as at sporting events or when you're on the edge of a canyon. They clearly compress distances, making distant objects look closer to each other than they actually are.

Super Telephoto Lenses

Ranging from 300mm to 1000mm, these lenses display significant foreshortening and have a very narrow angle of view. Apart from the 300mm, the super telephotos are specialist lenses. If the weight doesn't bother you then the price probably will. A 300mm lens magnifies the subject six times more than a standard lens and is commonly used by wildlife and sports photographers. For serious bird photography (that is, if you want to take pictures where you can actually see the bird) a 500mm lens, at the very least, is required.

Zoom Lenses

Zoom lenses offer convenience and flexibility by giving an unlimited choice of focal lengths within the given range of the lens. The many and varied focal length options have made zooms extremely popular and the ideal choice for the traveller. A standard outfit would typically include a 28mm wide-angle lens, a 50mm standard lens and a 135mm telephoto lens. Use a 28–150mm zoom and you can carry one lens instead of three, and you have the added bonus of all the focal lengths in between. This allows various framing possibilities from a fixed position, including the ability to hold a moving subject in frame without having to move with it, so that it appears the same size. This is very useful for action and wildlife photography. Many zooms also have a 'macro' setting, which allows close focussing.

Extreme focal lengths are now available, including 28–300mm and 80–400mm. They're generally heavier, larger and have greater minimum focussing distances to the more moderate zooms. Two zooms, such as a 24–90mm and 70–210mm, will cover most subjects. If that's one lens too many, and the 28–200mm doesn't suit you either, a wide to medium zoom such as a 35–105mm or 28–80mm is the best single lens option. Most new cameras are packaged with a zoom lens around these focal lengths.

The main drawback with zoom lenses is that they're slower than comparable fixed focal lengths.

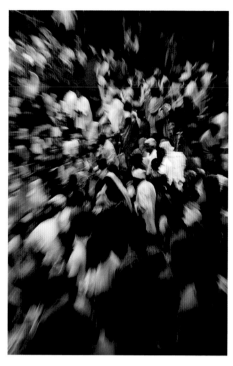

Pilgrims bathing at Trimbakeshaw Temple, Nasik, India

One fun effect that you can create with zoom lenses is achieved by zooming during the exposure. Choose a point of interest at the centre of the composition and select a shutter speed around 1/30. Start zooming before you press the shutter.

▲ 35mm SLR, 24-70mm lens, 1/30 f4, Ektachrome E100VS

This often results in unsharp pictures as a result of camera shake – especially at the tele-photo end of the zoom range and when using the close-focussing feature (see p96). Fast film can help solve this problem and is a good solution if you're taking colour prints. For colour slides you have to weigh up the advantages of fast film against the disadvantages of increased grain and loss of image quality (see p47). Consider complementing your zooms with a fast standard lens, such as a 50mm f1.4. This will increase your options in low-light situations. More compact than a zoom, it's easier to slip into a bag for those times when you want to take your camera but are put off by its weight and bulk.

Bear in mind the possible security consequences of placing all your eggs in one basket. If your 24–70mm lens is damaged or stolen your entire wide-angle to short telephoto range is gone. It's the kind of thing that comes to mind when you put your lens down on a wobbly rock and watch it roll away.

Macro Lenses

If you have a special interest in photographing very small things, such as insects or indi-vidual flowers, consider equipment made for macro photography: macro lenses, extension tubes or close-up filters. Macro lenses are described by the degree of magnification pos-sible. A macro lens with 1x magnification is capable of 1:1 reproduction (ie, it reproduces objects at life size). A lens capable of 0.5x magnification reproduces objects at half life size. Macro lenses are available in various focal lengths, including 50mm, which can be used as a standard lens for 'normal' photography. Extension tubes go between the camera body and the prime lens, which determines the magnification. With a 35–80mm zoom, magnification of 0.3x to 0.5x is possible. The least expensive, but optically inferior, option is close-up filters, which screw on to the front of a prime lens. Available individually, or as a set of three with magnifications of 0.1x, 0.2x and 0.4x, they can be used in any combination for a magnification up to 0.7x.

Teleconverters

Teleconverters are optical accessories that fit between the camera body and the lens to increase the focal length of the lens. They're available to increase magnification by 1.4x or 2x. Used with a 200mm lens, a 1.4x teleconveter turns your lens into a 280mm, and a 2x converter increases its focal length to 400mm. Used with a 70–210mm zoom lens a 2x teleconverter will change the focal length to 140–420mm. They provide an ideal solution for people who need access to focal lengths in the super telephoto range for a one-off event such as an African safari. Teleconverters will save you a lot of money, packing space and weight – but you can't have all that without giving something up. It's inadvisable to buy a cheap teleconverter because the inferior optics will have a noticeable effect on the sharpness of your pictures. And why put a cheap piece of glass between your good lens and the film or sensor?

As with zooms, the main drawback, even with high-quality teleconverters, is loss of lens speed, or light-gathering power. With a 2x converter your 70–210mm f3.5/5.6 suddenly becomes a painfully slow f7–f11. It's fine in bright, sunny conditions, but it won't take much variation in the sun's brightness for you to be reaching for fast film or a tripod.

FILTERS

Filters are optical accessories that are attached to the front of the lens, either via a filter holder or screwed directly onto the lens. Every lens has a filter size and it's ideal if your different lenses have the same filter size to reduce the number you need to carry. Filters are available for a wide range of technical and creative applications, but the filters discussed here are those favoured by professional travel and landscape photographers. If you want to keep your gear simple, only two – the skylight and polariser – are really necessary for general travel photography (using colour film or digital sensor). The white balance function on digital cameras also alleviates the need to carry colour correction filters (see p72).

If you do carry four or more filters, consider carrying them in a filter pouch. Although filters are neatly packaged in individual cases, a pouch is much more practical because it takes up less room and gives quicker access.

The use of filters should be handled carefully; they don't automatically improve pictures, and often they do the opposite. Good filtration should not be noticed. It's good practice not to stack, or to use more than one filter at a time – making the light pass through more layers of glass than necessary will result in loss of image quality. Also, when using wide-angle lenses stacking screw-in filters may cause you to photograph the filter mount itself, which will show up in the photograph as a vignetting or darkening of the corners.

Skylight (1B) & Ultraviolet (UV) Filters

Technically, skylight filters reduce the excessive bluishness that often occurs in colour photography outdoors, especially in open shade. UV filters absorb ultraviolet rays, which can contribute to hazy and indistinct outdoor photographs.

▸ A skylight or UV filter should be on every lens you own.

Filters also protect your lenses from dirt, dust, water and fingerprints. Lenses are expensive, filters aren't. It's much better to clean a dirty big fingerprint off a filter than off a lens.

Polarising (PL) Filters

A polarising filter is an essential item in any camera bag. Polarisers eliminate unwanted reflections by cutting down the light reflected from the subject. This increases the colour saturation and the contrast in the picture, intensifying colours and increasing contrast between different elements. The level of polarisation is variable and is controlled by rotating the front of the filter and the camera lens in relation to the position of the sun. As you view your subject through the lens you can see exactly what effect the filter will have at different points in the rotation. A polariser has its most marked effect when the sun is shining and is at ninety degrees off axis with the sun. It has its minimum effect when the sun is directly behind or in front the camera.

Although the effect produced by polarisers can be very seductive in the viewfinder, they shouldn't be treated as standard filters. Don't leave them on your lens. They don't enhance every photo, and should be used only as a creative tool. Additionally, they reduce the amount of light reaching the film by two stops. On lenses wider than 28mm it's important to note the position of the filter, particularly in clear areas of the picture such as the sky. If it's not positioned properly one part of the sky may appear darker than another, which translates to very unsatisfactory prints or slides. Also, when the contrast of a scene is already high, such as white snow against a deep blue sky, over-polarisation can result in the sky recording as an unnatural-looking black.

There are two types of polarising filters, the standard PL and the circular polariser (PL-CIR). The PL-CIR is designed to avoid problems with through the lens (TTL) auto-focussing. Check your camera manual, but if in doubt, use a circular polariser.

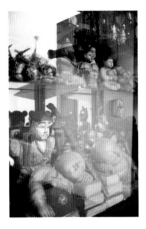
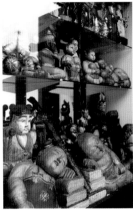

Shop window, Penang, Malaysia

Without a polarising filter this is an ineffective photo. The reflection from the window reduces colour and contrast.

◀◀ 35mm SLR, 50mm lens, 1/60 f11, Kodachrome 64

Add a polarising filter and there's still a little reflection, but it's been minimised and moved away from the main subject area.

◀ 35mm SLR, 50mm lens, 1/60 f5.6, Kodachrome 64, polarising filter

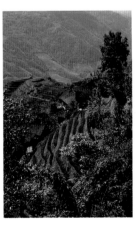
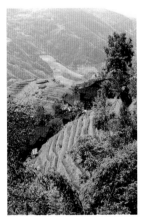

Longshen village, China

In the middle of the day the leaves and village roofs reflect the bright sunlight and all colour is lost.

◀◀ 35mm SLR, 50mm lens, 1/125 f11, Ektachrome E100VS

A polarising filter cuts the glare from the reflective surfaces and intensifies the colours.

◀ 35mm SLR, 50mm lens, 1/125 f5.6, Ektachrome E100VS, polarising filter

80 Series Filters

The 80A, 80B and 80C filters are blue-coloured, colour-conversion filters. They're used to reduce the yellow/orange cast that occurs when using daylight film with incandescent light. If you're going to take a lot of interiors using the available light (rather than flash) and don't like the colour cast, the mid-strength 80B is a good option. It reduces the light reaching the film by one stop.

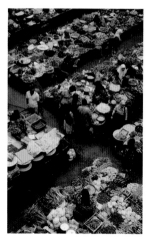

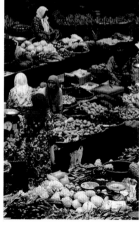

Central Market, Kota Bharu, Malaysia

Indoors at Kota Bharu's Central Market there seems to be plenty of daylight, but incandescent lighting is dominant. Daylight film records the scene with a yellow cast.

◄◄ 35mm SLR, 50mm lens, 1/60 f8, Kodachrome 200

With an 80B filter, the colour cast is reduced and colours appear more natural.

◄ 35mm SLR, 50mm lens, 1/60 f5.6, Kodachrome 200, 80B filter

81 Series Filters

The 81A, 81B and 81C filters are amber-coloured, light-balancing filters referred to as warming filters. Essentially strong skylight filters; they're commonly used to reduce the bluish cast from shadows under a clear sky, for portraits in open shade and in snow scenes. The 81C is the strongest of the three and is the one to carry as a good general warming filter. It reduces the light reaching the film by two-thirds of a stop.

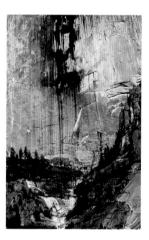

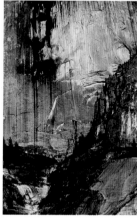

Half Dome detail, Yosemite National Park, USA

An 81C filter warmed up the colours of Half Dome's sheer rock wall rising above Mirror Lake. Until you're really sure what effect a filter will have, try shooting frames with and without so you can see the difference when you have the film developed.

◄◄ 35mm SLR, 100mm lens, 1/30 f16, Ektachrome E100SW, tripod

◄ 35mm SLR, 100mm lens, 1/30 f11.3, Ektachrome E100SW, tripod, 81C filter

82 Series Filters

The 82A, 82B and 82C filters are blue-coloured, light-balancing filters referred to as cooling filters. They reduce the warm tones of early morning or late afternoon light to give a more natural look to portraits.

Graduated Filters

Graduated filters are clear in one half and coloured in the other half. The density of the colour decreases towards the centre of the filter to prevent the boundary between the two halves showing up in your photograph. Available in many colours, they are special-effect filters that have to be used very carefully or the result will be unnatural. For example, if you put a sunset coloured filter on to change the colour of the sky to orange, but the shadows in the picture are short, the use of the filter will be obvious and the effect amateurish.

The most useful graduated filter is the grey, or neutral density (ND), filter. ND filters don't add colour to the image, but reduce the light reaching the film in half the scene. It's used by landscape photographers to even out exposure differences where the contrast between two areas of a scene is too high for the film to record detail in both areas (see p89-99).

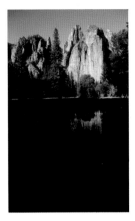 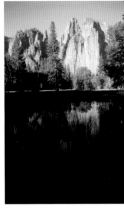 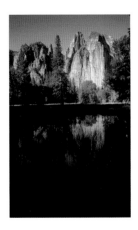

Reflection, Yosemite National Park, USA

By exposing for the rock wall good colour and detail was ensured, but the reflection in the water can hardly be seen.

▲ 35mm SLR, 35mm lens, 1/15 sec f8, Ektachrome STX, tripod

Exposing for the water records the reflection correctly but the colour and detail in the rock wall is lost.

▲ 35mm SLR, 35mm lens, 1/4 sec f8, Ektachrome STX, tripod

A graduated neutral density filter solves the problem by evening out the light levels between the light and dark areas, ensuring good colour and detail in both the rock wall and its reflection.

▲ 35mm SLR, 35mm lens, 1/4 sec f8, Ektachrome STX, tripod, Graduated ND filter

When using graduated filters it's important not to stop down too much, especially with wide-angle lenses, as this can result in a sharp line across the picture. If your camera has a depth-of-field preview button use it to ensure the line isn't visible.

Graduated filters are much more useful and easier to control in the square, slip-in holder style than the screw-in style. It allows you to move the filter up and down for more accurate placement of the line between the coloured and clear areas.

TRIPODS

There's no question that a good tripod is an extremely important piece of equipment for the serious travel photographer. Whether or not you actually take one comes down to the

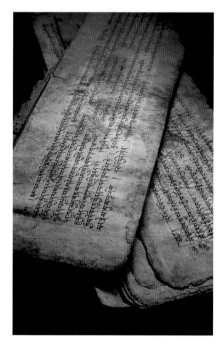

Pages from the Tibetan Book of Prayers, Lo Manthang, Nepal

I could have taken this image without a tripod, but the risk of camera shake was high and the depth of field zero. The tripod allowed me to select the aperture needed to attain pin sharpness from front to back; it didn't matter what the shutter speed was.

▲ 35mm SLR, 35mm lens, 1 sec f8, Ektachrome E100VS, tripod

kind of pictures you hope to take and if that overrides the hassle of packing and carrying the extra weight. You can take the majority of travel pictures without a tripod. During most of the day there's plenty of light and hand-holding the camera will present few problems. In low-light conditions indoors or on city streets, switching to fast film will let you continue hand-holding the camera. But if you want to use fine-grain films in low light indoors or out, maximise depth of field and use slow shutter speeds for creative effects, a tripod is needed.

The most common travel subjects that call for a tripod are landscapes and cityscapes, which nearly always look best on fine grain film. Many of the most successful pictures of these subjects are taken early or late in the day when light levels are low and maximum depth of field is required to render the whole scene sharp. If you have a special interest in landscape photography you'll need a tripod. Look for a tripod that you're happy to carry – they're useless if you keep leaving them behind. Anything too flimsy will let you down by not keeping the camera steady. Check them out at full extension and with your camera and longest lens attached. Make sure you can splay the legs for ease of use on unlevel ground. If you're budget allows, a carbon-fibre tripod will take a load off your back.

Tripod Heads

Tripod heads attach to the camera base and allow movement of the camera in any direction. Buy a reasonably good tripod and you'll have a choice of heads. It's worth checking out the options to find one that you feel comfortable with. You'll have a choice between a ball head and a tilt/pan head. The ball head is ideal for travel photography because it's more streamlined and easier to pack. Make sure that switching between horizontal and vertical positions is smooth, that it locks into position easily, and that it is strong enough to support your biggest lens in both positions.

Another feature worth its weight in gold is the quick-release plate. The release plate is attached to the base of the camera and slides into the tripod head and is locked in position. This saves a lot of time attaching and removing the camera from the tripod.

Other Camera-Support Options

If you don't want to take even a small tripod there are several options worth considering. Table-top tripods support the camera around 15cm above the surface. These tiny tripods are suitable for compact cameras that have auto exposures running to several seconds and for small SLRs with wide-angle or standard lenses. They need to be used in conjunction with a wall or table…unless you want to take all your low-light pictures lying on the ground looking up.

Monopods are a single-leg camera support. They're well suited for street and action photography and are often used by sport photographers. They can provide support in crowded places where setting up a tripod would be impractical. The down side is that they're longer than many tripods because they're made to extend to eye level.

Alternatively, you can improvise a camera support. Jackets or sleeping bags can be bundled up and the camera nestled into the folds. A pile of stones will do a similar job. These suggestions will work better using SLRs with zoom or telephoto lenses so that the front of the lens can be positioned clear of the support. When you've finished getting organised, just hope that the elements of the scene that attracted you haven't disappeared. You can also try bracing yourself against trees, buildings, fences or anything else that is solid and in the right place. It's worth practicing some hand-held low-light photography, shooting at speeds of 1/15 of a second and slower to find out how steady your hand is – and just how far you can push your luck (see p96). These compromises may or may not work for you, but don't expect the consistent sharpness, speed and ease that the use of a tripod provides.

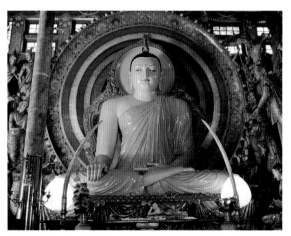

Buddha statue at Gangaramaya Temple, Colombo, Sri Lanka

Caught without my tripod in a low-light situation I made do by placing my camera bag on a stool and nestling the camera into the soft top cover. Obviously, angle of view is limited by what's lying around to place your bag on. Precious minutes can also be lost trying to get the camera to sit straight, so it's not a practice I'd recommend as standard.

◄ 35mm SLR, 24-70mm lens, 1/3 f2.8, Ektachrome E100VS, on stool and camera bag

AUTOWINDERS

Most modern compact cameras and SLRs have built-in autowinders that advance the film automatically. If you own an SLR that doesn't have this feature check your camera manual to see if it's possible to attach an accessory autowinder. If you can, it's well worth spending the money, especially if you're interested in photographing people, wildlife or action. You can shoot without having to remove your eye from the viewfinder between frames, which lets you keep your eye on the subject and maintain your composition. The small price to pay for this convenience is a little extra weight and the need to carry a few more spare batteries.

HAND-HELD EXPOSURE METERS

Most modern cameras have built-in exposure meters that measure the amount of light reflected from the subject. You can do the same thing with an accessory light meter, which some photographers prefer to do. For the traveller there isn't really much point carrying around the extra piece of equipment (see p89).

FLASH UNITS

Available light is the primary source of illumination for travel photographs, but it still pays to carry a compact flash unit (also called a flashgun or speedlight). There will be times when it's inconvenient, impractical, prohibited or simply too dark (even for fast films) to set up a tripod.

All flash units have a guide number (GN) that indicates their power with 100 ISO film. Guide numbers range from 10 to 50. The higher the guide number the more powerful (and expensive) the unit. The majority of new cameras have built-in flash units and these provide a convenient light source, ideal for candid photos such as in restaurants and at parties, but they have limited value for creative photography (see p114). Remember to always work within the limitations of the flash. Most have a GN of 10 to 15 and illuminate subjects between 1m and 5m from the flash.

If you don't have a built-in flash, or need more power, there are many accessory flash units to choose from that are either mounted onto the camera via a hot-shoe or are off-camera on a flash bracket, connected to the camera with a flash lead. Manual flash units are available, but far more popular are automatic and TTL units.

Manual Flash Units

Manual flash units deliver a constant amount of light and require a simple calculation to determine the aperture setting to achieve correct exposure. The shutter speed is irrelevant (except for the synchronisation speed – see p114) because the flash duration is very fast, typically 1/10,000 of a second or faster. With 100 ISO film, divide the GN of the flash unit by the subject's distance from the camera. For example, if the GN is 32 and the subject is 8m away, then the aperture will be f4. The intensity of flashlight falls off rapidly as it travels away from the unit, so the further away the subject is the wider the required aperture. Most manual flashes have a scale on the back of the unit that shows the aperture required based on the film's ISO rating and subject distance. This saves adjusting the GN if you're using a film other than 100 ISO.

Automatic Flash Units

Automatic flash units, which can be used on any SLR, have sensors that read the amount of light reflected from the subject and quench the flash as soon as the correct amount of light has reached the subject. Most units offer a selection of f-stop settings and indicators that confirm correct exposure, or alert you to over- or under-exposure.

Through the Lens (TTL) Flash Units

TTL flash is a more sophisticated form of automatic flash. The sensor that determines the exposure is in the camera body, not on the flash unit. This means that the light that actually exposes the film is measured automatically, taking into account the aperture setting and filters on the lens. Any aperture can be used (restricted only by the unit's capacity and the distance from the subject) and the need for film speed and aperture settings on the flash unit is eliminated.

Camera manufacturers make dedicated flash units with TTL functions for use with their cameras, and sometimes only for a specific model. Independent flash manufacturers produce units that can be dedicated to most cameras via an adaptor. To simplify flash work, TTL flash units are recommended (if your camera has TTL flash capabilities). Look for a unit with a manual mode that will let you experiment further with the possibilities of flash.

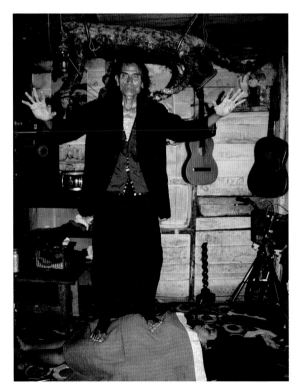

Medicine man, Banjarmasin, Kalimantan, Indonesia

I prefer to use available light whenever possible, rather than flashlight. However, for those occasions when I happen upon a man who's just eaten razor blades and is standing on his wife's stomach (and she's lying on a bed of rusty nails in a very dark room featuring a stuffed wild cat of some sort)...well, I can be talked into using my flash.

◄ 35mm SLR, 24mm lens, 1/60 f8, Kodachrome 64, direct flash

BUYING GUIDE FOR FILM CAMERAS

The old adage of 'you get what you pay for', can certainly be applied to camera equipment. Higher prices usually mean more features, better quality components and optics, and better construction. Shop around because retail prices can vary considerably, especially when a model is about to be superseded. Always check the warranty. This is particularly important if buying outside your own country or if you're going on a long trip and may require repairs while travelling. If you do buy camera equipment overseas, leave yourself time to put a roll of film through to check everything is working (and to sort the problem out if there is one).

Basic Compact Cameras

The 35mm compact range starts with simple point-and-shoot cameras with a fixed wide-angle lens. The flash fires when the light is low, and can't be turned off. The auto-focus has one sensor in the middle of the frame. Prices range from US$50 to US$100. They're not recommended for anyone interested in taking good pictures. Spend a little more money and you can add a zoom lens or features that allow some flash and exposure control. It's not until you move into the advanced compact bracket that you get all the features in one camera.

Advanced Compact Cameras

More highly recommended is the next level of compacts, available in APS (Advanced Photo System) and 35mm formats. In automatic mode they are point-and-shoot cameras, but they have a number of features that give some control over composition and exposure. Cameras in this category range in price from US$150 to US$300 and should feature:

- moderate zoom lens around 38mm-90mm
- built-in flash with optional settings for red-eye control, fill-flash, night flash and flash off
- focus and exposure lock for accurate focussing and exposure of the main subject
- mid-roll rewind
- multi-point auto-focus sensors to handle off-centre subjects
- self-timer

35mm SLR Cameras & Lenses

So, you want to buy a new SLR? Is that with 10-segment 3D matrix metering, 14-segment honeycomb-pattern metering or six-segment multi-pattern metering? Or maybe you'd prefer a 35-zone evaluative system? And, what about the Vari-Brite focus-area display, on-demand grid lines, predictive auto-focus and eye-controlled focus? Buying a new SLR could easily be an unnerving experience. A glance at the glossy brochures will reveal so many choices you may want to run back to the old camera you're trading in or stick to the compact you've had for years. However, with a bit of research and the help of a good salesperson you'll have no trouble finding the perfect camera for you.

Apart from the features, compare the weight, size and feel of the camera. If it's too heavy you may be inclined to leave it in the hotel room. Don't compromise lens quality for camera features. The lens determines image sharpness, contrast and colour rendition. Buy the fastest lens you can afford for superior optics, strong construction and maximum flexibility in low-light situations. Many cameras are sold as a package with a zoom lens at the bottom end of the quality scale to keep the price down. Inquire about what other options are available.

Suggested SLR Systems

Outlined below are four suggested camera outfits for general travel photography. The camera body should come from the mid-range aimed at camera enthusiasts, and retail between US$200 and US$1000 with a zoom lens made by the camera manufacturer. These cameras are one step down from semi-professional equipment and one step up from the entry-level cameras. In this price range cameras have a host of features, they are well built and should withstand the rigours of travel and perform reliably in most conditions. Look for a camera whose features include multi-zone auto-focus, multiple exposure modes, spot metering, built-in flash, automatic film advance and rewind, mid-roll rewind and depth of field preview button. Confirm that all automatic features can be overridden with manual settings. The suggested systems should all fit into a compact camera bag (except the tripod) when the equipment is removed from its individual cases, along with 20 rolls of film. There are numerous other camera–lens combinations, so use this as a guide as you consider your own budget, needs and photographic goals.

BASIC SYSTEM

The minimum SLR outfit for those who want more than a compact can offer, but with minimum weight and bulk.

▸ 35mm SLR camera body
▸ 35-80mm f4-5.6 or 28-105mm zoom lens f4-5.6
▸ skylight or UV filter
▸ polarising filter

STANDARD SYSTEM

A popular system with many travellers. This is the recommended minimum outfit for covering most situations.

▸ 35mm SLR camera body
▸ 28-80mm f3.5-5.6 zoom lens
▸ skylight or UV filter for each lens
▸ 70-210mm f4-5.6 or 70-300mm f4-5.6 zoom lens (if wildlife is a priority subject)
▸ polarising filter to fit all lenses

STANDARD PLUS SYSTEM

The addition of a fast standard lens and tripod create flexibility in low light and greater control over depth of field.

▸ 35mm SLR camera body
▸ 28-80mm f3.5-5.6 zoom lens
▸ 70-210mm f4-5.6 or 70-300mm f4-5.6 zoom lens (if wildlife is a priority subject)
▸ 50mm f1.4 fast standard lens
▸ skylight or UV filters for each lens
▸ polarising filter to fit all lenses
▸ compact tripod

ADVANCED SYSTEM

A versatile outfit for the traveller who places a high priority on picture-taking and is not concerned with the weight and bulk of the camera bag. The extra body is a great backup, but also increases speed and flexibility while shooting. The fast lenses and tripod will increase picture opportunities and give greater control over depth of field in the majority of low-light situations. The bounce-flash kit provides natural-looking flash pictures.

▸ two 35mm SLR camera bodies
▸ 28-80mm f3.5-5.6 zoom lens
▸ 70-210mm f4-5.6 or 70-300mm f4-5.6 zoom lens (if wildlife is a priority)
▸ 50mm f1.4 fast standard lens
▸ 24mm f2 fast wide-angle lens
▸ skylight or UV filter for each lens
▸ polarising filter to fit all lens
▸ compact tripod
▸ compact dedicated flash with tilt head
▸ bounce-flash reflector kit

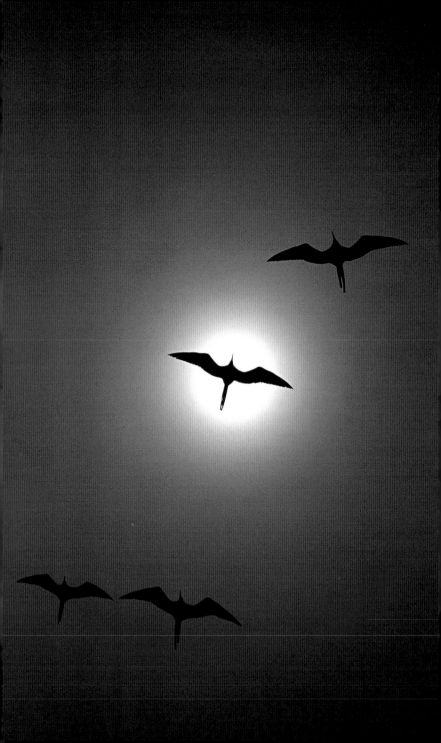

ACCESSORIES

Once you've got your equipment organised, you'll need a convenient and practical way of carrying it. Then, when you've got your camera bag, there are a few other bits and pieces worth throwing in.

CARRYING EQUIPMENT

If you've got anything more than a simple SLR outfit, the choice of carrying equipment is very important for comfort, security and ease of access.

Bags

Lots of bags look good but are not necessarily functional or comfortable. The main styles available are:

▶ **Day-pack/backpack-style bags** Ideal for carrying lots of equipment, but access is slow because the bag has to be removed from your back. Popular for trekking.

▶ **Hard-sided cases** These offer the greatest protection for equipment, but are very uncomfortable to carry around. Access is slow and all your gear is displayed when you open them up. Ideal if you're carrying a lot of equipment and need to check it in on planes (but carry a soft bag for use at your destination).

▶ **Soft shoulder bags** Quick access and generally comfortable to carry. These conform to the body and adapt easily as the gear in the bag changes. However, they offer the least amount of protection from knocks.

When buying a bag take all the equipment you intend carrying on your travels and try out the options in the shop. Aim to fit all your gear and film into one bag, but ensure that it's easily accessible. It can then be carried onto planes as hand luggage, and you only have one bag to worry about. Try not to select a bag that looks so good it's worth stealing. Look for bags with wide straps and accessory shoulder pads – they make carrying a weighty bag much more comfortable.

It's important to have a trial run with your bag of choice loaded up with everything you intend to take. Don't just wander around the lounge room for five minutes. Carry it and use the equipment to see how comfortable and easy it is.

Many travellers prefer to carry their camera and lenses in their regular day-pack. Unless you're prepared to carry your camera on your shoulder whenever you're out, having to remove the camera from the day-pack every time you want to take a photo is slow and inefficient.

Pouches

If you only have one camera and a zoom lens, consider carrying it in a pouch worn on a belt. Pouches provide quick access and take the place of the camera-maker's case. Film, and other items less regularly used, can then be carried in a day-pack.

Straps

Camera straps should be wide. Those provided by the camera-makers are not always comfortable, especially for cameras with heavy telephoto and long zoom lenses.

Silhouetted magnificent frigate birds,
San Salvador Island, Galápagos, Ecuador
◀ 35mm SLR, 24-70mm lens, 1/250 f11, Ektachrome E100VS

Jackets & Vests

Photographer's jackets and vests have numerous pockets, which distribute the weight of the gear evenly over the shoulders. Quick access is assured…that is, if you can remember in which of the 400 pockets you have put what you need. They're useful in crowded situations and permit greater agility in more adventurous environments than a bag swinging from the shoulder.

CLEANING KIT

Lens tissues and a blower brush are sufficient for most cleaning requirements. For really stubborn marks on lenses, a lens-cleaning fluid may be required. Generally, though, it's not worth carrying on the road.

BATTERIES

▶ **Always carry spare batteries for each piece of equipment.**

Carrying spare batteries becomes more important the further off the beaten track you go, especially if your camera uses lithium batteries (they last longer but aren't readily available in smaller places). The most common reason a camera stops working is that the batteries fail. Often it's because the battery is getting old and a build-up of dirt is interrupting the flow of energy. If you don't have spares, remove the batteries, wipe the battery ends and the contacts in the camera, and try them again. See p71 for specific advice on batteries for digital cameras.

CABLE RELEASES

A cable release is an accessory that lets you fire the shutter without physically touching the camera, reducing the risk of camera shake. If you have your camera on a tripod (or a pile of stones) you should use a cable release. If you don't have one, or your camera doesn't accept one, use the self-timer. By giving the camera 8–10 seconds to steady itself after the shutter release is pressed, sharper pictures will result. Don't forget though, in 8–10 seconds you could have recomposed a different shot by changing lenses, zooming in or out, changing orientation from horizontal to vertical or, worse still, the sun could have dipped below the horizon or the mountain could be engulfed by cloud.

LENS HOODS & EYE-CUPS

Lens hoods are essential and should be fitted to every lens if they're not built in. Their function is to prevent stray light entering the lens, which can cause flare, reduce sharpness and affect exposure settings.

If your camera doesn't have a built in eye-cup around the eye-piece, buy one as an accessory. It prevents light entering the eye-piece so that the viewfinder remains at its optimum brightness for accurate focussing.

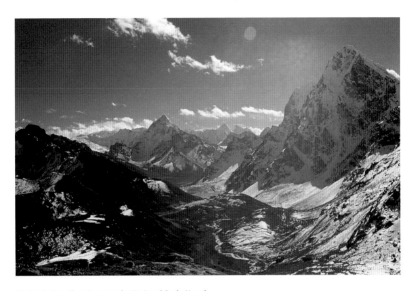

Chola Khola valley, Sagarmatha National Park, Nepal
Even if the sun isn't in the frame, shooting into the light can still cause flare and degrade the sharpness of the images.

▲ 35mm SLR, 24-70mm lens, 1/125 f11, Ektachrome E100VS, without lens hood
▼ 35mm SLR, 24-70mm lens, 1/125 f8, Ektachrome E100VS, with lens hood

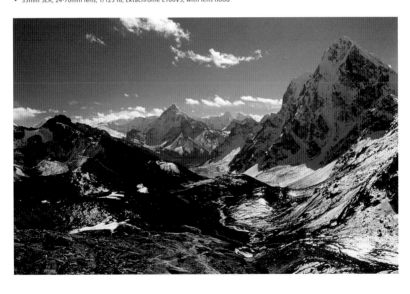

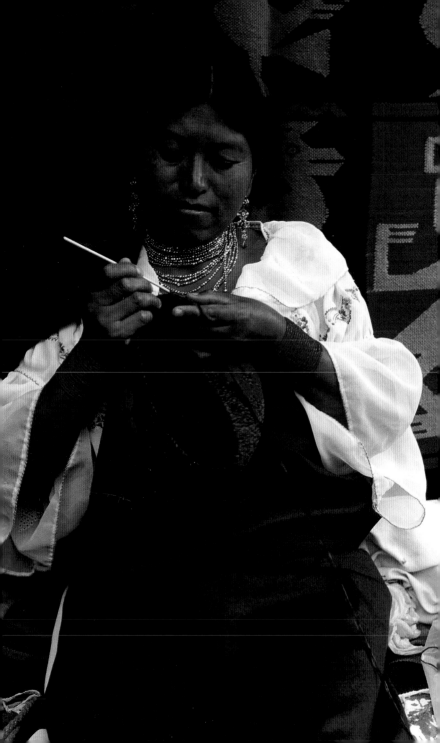

FILM

▶ **Choice of film is an important creative decision and should not be left to the last minute.**

The film you choose will have a dramatic impact on how your images look. It will determine the kinds of pictures you can take successfully, when and where you can take them, and what other equipment you may need, such as flashguns and tripods.

Kodak, Fujifilm and Agfa all make excellent films and professional photographers will argue tirelessly for the films they think are best. In some cases one film might be more suited to a particular application or subject than another. Fujichrome Velvia is regarded as an excellent film for landscapes and Kodak Portra is made specifically to accurately reproduce skin tones. Additionally, film is manufactured with a particular colour balance. The majority of films are balanced for daylight and electronic flashlight. When daylight film is used in situations where incandescent light is the dominant light source the print or slide will have a yellowish or warm cast. This can be overcome with flash, filtration, or by using a film balanced for tungsten lighting.

For the traveller, it's impractical to carry different films to cover the range of subjects and lighting conditions you'll want to record. Try a few different films to see for yourself how they react to different subject matter and under different lighting conditions and settle on the one film that gives you the most pleasing results.

PRINTS OR SLIDES?

The first decision to make is whether you want prints or slides, colour or B&W, or a combination. It's obviously a personal choice and depends a lot on what you want to do with your pictures and how you want to show them when you get home. Shooting two types of film at once, eg, for colour prints and slides, won't be easy unless you have two cameras. The time spent swapping film will lead to a lack of continuity in your final presentation. But even if you have two cameras, why take everything twice? You can always make prints (colour and B&W) from slides or slides from negatives.

Be clear about your main priority for taking pictures, and film choice will be easier. If you're simply recording your trip for yourself, then colour negative film, from which colour prints are made, is the most suitable choice. If you intend to submit your work to a photo library or hope to publish your work, then colour slide film is the way to go.

Colour Prints

Colour prints, displayed in an album, are easy to show others and, because they're so accessible, they get looked at a lot more often than slides after the initial burst of interest wears off. Reprints, to send to people you've photographed and travelled with, and enlargements of your favourite photos, are inexpensive. Minilabs now exist in most cities and towns, allowing you to develop and print film quickly and cheaply. You can enjoy your photos and get feedback immediately, and learn from your successes and failures as you travel.

Woman crocheting, Otavalo Market, Ecuador
◀ 35mm SLR, 24-70mm lens, 1/60 f6.3, Ektachrome E100VS

On the technical side, exposing negative film is much easier than slide film, as it has wide exposure latitude and exposure mistakes can often be corrected in the printing. If you're using a fully automatic compact point-and-shoot camera, colour negative film is clearly the best choice.

The main disadvantage of colour negative film is that the amount of control you have over the finished print is limited. Unless you go to the extra expense of using a professional lab to print to your directions or you print your own negatives, you may be disappointed that the intensity of colour you remembered photographing is missing. Minilabs generally print everything as close to average as possible, so most prints have a sameness about them.

B&W Prints

The emphasis in this book is on the use of colour films, but B&W films are still widely available and popular. Processing B&W is not as convenient as colour negative films (few minilabs offer a B&W service, instead sending it off to a professional laboratory). The convenience of minilab processing is available if you use one of the B&W chromogenic films that can be developed and printed with the same chemicals and paper used for colour negative films. The prints often have a colour cast, which can result in them looking slightly blue or sepia brown. Good B&W prints are possible off chromogenic negatives when they're printed onto B&W paper.

Colour Transparencies

A colour transparency, or slide (also called a trannie or chrome), when properly exposed and projected onto a white screen in a very dark room, is the closest you can get to reliving the depth of colour and range of tones that you saw when you took the photo. Most professional travel photographers shoot transparency film because it allows total flexibility in end use, and it's also the standard requirement of most publishers and photo libraries. Most importantly, the final look of the image is determined by the type of film used and through exposure choices made by the photographer. The slide is a final product and therefore an expression of the photographer's vision and intentions. It doesn't need to be interpreted by a printer, as a negative does, before it can be viewed.

It's important to understand that different films record colour differently, and that this characteristic is especially relevant to colour transparency film. The variations between films can be quite dramatic and aren't just apparent from one manufacturer to another. A particular Kodak 100 ISO colour slide film will not only record colours quite differently from a Fujifilm or Agfa 100 ISO film, but differently from another Kodak 100 ISO film.

When you choose one slide film over another you're actually making a creative decision that can greatly affect how your pictures look. The film type determines the way colour is recorded and the film speed (see p47) determines the overall quality and sharpness of the image.

Colour prints can be made from slides, but are more expensive than prints from negatives, and as contrast is increased in the process they're often disappointing and look too dark. Good-quality prints from slides can be made at a considerable increase in cost by a professional laboratory, but are well worth it if you intend to display a framed print of your favourite photograph.

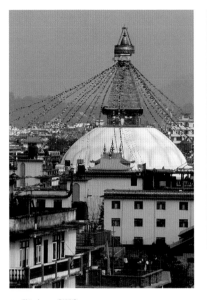

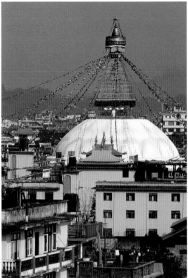

▲ Ektachrome E100G

▲ Ektachrome E100VS

▼ Ektachrome EBX

▼ Fujichrome Sensia

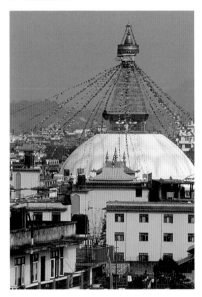

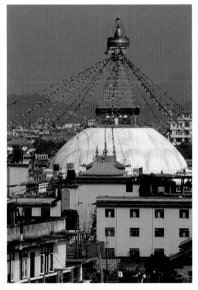

Bodhnath Stupa, Kathmandu Valley, Nepal

Same subjects, same light: different film, different colour. Colour films reproduce colours differently. Try various films to find the one that gives you the most pleasing results.

35mm SLR, 70-200mm lens, 1/200 f10, tripod

Transparency film is not recommended for travellers using automatic point-and-shoot cameras. To ensure consistent results an SLR with a reasonably sophisticated built-in exposure meter is required.

Colour slides need to be projected if you wish family and friends to see them, and that requires extra equipment and preparation. Not to mention the fear you'll put into your friends when they're invited over to see the slides of your latest trip (but more on getting over that later). However, nothing beats a projected slide for brilliance and colour.

PROFESSIONAL OR AMATEUR FILM?

Most amateur (or consumer) colour slide and negative films have a professional equivalent (identifiable in most retailers as it's stored in refrigerators), but both have the same chief characteristics of colour, sharpness and grain.

All colour films have emulsions made from chemical compounds that change slowly over time, which results in a process known as ageing, where the colour balance and speed of the film changes. The film manufacturers allow for this based on the way film is used by the two customer groups. It's expected that there will be quite a delay between manufacture and processing of consumer film, as it sits first on the retailer's shelf and then for some weeks or months in the customer's camera. During this time the film ages so that it's close to its optimum during the period of its expected use.

Professional films are aged by the manufacturer and then kept in refrigerated storage so that they're released and used much closer to their intended optimum colour balance and speed. This is important for some professional applications where consistency from roll to roll is required. Many professionals buy large quantities at once to ensure this consistency; saving time and money.

For the traveller, amateur films have many advantages. It's impossible to keep film refrigerated on the road, so the batch consistency of professional film can't be guaranteed. Also, on a long trip amateur film is considerably cheaper. Processing costs are the same for professional and amateur film.

As with choice of film, it's well worth trying and comparing a couple of different amateur and professional films to establish which will best meet your needs.

FILM SPEED

All film has an International Standards Organisation (ISO) rating that designates the speed of the film. Film is light sensitive and the more sensitive it is to light the higher the film speed or ISO.

Film speed is recorded numerically. For example, there are 64 ISO, 100 ISO and 400 ISO films. Doubling of the number shows the doubling of film speed, 100 ISO film is twice as fast and twice as sensitive to light as 50 ISO. The 50 ISO film requires twice as much light to achieve the same exposure as the 100 ISO film.

Film is also classified more informally into slow, medium and fast. Slow films have ratings of 25 or 50 ISO. Medium (or standard) speed films are rated at 64, 100, 160 and 200 ISO, and fast films include 400, 800, 1000, 1600 and 3200 ISO films.

Film speed is also a good indication of the potential overall image quality that can be expected. Slow films have a finer grain than fast films and result in much sharper images with excellent detail and colour rendition. This is particularly noticeable when making prints larger than 20cm x 25cm. As the image is enlarged the grain is magnified and, unless the effect has been sought for artistic reasons, the print will acquire an unsatisfactory soft, textured effect.

The choice of film speed comes down to the conditions you expect to be shooting in, personal preference, and the expected or desired end use of your photographs.

If you use a compact point-and-shoot camera for colour prints, 400 ISO film is ideal. The extra sensitivity to light over the slower films means that you can hand-hold your camera in most situations and that the effective range of the built-in flash is extended.

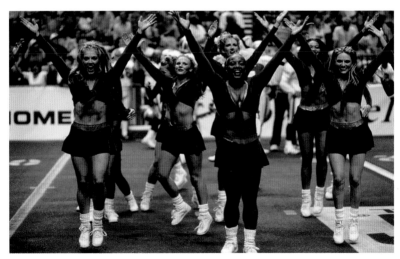

Cheerleaders at indoor football game, Nashville, USA

It can be really tough when the light is low, you can't use flash or tripod and your subject is leaping about. Fast lenses and films that are made to be pushed are invaluable in these situations.

▲ 35mm SLR, 100mm, 1/125 f2, Ektachrome E200 rated at 800 ISO (a two-stop push)

If you use an SLR and are interested in getting the most out of your equipment and film and intend enlarging your favourite pictures, select 100 ISO as your standard film speed. It's suitable for the majority of picture-taking situations. However, different situations call for different speed films. If you have a special interest in landscape photography and will be carrying a tripod, then a very fine grain 50 ISO would be best. If your interest is in photographing sport or theatre, you'll need greater quantities of faster film. Carry a few rolls of 400 for low-light situations or explore the possibilities of 'push processing'.

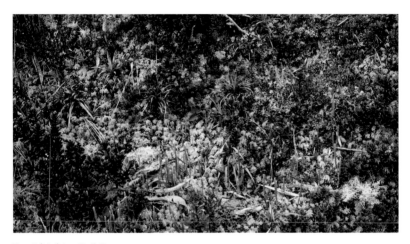

Forest detail, Inca Trail, Peru

Same subject, same light: different grain, different quality. The 25 ISO film displays very fine grain (hardly noticeable), has captured the subject's intricate detail and is extremely sharp. The 1600 ISO film is clearly grainy, lacks detail, is less sharp and has more contrast.

▲ Kodachrome 25 ISO
▼ Fujichrome 1600 ISO

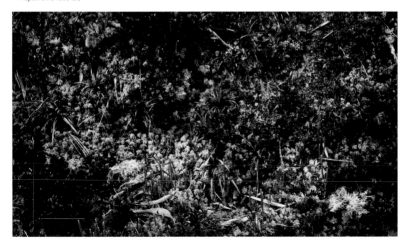

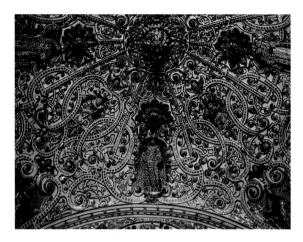

Interior roof detail, Santo Domingo Church, Oaxaca, Mexico

When you're allowed to take photos but prohibited from using flash or a tripod, fast film allows hand-held photography in very dimly lit places.

◀ 35mm SLR, 50mm lens, 1/60 f1.4, Ektachrome E200 rated at 800 ISO

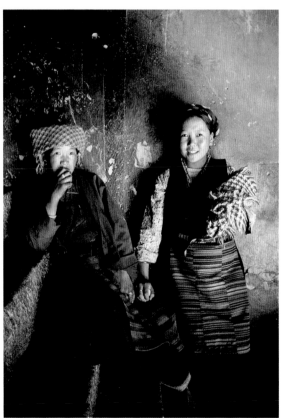

Tibetan girls on stairs, Sera Monastery, Lhasa, Tibet, China

There wasn't much room to move on the steps leading up to the second floor of the Sera Monastery, and these girls were standing back to let others pass. The low light level meant that with my standard film an exposure of a 1/15 sec would be required, which would almost guarantee an unsuccessful picture due to camera shake and subject movement. By using fast film, I was able use the available light and retain the atmosphere of the location while hand-holding the camera.

◀ 35mm SLR, 24mm lens, 1/60 f2, Kodachrome 200 rated at 400 ISO

PUSHING & PULLING FILM

Pushing and pulling film is a technique that allows you to vary the ISO of colour slide and B&W film, at the time of exposure, for practical and creative reasons.

The most common technique is to 'push' film one or two stops by exposing it at a higher ISO setting than its actual film speed. (Eg, with 100 ISO film in the camera, set the ISO on 200 for a 'one-stop push', or on 400 for a 'two-stop push'.) The camera meter is tricked into thinking that you're using faster film so that less light is required for correct exposure. The entire roll must be exposed at the new setting and the film lab must be informed so that the developing time is extended. If you don't inform the lab you'll end up with transparencies that are underexposed, or too dark. If you 'push' your standard films, carry stickers or devise a foolproof method of identifying the pushed film.

Pushing film creates opportunities to take pictures in low levels of available light, instead of resorting to flash, using a tripod or having to hand-hold your camera at shutter speeds that risk camera shake (see p96).

It also allows you to carry only one film stock and push the film as necessary in low-light situations, rather than having to estimate in advance how much fast film you should carry on a trip.

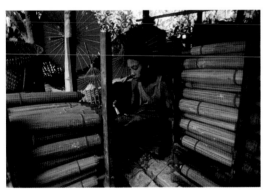

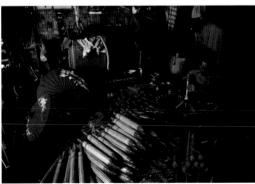

Umbrella workshop, Pathein, Myanmar

Working in a covered but open-sided building, this young boy was facing the light. There was enough light to use my standard 100 ISO film with my fastest lens – always my first choice.

◄ 35mm SLR, 50mm lens, 1/60 f1.4, hand-held, Ektachrome E100VS

The workshop owner was working in a dimly lit area, which required an 1/8 sec exposure with the 100 ISO film. Flash would have eliminated the ambience of the location and although a tripod could have been used, I find it limits the spontaneity possible when working with people. Switching to my camera body loaded with 200 ISO film, but rated at 800 ISO, I was able to hand-hold the camera and move around my subject as he worked. Workshops like this one are often dark, but in low-light situations the grain of the film enhances mood and sense of place.

◄ 35mm SLR, 24mm lens, 1/30 f2, hand-held, Kodak E200 rated at 800 ISO (a two-stop push)

Be aware that when film is pushed, contrast and grain are both increased, which is why pushing film is not recommended in good lighting conditions. It's an ideal technique when working indoors and in low light. The increase in grain often adds to the mood of the shot.

'Pulling film', rating film below its actual ISO, isn't a technique commonly used, but it can be useful if film is accidentally exposed incorrectly. If you change from 100 ISO film to 400 ISO film but forget to change the setting on your camera, your pictures will be over-exposed. Inform the lab and in the processing they'll compensate for the error.

Rating film incorrectly has become less of a problem since DX coding, which reads the speed of the film and sets it automatically when it's loaded into the camera. DX coding has become a standard feature on modern cameras.

REMOVING FILM MID-ROLL

There are several reasons to take film out of the camera before it's finished. You may want to change from a slow to fast film, 'push' one of your standard films, switch from colour to B&W, or remove the film before the security check at the airport. If your camera rewinds the film automatically, check that it has a mid-roll rewind facility that doesn't wind the film all the way back into the cassette. If not, you can buy a small plastic gadget for retrieving the film leader from the cassette. Most minilabs have one of these tools and may do it for you. Just remember to immediately label the cassette with the number of exposed frames already taken.

HOW TO REWIND A PARTIALLY USED FILM

‣ Note the frame number of the last photo taken.
‣ Rewind the film until you feel and hear it come loose from the take-up spool.
‣ Write the frame number on the leader.
‣ Crease the last centimetre of the film leader to guard against loading the film accidentally.

HOW TO RELOAD THE FILM

‣ Note the frame number of the last photo taken.
‣ Set the highest shutter speed on the camera.
‣ Stop the aperture right down.
‣ Put the lens cap on or place the lens against a dark object such as a camera bag.
‣ Advance the film to the last frame used, plus one.

X-RAYS

▶ **Ideally, film should not be x-rayed**

Unprocessed film is light and heat sensitive and exposure to x-rays can fog the film. The amount of damage results from a combination of the ISO rating, the strength of the x-rays and the number of times the film is scanned. The good news is that Kodak have done extensive tests and found that slow- and medium-speed films can handle up to 16 passes through the x-ray machines used to check hand luggage at modern western airports. The more light sensitive, faster films, from 400 ISO, are much more susceptible to x-ray damage. Limit their exposure to four or five passes.

Be aware that in many developing countries airports are still using old technology and the dose of the x-ray may be set at higher than acceptable levels. The danger for medium and slow ISO films is the cumulative effect of x-rays. One or two passes through the scanner may not matter, but five or six may take the levels over the acceptable threshold and fog the film. It's very easy to clock up half a dozen security checks even on a short trip.

▶ **Never pack film in your check-in luggage.**

High dose CT (computerised tomography) scanners are now widely used for check-in luggage at airports around the world and have been proven to fog film with just one pass. Carry all unprocessed film in your hand luggage. If your travels will take you through many security checks, or you're confronted with a machine that you're not confident is 'film safe', ask for a hand inspection.

Hand inspections are not usually a problem, even with the recent focus on airport security, but there are ways of making the request less painful for the security staff. Take all film out of the boxes and plastic containers and carry it in a clear plastic bag or box (I use Tupperware containers). Before you get to the security check remove your film and put your camera bag through the machine, making sure there's no film in your cameras. This indicates that you're doing your best to comply with security requirements and packaging of the film in clear containers makes the security staff's job easier. It's also worth getting to the security check with plenty of time to spare so you have time to wait if the security staff claim to be too busy to hand-check bags. Remember, they're only doing their job, and after all it's for your protection, so be patient and courteous.

Lead-lined bags may give you some peace of mind if a hand-check is refused. The lead lining stops the x-ray penetrating the bag, but may cause the inspector to increase the dosage. If you're lucky, the presence of a solid black package in your bag will simply lead to a hand-check after the x-ray.

HOW MUCH FILM TO TAKE?

▸ **The cost of film adds up when you use lots of it, but it's better to take too much than too little.**

Run out of film and you'll never forgive yourself. Compared with the other costs of travel, film and processing are relatively cheap, especially given the years of pleasure you'll get from the photographic memories. It's best to take as much as you can with you, especially if travelling to out-of-the-way places. Even if the more remote locations have the exact film you want, when you want it, it may not be fresh or it may not have been handled properly, and it will often be very expensive. Excess film can always be used when you get home, stored in the freezer for your next trip, or sold to a fellow traveller that miscalculated their requirements.

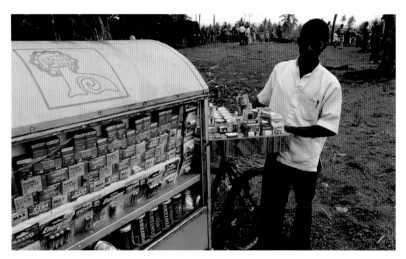

Film and beer seller, Pinnewala, Sri Lanka

Do you really want to buy your film from the front of a bike? This young man is providing an excellent service to badly prepared travellers – make sure you're not one of them.

▲ 35mm SLR, 24-70mm lens, 1/125 f5.6, Ektachrome E100VS

It's almost impossible to recommend how much film to take. You'll need more if you're rushing around from sight to sight than if you intend to sit on the same beach for days. A quick survey of regular travellers suggests that two to three rolls of 36 exposures a week is adequate to record a trip, but five to six rolls a week would suit someone with a keen interest in photography. (I budget for 10 rolls a day on an assignment and two rolls a day on a family holiday.)

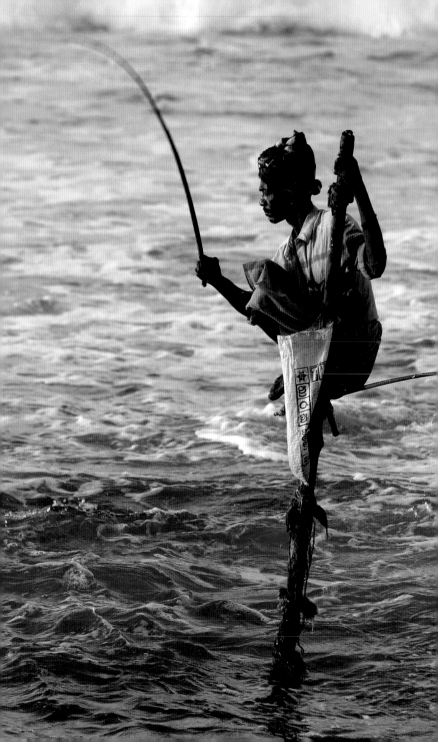

DIGITAL PHOTOGRAPHY

Digital photography has well and truly arrived. Although still in its infancy, digital camera sales have exploded in the last couple of years. Competition between camera, film and electronic manufacturers to produce digital cameras for the consumer market has seen the release of a staggering number of camera models. This has led to rapid gains in image quality and an increasing number of features. The dramatic increase in sales saw prices drop in 2003 to the point where reasonably sophisticated compact digital cameras became not only affordable but comparable in price to compact film cameras. Everyone in the market for a new camera is now asking if digital capture is right for them. Many already think it is. According to a study by research company InfoTrends around 53 million digital cameras will be sold worldwide in 2004. They expect this number to grow each year and predict around 82 million digital cameras will be sold in 2008. This is a staggering jump from the 11 million units sold in 2000. It's worth noting that although film camera sales have declined each year since 2000, around 57 million units were sold in 2003.

DIGITAL OR FILM?

Remember, it's everything that goes on before the shutter is pressed that makes great photos, not the type of camera used.

▶ **A properly exposed, nicely lit and well-composed image is the aim, whether it's captured on the silver halides of film or the pixels of a sensor.**

As with film-based cameras, the choice of digital equipment is important in ensuring that your creative intentions are fulfilled, rather than impeded. Just as some photographers reach their goals with one camera and one lens, while others need three cameras and six lenses, the choice of digital or film is just another creative option available to help you capture and present images that reflect your personal photographic vision.

Images, captured digitally or on film, can certainly be enhanced through skilful image manipulation using image-editing software and a computer, just as a skilled craftsperson can bring a negative to life in the darkroom. However, that can only happen if all the required information is captured in the first place. It's a mistake to think that badly executed digital images can be 'rescued' in Photoshop (or other image-editing software programs) to produce stunning prints displaying the full tonal range and colour of the original scene. 'Photoshopping' to correct mistakes should be a last resort and not part of your standard photographic practice.

Travelling with a digital camera is becoming easier all the time. Retail outlets now stock memory cards and offer image transfer, printing and copying services in more and more remote places. Portable storage devices allow thousands of images to be taken without

Stilt fisherman, Koggala, Sri Lanka
Squatting on a small cross beam on a pole embedded in the ocean floor, the stilt fishermen of Sri Lanka's west coast were a challenge to photograph. I knew I didn't get decent pictures from an afternoon session where the light was very flat, so went back the next morning. The shot that finally worked focussed on one fisherman from an elevated viewpoint that eliminated the horizon (which when included was cutting the composition in half). The upright angle of the fishing rod kept the composition tight. The slight bend and blur at the end of the rod from the tension of a caught fish was the finishing touch.

◀ Professional DSLR, 70-200mm lens at 200mm,
1/250 f5.6,100 ISO, 3072 x 2048, RAW

having to carry enough memory cards to cover an entire trip. The reduced weight and space savings of not carrying film, not to mention the elimination of x-ray hassles, are big enough incentives for the travelling photographer to at least investigate if digital capture is the way to go.

Some people treat memory cards like traditional film, buying another card when the first one is full. This practice defeats two of the key economic benefits of digital capture: the reuse of the memory card and the ability to delete unwanted images. It's scary pressing a button that says 'Delete All Images', even after you've had prints and a copy of the files made. Confidence in the technology is required. It's well worth allowing the time to experience each step of the digital process at home to become comfortable with how it works before you hit the road. You'll then be able to take advantage of the services that photo retailers and Internet cafes provide. Feeling uncertain about the technology doesn't help the creative process.

What's so Good about Digital?

Digital photography has certainly captured people's imagination, and with good reason – it has a lot going for it. But of course, you can't have all the wonders of digital capture without having to put up with some downsides.

ADVANTAGES

- instant review of image lets you check the shot and gives you the opportunity to re-shoot if you're unhappy with the result
- no film or processing costs
- you can shoot a limitless number of images
- unwanted images can be deleted and best pictures only are printed (no need to pay for the whole roll to be printed)
- white-balance feature eliminates the need to carry filters to correct colour under artificial light
- you can adjust the ISO rating from frame to frame
- elimination of film weight and bulk (the more film you normally carry the more you'll benefit)
- no x-ray hassles
- you can match the image file size to output requirements – print or email
- you can compose close-ups effectively with Liquid Crystal Display (LCD) screen
- images can be downloaded directly to a computer, eliminating the need for scanning
- ideal for web use, emails and business presentations
- date, time and shooting data such as shutter speed, aperture and focal length is recorded automatically
- sound annotation feature on some cameras allows spoken notes to be recorded against images
- you can shoot in colour, B&W or sepia from frame to frame
- prints can be made within minutes of taking the photographs
- images can be emailed or posted to a website instantly
- cost of making prints is comparable to making prints from negatives (although this varies considerably from country to country)
- great learning tool because of its immediacy
- it's a lot of fun

DISADVANTAGES

- very easy to delete files accidentally
- computer hardware, peripherals and software need to match the photographer's output

- computer time required to manage digital files
- delay or lag time between pressing shutter and image capture while the camera focusses and sets exposure and white balance is annoying and can result in missed photo opportunities (the delay varies from 0.3 to 1.5 seconds on the majority of cameras but over two seconds with subjects that are difficult to focus)
- many digital cameras take time, typically two to five seconds, to power up from the off setting (some recently released cameras are as quick to start up as a film camera)
- Digital Single Lens Reflex (DSLR) cameras currently cost more than film cameras with comparable features
- diligent management of battery power and constant recharging of batteries is necessary
- dust on the sensor of a DSLR effects every image and is often not seen until images are viewed at 100% enlargement on a computer monitor
- high power consumption of sensors, LCD screens, auto-focus, flash and the review and delete functions, which chews up batteries
- lag time demands a change in technique to compensate
- lens multiplier factor (see p81) requires a re-evaluation of the lenses SLR owners have, and will probably result in new lenses being purchased (except in the case of the very expensive professional cameras with full frame sensor)
- memory cards are susceptible to electromagnetic fields
- print size is limited by camera's resolution

Computer Considerations

A computer isn't necessary to take or print digital pictures. However, if you really want to enjoy all the possibilities that the medium has to offer, a computer is an integral part of the digital photographer's set-up. Digital images contain a lot more information than text files and require a considerable amount of computer memory or RAM (Random Access Memory) to process the images quickly. A decent amount of hard drive capacity is also important to handle the software requirements for cataloguing and enhancing images. Working with image files on a slow computer soon gets tedious. If you already have a computer, check that it has the right cable connector ports. If it's over three years old, and wasn't purchased with digital photography in mind, you'll probably need to upgrade. Exactly what computer specifications you need depends on how many pictures you take and your degree of involvement with the process, but a recommended minimum computer set-up for working with images is:

- 1 gigabyte (GB) hard drive
- 256 megabytes (MB) of RAM (but 512 MB is much better and 1 GB is ideal)
- built-in compact disk writer (CD-RW) and/or digital versatile disk (DVD-RW) writer.

DIGITAL CAPTURE

The world of digital imaging can seem a little daunting at first, but it needn't be. Here's a simple summary of what happens after you press the shutter on a digital camera.

▸ The lens focuses the light onto an image sensor made up of light-sensitive cells (instead of film).
▸ The light is converted into electronic data and processed by software built into the camera to create an image file.
▸ The image file is saved to a removable and reusable memory card, sometimes called digital film.
▸ The image can be reviewed immediately on the camera's built-in screen.
▸ You can delete the image if you're not satisfied with it.
▸ Once the memory card is full you replace it with another card or transfer the images to a storage medium such as a computer hard drive or CD.
▸ You delete the images from the memory card.
▸ You reuse the memory card.
▸ Prints can be made directly from the memory card before deleting the files or from a computer or CD anytime.

There is, of course, a lot more to know about digital image capture, especially if you're in the market for a new camera. You don't have to be a tech head to understand the technology. However, to ensure you get the right camera for your creative goals there are a few basic concepts (and lots of new jargon) to get your head around. Understanding the different types of digital cameras and their host of features and functions will help you make the right choice.

Sensors, Pixels & Resolution

At the heart of a digital camera is the image sensor, which takes the place of film. The size and quality of the sensor are key variables that affect the price of the camera, the maximum print size possible and the underlying characteristics of the digital image file produced, in terms of colour and sharpness. The sensor converts light into numerical data so that it can be processed, stored and retrieved using computer language. Various sensors are manufactured, but the most common in digital cameras are the CCD (Charge Coupled Device) and the CMOS (Complementary Metal Oxide Semiconductor). Essentially, sensors are semiconductor chips made up of a grid of tiny light-sensitive cells called photodiodes. Because photodiodes are monochromatic devices, a coloured filter is placed over the sensor to enable colour to be recorded. When light hits the photodiode an electrical charge is generated. Each photodiode records the brightness and colour of the light and generates a corresponding pixel that is placed in a grid. The number of pixels in the grid determines the amount of information recorded. The degree to which this information displays detail, sharpness and colour accuracy is described as resolution. High-resolution images are made from millions of pixels that allow fine detail, sharpness and accurate colour to be recorded. Low-resolution images are made from fewer pixels and therefore cannot reproduce all the data originally captured.

A camera's resolution is determined by multiplying the number of photodiodes on the vertical and horizontal axis of the sensor. This equation usually results in a total pixel count in the millions and is described in megapixels (MP). One million pixels equal a megapixel. For example, a camera with a sensor containing 1536 x 2048 pixels has a pixel count of

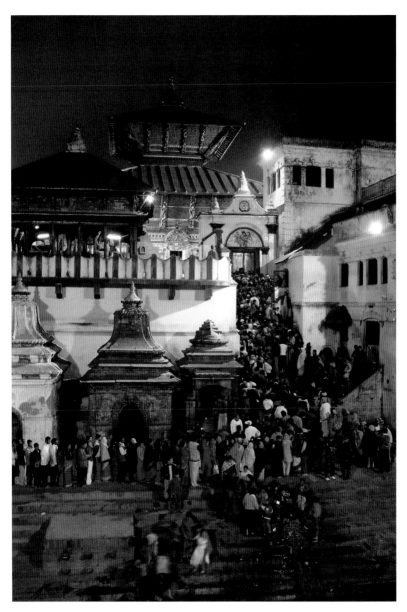

Pashupatinath Temple, Kathmandu Valley, Nepal

Compact digital cameras can produce excellent results. By placing the camera on a tripod, using the manual override option to select a slow shutter speed and turning off the flash, the mood and movement of early evening at the Shivaratri Festival is conveyed.

▲ Standard compact digital, 5.5-21.8mm lens at 5.5mm, 1/2 f2.8, 200 ISO, 1728 x 2304, 4 MP JPEG, tripod

3,145,728 and is described as a 3.2 MP camera. This number is usually displayed on the camera body and is an initial indicator of price as well as the image quality and maximum print size that the camera can be expected to produce. However, it's only an initial indicator. It's important to understand that cameras can't be compared on pixel count alone. The actual quality of the information recorded in the image file is affected by manufacturing variables including the build quality and physical size of the sensor; the quality, size and spacing of the actual pixels; the way the data is processed by the camera's image processor; and the quality of the lens. In other words, all equivalent megapixel cameras aren't exactly the same.

You'll also notice a discrepancy in a camera's technical specifications between sensor resolution and image resolution, sometimes described as effective pixels. This is because part of the sensor is masked with black dye as a reference point for establishing an accurate black level. Part of the sensor may also be required for other functions such as recording time and date. It's the number of effective pixels that matters.

Sensor Characteristics

Unlike film – which can be changed to suit the lighting conditions, subject and the photographer's creative intentions – the image sensor is built into the camera. Consequently, the inherent characteristics of the sensor will be imparted onto the image files. The integral look of the file does vary from sensor to sensor, although varying degrees of customisation are possible with advanced cameras. This is particularly evident when comparing compact cameras with DSLRs because of the latter's much larger photodiodes. Manufacturers determine how they feel an image looks best through variations in colour balance, saturation levels, automatic white balance and sharpness. The sensor's inherent characteristics should be an important consideration when buying a camera – you will need to override the settings or adjust the image with editing software if you want to change them. Look for the differences when comparing cameras in a shop, especially if the salesperson is making prints for you. You can also check out technical reviews on websites that have tested sensor characteristics and provide information on colour rendition.

Sensor Size

Sensor size is an important contributor to digital image quality. Basically, the bigger the better. The compact camera range, from point-and-shoot through to high-quality advanced compact cameras, features sensors that range in size from 6mm to 11mm diagonally. Sensors in DSLRs measure 22mm to 44mm diagonally. The 44mm sensors are known as full-frame sensors because they're the same size as a 35mm film frame (24mm x 36mm) and are only used in a couple of high-end professional cameras.

Sensor size also determines a lens's angle of view and lens multiplier factor (see p80).

Keeping the Sensor Clean

Sensors are electrically charged components and consequently attract dust. This is only an issue for DSLR cameras when the sensor is exposed while lenses are being changed. The main concern is that any dust or dirt on the sensor will appear in every image. It can be removed with editing software but imagine how much time that could take after a trip.

Note also that you're not going to see the result of dust on the sensor on the camera's LCD screen. It's not until you view the image at 100% magnification in photo-editing software that the problem will reveal itself. Check the sensor under a bright light source; a flashlight will do the job. Ideally, you'll be able to remove dust with a blower brush without touching the surface. More stubborn particles may require sensor swabs and cleaning fluid made specifically for cleaning sensors. Prevention is the best aim. Avoid changing lenses in dusty environments and windy conditions (easier said than done when on the road).

ISO

Image sensors, like film, are light sensitive. Unlike film, which has its sensitivity predetermined and requires the entire roll to be exposed at the same ISO setting, a sensor's ISO sensitivity can be electronically varied from shot to shot to suit the lighting situation or creative intent of the photographer. The settings are described as ISO equivalents, allowing the photographer to understand the sensor's sensitivity by relating it to the familiar ISO rating of film (see p47).

Most compact cameras offer a small range of ISO equivalent options or automatically alter the setting to suit the conditions, typically offering 100, 200 and 320 ISO equivalents. More advanced compact and DSLR cameras extend the range to offer lower (25, 50, 64 and 80) and higher (800, 1600, 3200 and 6400) ISO equivalents. Some cameras restrict the file size or image quality to small or lower resolution images with 800 or higher ISO settings (see p62). As with film, the best quality images are made at the lowest ISO equivalent settings and 100 or 200 ISO is a good standard setting for general travel photography.

Noise

Noise is the digital equivalent of grain (see p47). As with high ISO film, high ISO equivalent settings on a digital camera can cause image degradation that is undesirable (unless intended for creative reasons). This is known as noise. Noise occurs when high ISO settings are used in low light conditions because the sensor can't record the available light. This results in interference during the conversion of data to pixels, and gaps will appear, which the processor fills with white or coloured pixels. These are known as error pixels. Larger sensors produce less noise across the ISO range and allow higher ISO settings to be used before noise becomes visible. You can use this fact to test the quality of the sensor when buying a camera: take pictures with your preferred cameras at their highest ISO setting in low light levels using exposures of at least five seconds, and compare the results.

Compression

The creation of high-quality digital images requires the capture and storage of a lot of information, often resulting in large image files that use up a lot of space on storage devices. In order to maximise memory card storage capacity, image files are reduced in size through a mathematical process known as compression. Images can be compressed using lossless or lossy compression routines. Both systems reduce image files by discarding some of the data. Lossless compression doesn't reduce the file size as much as lossy compression, so less space is saved, but, as the name suggests, there is no loss of image quality. When the file is restored back to its original size in image-editing software all the information captured in the image is visible. Lossy compression allows the files to be reduced in varying degrees, discarding more and more data as compression is increased. When the file is decompressed the discarded data is added back into the file through a process known as interpolation. This can cause image quality to deteriorate, especially when high levels of compression have been applied. It's also important to understand that each time an image is compressed using a lossy compression process more data is lost.

File Formats

The data captured by a camera to create a digital image is stored in a file format so that it can be retrieved and processed using photo-editing software. There are many file-format options but the most commonly used in digital image capture are TIFF (Tagged Image File Format), JPEG (Joint Photographic Experts Group) and RAW.

TIFF is an industry standard file format commonly used for storing images intended for print publishing. Some advanced compacts and DSLR cameras offer TIFF storage as the highest quality option. TIFF files are usually uncompressed and are subjected to extensive post-capture processing. Consequently, they quickly use up space on a memory card and take longer to be saved, increasing the delay between shots.

Most digital cameras utilise the industry standard JPEG file format and compression routine. JPEG files are compressed using lossy compression that offers quick in-camera processing and allows large numbers of images to be stored on memory cards. Most entry-level compacts only provide one 'resolution' or 'quality' setting. Better quality models provide separate 'resolution' and 'quality' settings; 'resolution' adjusts the size of the pixel array, while 'quality' sets the level of JPEG compression. The degree of compression can be varied through a camera control or menu option usually labelled 'Image Quality'. This option allows images to be stored in a range of file sizes or compression levels usually described as Low, Medium and High. The highest resolution files are compressed the least. The smallest files are heavily compressed. The greater the compression the lower the quality of the image file (see opposite).

If you want to get the absolute best results from your digital camera, capture your images using the RAW file format, an option available on some compact and all DSLR cameras. Often described as a digital negative, it's the format preferred by professional photographers. RAW files are not processed by the camera's software, which compresses the data and makes adjustments that are embedded irremovably in the image file. Instead, RAW files are compressed using a lossless process, so they retain all the information originally captured but are saved to the memory card quickly. Adjustments such as contrast, saturation, sharpness and white balance are made by the photographer after the image has been downloaded to a computer. Creative decisions can then be tailored to each image using the much greater functionality of image-editing software.

Shooting RAW files requires a considerable amount of post-capture computer time and more than a basic understanding of image-editing software. RAW files must be processed or converted before they can be opened in photo-editing programs. Cameras with RAW file capture are sold with proprietary software for that purpose. Your investment in time and equipment will be rewarded with digital files and prints that maximise the capabilities of your camera.

Image Quality & File Size

Even if you intend to set your digital camera on auto everything, time should be taken to understand and control the Image Quality or File Size setting. Selecting the correct image-quality setting at the point of capture is critical to what you can do with the image file post capture and is particularly important in relation to printing options. Additionally, your choice will determine how many photographs can be stored on the memory card you're using. This process is one of the major differences between shooting digitally and shooting with film.

On all cameras, small or low-resolution files allow the maximum number of images to be stored and are ideal for emailing and web use. However, they are unsuitable for printing. High resolution images or large files result in the smallest number of images being stored on a memory card, but allow the largest photo-quality prints to be made. The maximum size of the print is primarily determined by the number of pixels captured by the camera. The biggest file size on a 4 MP camera will generally allow bigger prints to be made compared to the biggest file size on a 3 MP camera. Remember also that variables other than pixel count determine image quality (see p58). General photo techniques, including the ISO, aperture and shutter speed combination, play their usual role in attaining a quality image. Knowing exactly how the images are to be used means the 'quality' setting can be selected with confidence. This decision can be made image by image. If in doubt, shoot at the highest quality setting. Large files can always be made smaller for email or web use through image-editing software, but making small files large creates unsatisfactory results.

Camera Megapixel Rating	Camera Pixel Resolution	Maximum Print Size in Centimetres	Maximum Print Size in Inches
0.3	640 x 480	5.3 x 4.0	2.1 x 1.6
1.3	1280 x 1240	10.9 x 8.6	4.3 x 3.4
2	1600 x 1200	13.5 x 10.2	5.3 x 4.0
3	2000 x 1500	17.0 x 12.7	6.7 x 5.0
4	2448 x 1632	20.8 x 13.7	8.2 x 5.4
5	2560 x 1950	21.6 x 16.5	8.5 x 6.5
6	3008 x 2000	25.4 x 17.0	10.0 x 6.7
8	3264 x 2448	29.2 x 19.3	11.5 x 7.6
11	4064 x 2704	34.3 x 22.9	13.5 x 9.0
13.5	4500 x 3000	38.0 x 25.4	15.0 x 10.0

This table shows the maximum print size recommended for high-quality photo prints from 0.3 MP to 13.5 MP cameras set on the highest JPEG image quality setting. The table is adapted from data provided by the Digital Image Submission Criteria (DISC) working group (see Useful Websites, p256). The table assumes the full frame of the image is used. If you crop the image the maximum print size will be reduced unless you're willing to sacrifice print quality. Opinion varies as to the maximum-size photo-quality print that can be achieved from each MP value. Camera manufacturers are generally more liberal in their recommendations, and their claims vary considerably from camera to camera. Treat this table as a starting point for your own research and tests.

Memory Cards

Most digital cameras store images on removable and reusable memory cards instead of film. Sometimes referred to as digital film, memory cards are available in various formats, storage capacities, qualities and prices.

Formats

The memory-card format that a camera uses is determined at the manufacturing stage. Most cameras have a single memory-card slot built into the camera body, but there are models that have slots for two different cards. The memory-card slot is compatible with one type of memory-card format. Common formats include Secure Digital (SD), Multimedia Memory Card (MMC), Memory Stick (MS), CompactFlash (CF), CompactFlash Type 11 (CF11) and Extreme Digital (xD).

Another storage option you'll come across is the Microdrive. It's not a card format but a miniature hard disk based on the dimensions of a CompactFlash Type 11 card and compatible with most cameras that accept CF11 memory cards.

Storage Capacity

The storage capacity of memory cards is described in megabytes and gigabytes. Cards are available in a range of capacities including 2, 4, 8, 16, 32, 64, 128, 256 and 512 MB and 1, 2, 4, 6 and 8 GB. Not all formats are available in every size. Greater storage capacity equals higher price. The actual number of images that can be stored on a memory card varies depending on the image quality or file size selected, the content and complexity of the image, and specification differences from camera to camera.

		MP RESOLUTION					
		0.3 MP 640 x 480	1 MP 1200 x 900	2 MP 1650 x 1200	3 MP 2000 x 1500	4 MP 2400 x 1700	5 MP 2750 x 1900	6 MP 3000 x 2000
CARD SIZE	16 MB	120-130	30-45	17-19	11-13	8-9	6-7	5-6
	32 MB	230-260	61-90	34-39	23-26	16-19	12-15	10-12
	64 MB	450-520	122-180	68-78	47-53	32-39	24-30	20-24
	128 MB	900-1040	244-360	136-156	95-106	64-79	48-61	40-49
	256 MB	1840-2080	489-720	272-312	191-213	128-159	96-122	80-98
	512 MB	3600-4100	978-1440	544-625	382-426	256-319	192-244	160-197
	1 GB	7000-8000	1956-2880	1088-1251	764-853	512-638	384-489	320-394
	2 GB	n/a	3900-5760	2200-2500	1520-1700	1000-1250	750-970	640-750
	4 GB	n/a	7800-11500	4400-5000	3000-3400	2000-2500	1500-1930	1250-1500

This table shows the approximate number of digital images that various size memory cards can hold in different megapixel cameras. Image number range is based on high-resolution JPEG setting. Results vary considerably from camera to camera. Treat this table as a guide only. Refer to individual camera specifications for exact capacities.

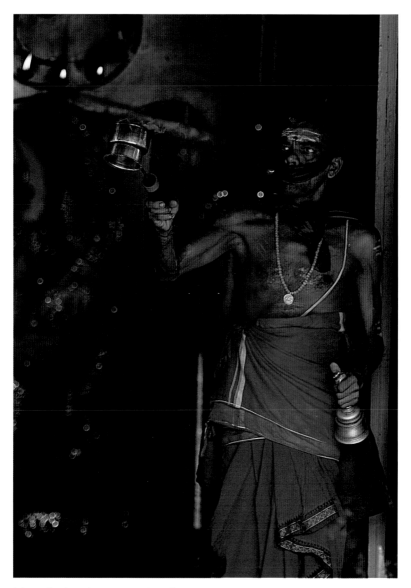

Priest performing puja, Kataragama, Sri Lanka

It was starting to look like a photo of the priest performing prayers was not going to happen. His activities were clearly focussed inside the temple and I was made to stand behind a rope much too far away from the action for my liking. When I'd all but given up he stepped into the light of the porch. A second later he was back inside and the puja was over. This was the only time the lens multiplier factor worked for me, extending my 70-200mm zoom to a 112-320mm zoom just long enough to get this shot.

▲ Professional DSLR, 70-200mm lens at 120mm, 1/100 f2.8, 100 ISO, 3072 x 2048, fine JPEG

Quality & Price

Memory cards are manufactured with varying component quality and technical specifications to suit different user budgets and needs. The more expensive cards in each brand range are made from higher quality components backed by a lifetime guarantee. They may also offer faster read and write speeds. Write speed determines how fast the image is recorded onto the card. Read speed determines how quickly the image can be reviewed on the LCD screen. These are important factors in ensuring that the camera is ready as quickly as possible to capture the next image. Additionally, the highest priced cards are guaranteed to work in extreme low and high temperatures and to withstand the rigours that professional camera equipment is often put through.

How much Memory Capacity to Take?

How much memory-card capacity to take on a trip is a difficult decision. Ultimately, it depends on the length of your trip, how many pictures you anticipate taking, the file size you select and how you intend to manage the image files. What's for sure is that the 8, 16 or 32 MB memory card that comes with the camera will be nowhere near enough for the travelling photographer. You'll want enough capacity on your card to store at least 72 images (refer to the table above). The decision can be made much easier if you have a clear plan on how to manage the files.

If you intend to rigorously review your pictures and delete the unwanted ones, you could probably select an appropriate film card to cover your needs. In this case, remember that you're only counting the good pictures. Judicious editing will mean that the memory card only needs to store your good pictures, not the ones that usually end up in the rubbish bin. An interesting option to make review and selection easier and more fun than scrutinizing your work on the camera's tiny LCD screen is to carry the AV cables that come with most digital cameras and let you connect your camera to a TV set. Most cameras are PAL and NTSC compatible so you can view your pictures anywhere you can access a TV set. If this plan works for you it's still strongly recommended that you carry a spare card (see p84).

However, you may prefer to review your pictures at the end of the trip in the comfort of your home. This will give you access to the benefits provided by a personal computer with its superior processing speed and large monitor. In this case, you may choose to carry enough memory card capacity for the entire trip. More highly recommended is the use of a portable storage device (see p83).

What Can Go Wrong?

One of the wonders of digital photography is that it's possible to capture an entire trip on one tiny bit of plastic as big as a postage stamp. Unfortunately, the digital advantage may be negated if any of the following happen:

▸ The memory card is removed before the camera has finished writing to the card. Always wait until the image has been saved before turning the camera off.
▸ The memory card is removed while the camera is turned on.
▸ The Compact Flash or Microdrive memory card is inserted carelessly. This can result in damaging the connector pins in the camera body, preventing it from accepting cards and resulting in an expensive camera repair.

- The memory card is damaged by an electromagnetic field. Keep memory cards away from TVs, computer monitors, microwaves and, especially, mobile phones.
- The Microdrive's spinning disk is damaged. When not in use Microdrives are very robust, but when reading or writing data they're susceptible to damage.
- The battery fails during writing.
- The memory card is damaged. They're not indestructible. When the card is not in the camera, store it in a purpose-made dust- and moisture-free container, out of direct sunlight and away from heat sources (just like film).
- The memory card is lost. They're very small and easy to misplace.
- The device containing the memory card is stolen. Unlike film, storage devices are expensive pieces of desirable hardware and need to be protected from theft.
- The memory card is rendered useless or corrupted through mishandling or by a computer virus.

The good news is that if the problem is a technical one, data-recovery software is cheap and effective. Some photo retailers provide a data-recovery service. Alternatively, download software from the Internet and do it yourself (see p256).

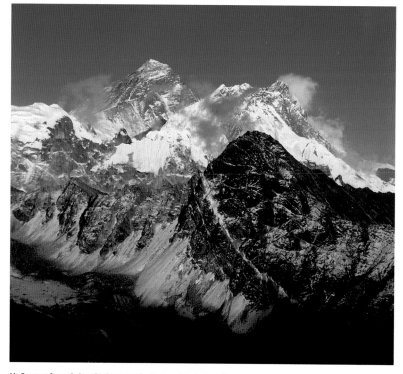

Mt Everest from Gokyo Ri, Sagarmatha National Park, Nepal

Adding another camera to my already weighty bag on a 20-day trek, just to see how good digital was for myself, didn't seem such a good idea at the start of the steep walk up Gokyo Ri. Cold conditions (-5°C) and high altitude (5483m) are a good test for any camera, and its batteries. The camera passed the test with flying colours and the opportunity to review the images during the evening more than made up for the extra weight.

▲ Advanced digital compact, 6.3-63.2mm lens at 14mm, 1/500 f6.3, 80 ISO, 2304 x 1728, 4 MP JPEG

CAMERA FEATURES

Users of film cameras will recognise many of the features built into digital cameras, such as different exposure modes, spot metering, flash options, subject modes, exposure compensation, auto bracketing and depth-of-field preview. However, there are a whole load of features that are unique to digital image capture.

Electronic Viewfinder

Most digital compact cameras have the familiar optical viewfinder that you hold up to your eye to compose images, but some advanced compact cameras feature an electronic viewfinder (EVF). Its main advantage is that it allows you to view through the lens, eliminating the need to switch to the LCD screen for close-ups. Additionally, the data display and the instant review image are shown in the viewfinder, so the camera doesn't have to be taken from the eye to see the shot you've just taken. EFVs do have some disadvantages: they display poor-quality colour, images have a granular-looking appearance, they can white-out or get filled with vertical white streaks when taking backlit shots and they use power.

Liquid Crystal Display (LCD) Screen

Digital cameras have an LCD screen on the back of the body. This is one of the most obvious physical differences between film and digital cameras. The screen allows images to be reviewed and on compact cameras it can be used as an alternative to the optical viewfinder as a compositional tool. The LCD also gives access to control menus and camera settings. LCD screen size varies from camera to camera. Most are between 4cm and 5cm wide. Generally, larger screens make viewing more comfortable. Some screens are more viewable in bright light than others – check the performance of an LCD screen in different lighting conditions.

If your compact camera has an optical viewfinder it's much better to get into the habit of composing images through the viewfinder rather than with the LCD screen. The screen can be hard to see in bright sunlight. More importantly, it's a major drain on battery power. However, most viewfinders typically show between 80% and 90% of the field of view, so there are occasions when composing with the screen is recommended, as the screen displays the same view as the lens. Use it for accurate framing generally and especially when your subject is less than one metre away. It's also necessary to use the screen when taking pictures with digital zoom because the effect can't be seen through an optical viewfinder. Some LCD screens are hinged and can be flipped out and rotated. This is a very useful feature as it allows you to adjust the screen to provide the best view when shooting in bright outdoor lighting where a fixed screen can be hard to view. It's also an excellent tool for quick variation of viewpoints. You can easily compose pictures using a very low angle (you only have to get on your knees, not your stomach) and in crowded situations you can hold the camera up over people's heads, just like the press photographers.

Image Review

Image review, or playback, is usually available in various formats. Images can be viewed individually; as a series of tiny images, usually called thumbnails or index display; or as a slide show where the pictures are displayed one after the other for a few seconds each. Images can also be magnified for a closer look at details such as facial expressions, and to confirm sharpness using a feature called playback zoom. The degree of magnification varies from model to model but all cameras let you move about the display to view different areas of the image using a four-way controller.

▶ **Concentrate on shooting; review later.**

Avoid getting into the habit of reviewing every image as you take it: most cameras take one or two seconds for the image to appear on the screen and while you're waiting (and looking at the photo you just took) you may miss an even better shot.

When reviewing images to decide which ones to delete, always use the magnification or playback zoom function to confirm that the image is in focus. Assessing how well focussed, or how sharp, an image is on an LCD screen takes time and practice. Even with powerful magnification review tools it's impossible on a 5cm screen to be absolutely positive of critical sharpness. If in doubt, don't delete. Wait until you can analyse the image properly on a computer monitor.

Histograms

It's also very hard to tell if an image is correctly exposed on a tiny LCD screen that changes in appearance with even the slightest alteration in viewing angle. Lots of practice will give you some confidence that your exposures are correct. Digital, as you'd expect, also provides a more immediate solution in the form of a histogram. Histograms are a graphic

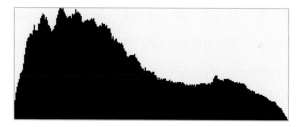

◀ **Histogram**

A graphic representation of the image below showing how the pixels are distributed across the tonal range of the image and their relative weighting in the shadow, mid-tone and highlight areas.

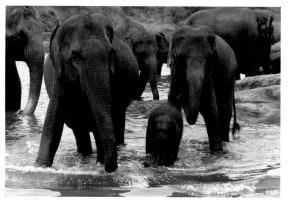

Elephants bathing, Pinnewala, Sri Lanka

Bathing time for the 60-odd elephants at the Pinnewala Elephant Orphanage is one of Sri Lanka's great sights. For two hours they drink, wash and play in the river, enthralling the hundreds of tourists gathered on the bank and in the riverside restaurants. Getting close isn't a problem, the trick is to isolate a moment of interest, such as this baby heading out of the water, escorted by two protective adults.

◀ Professional DSLR, 70-200mm lens at 70mm, 1/200 f4,100 ISO, 3072 x 2048, RAW

representation of the distribution of pixels in the image, showing their relative weighting in the shadow, mid-tone and highlight areas. The histogram is viewed on the LCD screen. For general photography the aim is to see pixels spread across the horizontal axis with most of them in the centre of the graph, indicating that detail has been recorded in the mid-tones, shadows and highlights. The histogram is an advanced feature and is not available on all cameras.

Metadata

Many cameras record and store information about each photograph as it's taken using EXIF (Exchangeable Image Format). Shooting data such as date, time, shutter speed, aperture, focal length (even when using zoom lenses), image-quality setting, image size and file format is recorded automatically. On advanced cameras this metadata is attached to the image file and can be reviewed on the LCD screen alongside the image. You can also access the EXIF metadata when the file is displayed on a PC. Go to File>File Info. This opens a dialogue box that either shows the metadata or allows you to insert general information. Click on the 'Section' box to access the EXIF metadata. This is a great learning tool and certainly beats taking notes.

Video Mode

A feature becoming more common across the range of compact digital cameras is Video Mode, allowing the capture of moving images. DSLRs can't capture video. The length of the clip that can be captured on compact cameras varies from around 15 seconds to continuous recording (limited only by the capacity of the memory card), depending on the camera. If capturing video on your digital camera is important check the frame rate specification. Anything below 15 frames per second (fps) will be visibly jerky. Fifteen fps offers borderline quality. You need about 20 fps for the clip to look as smooth as standard video footage.

Be aware that using the video mode drains batteries fast and fills memory cards.

Sound Annotation

Some cameras have built-in microphones to allow sound to be captured with video clips or to add brief spoken annotations to still images. Sound clips are usually limited to between five and 20 seconds. Important information can be captured at the time of shooting, which can be useful for identifying subjects and makes editing and cataloguing easier. It also means still photographers can now stand around talking to themselves, just like people with video cameras!

Burst Mode

To help overcome the annoying delay between shots most cameras have a burst mode, which allows the camera to take several pictures continuously. It varies from camera to camera, but on advanced compacts a typical burst produces two to three shots per second, with a maximum of five or six shots in one burst. To achieve this, images are either captured at a lower resolution or, preferably, high resolution images are stored in the camera's buffer memory and processed all at once at the end of the burst. The mode is very useful for action shots and any moving subject. It's also handy for portraits, where facial expressions change quickly. Remember, the camera has to process the files at some point, so plan ahead so that it's not writing to the memory card at the high point of the action.

Buffer Memory

Digital cameras have built-in, or buffer, memory where the raw data is processed into the final image file, after which it is written to the memory card. The amount of memory determines how many shots can be taken in burst mode before the images have to be processed.

AC Power Connecter

Cameras with an AC socket can be connected to the permanent electricity supply. This allows batteries to be recharged in the camera, and for electric power to be used when the camera is connected to the computer, minimising the possibility of disruption during image transfer.

Video Out

Cameras with a 'video out' socket can be connected directly to a TV. Images can then be viewed on a large screen using the camera's review mode. Is this the new slide show?

Batteries

You've probably already gathered that digital cameras use a lot of power. Unlike film cameras, you can't put a new battery in at the start of a month-long trip and expect it to last. It won't. Battery power is consumed at every step of the way, including turning the camera on and off, using the LCD screen, zooming and focussing, using an electronic viewfinder, reviewing and deleting images, firing the flash, using image-stabilisation lenses, writing images to the memory card, and transferring files from the camera. In other words – everything!

The latest models from quality manufacturers include power-saving facilities that have led to lower battery consumption in most cameras. Even so, managing battery power is a serious business when you're on the road and should be considered when you're shopping for a camera. Buy a camera that comes with a rechargeable battery – most do, but check. Definitely avoid cameras that only use common AA or AAA alkaline batteries because they're only good for around 20–30 shots. You're likely to come across three types of rechargeable battery; all have their strengths and weaknesses:

▸ The common AA Nickel Cadmium (NiCd) rechargeable batteries suffer from what's known as 'memory effect'. This results in reduced power levels if they're not fully discharged before recharging, which can be a bit inconvenient. However, they can be recharged up to 1000 times.

▸ Nickel Metal Hydride (NiMH) batteries have much greater capacity on each charge than NiCds, and they can be recharged at any time. They're only a bit more expensive than NiCds when you consider the total lifetime of the battery and are much cheaper to run than alkalines. The only downside is that they can only be recharged approximately 500 times.

▸ Many cameras use Lithium-ion (Lion) batteries. They're the most expensive but offer the greatest capacity per charge. Be aware that many cameras are supplied with a camera-specific Lion battery. This makes it especially important to carry spares – availability on the road can't be guaranteed.

Once you've got your camera with rechargeable battery don't leave home without:

▸ at least one spare rechargeable battery

▸ at least one set of non-rechargeable batteries if your camera uses AA or AAA cells (in case recharging is not possible)

▸ power conversion adaptor plugs

▸ the battery recharger and cables.

COLOUR & CREATIVE CONTROLS

Most digital cameras suitable for serious photography have a range of colour and creative controls that can be applied to suit the photographer's preferences. Less sophisticated cameras often offer a choice of three pre-sets. Higher-end cameras offer sliding scales for precise adjustment. If you're going straight to print from the memory card you may want to experiment with these controls. If you're going to upload the images to a computer it's advisable to leave most of the options in the auto or off position. Once recorded in the image file the results of the settings you chose can't be altered. Additionally, image-editing software offers more options and finer tuning than is possible in the camera. Requiring the camera to perform additional processing tasks also adds to the delay between shots and uses battery power.

Colour can be influenced with film cameras through choice of film type (colour, B&W, daylight or tungsten), film brand and filtration. Standard digital cameras allow basic colour selection options such as colour, B&W or sepia. Advanced cameras may also offer control over colour space, contrast sharpness and colour saturation. All cameras have white-balance control but in low-end models no adjustments can be made.

Colour Space

Colour space refers to the spectrum of colours that are available to create the image. Most digital cameras use the Red Green Blue colour space, known as RGB. This is predetermined by the manufacturer and is of little interest to compact-camera users. All DSLRs offer an alternate colour space known as Adobe RGB, which offers a broader colour range for the photographer to work with.

Saturation Control

Colour can be set to look natural or with varying degrees of saturation. Selecting the saturated setting on a standard compact camera increases the strength of colour in the image. Many compact digital cameras have inherently high saturation settings, which can be brought back to a more normal level by lowering the saturation control. More advanced cameras allow more precise variation in saturation.

White Balance

All digital cameras have an auto white balance function that adjusts the colours to ensure that white is recorded as white under all lighting conditions. Most cameras also have a range of pre-sets that typically include tungsten and fluorescent lighting settings. An increasing number of models include a pre-set for cloudy or shade conditions and some have several settings for balancing the different types of fluorescent light. Some recent models include 'sunset' and 'flash' pre-sets. Many of the more expensive models include a 'custom' or 'one-touch' setting which lets the photographer measure the colour of the ambient light and apply a suitable correction.

Contrast Control

Contrast refers to the difference between the lightest and darkest parts of the image. The contrast control allows the photographer to change the number of intermediate tones between the darkest shadows and brightest highlights recorded. A high-contrast image

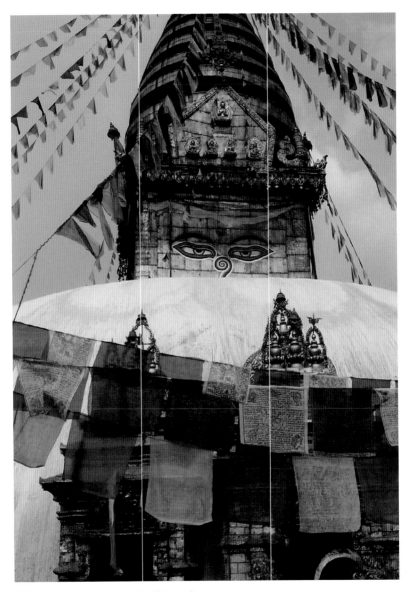

Swayambhunath Stupa, Kathmandu Valley, Nepal
Three images captured at the high-, medium- and low-resolution settings on a 4 MP compact camera enlarged to 20cm x 25cm (8in x 10in).

▲ Digital advanced compact,
6.3-63.2mm lens at 7mm, 1/350 f4.8,
100 ISO, 1728 x 2304,
high resolution (Best) JPEG

▲ Digital advanced compact,
6.3-63.2mm lens at 7mm, 1/350 f4.8,
100 ISO, 1242 x 1656,
medium resolution (Better) JPEG

▲ Digital advanced compact,
6.3-63.2mm lens at 7mm, 1/350 f4.8,
100 ISO, 900 x 1200,
low resolution (Good) JPEG

has a greater number of B&W pixels than an image with normal contrast. One problem with compact cameras is their limited dynamic range, or range of light levels that the sensor is able to record. This can result in blown-out, or overexposed, highlights and blocked-up, or underexposed, shadows in photographs taken in bright outdoor light. The dynamic range can be extended slightly by reducing the contrast setting. Varying the contrast in the camera is only recommended if images are to be viewed on a monitor or printed directly from the memory card.

Sharpening Control

Images can be made to appear sharper or softer through the use of a filter which increases or decreases the contrast between objects in the image. If used to excess, the sharpening control can produce white or black lines along edges of high contrast. This degrades picture quality. Its use is only recommended if images are to be viewed on a monitor or printed directly from the memory card.

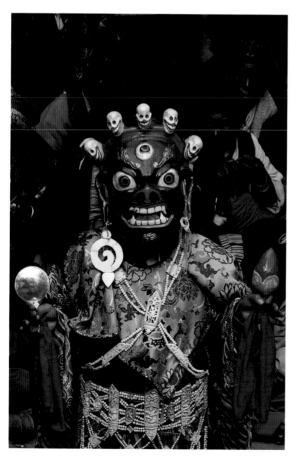

Masked dancer at Mani Rimdu Festival, Tengboche, Sagarmatha National Park, Nepal

Most compact digital cameras have a delay between the moment the shutter is pressed and when the exposure is made. This is quite annoying at first, especially when the subject is moving. The delay can be significantly reduced by a change in technique. Focus on the subject, which requires pressing the shutter button halfway, and keep the focus locked until you're ready to take the photo.

◀ Advanced compact digital, 6.3-63.2mm lens at 61mm, 1/350 f3.6, 80 ISO, 1728 x 2304, 4 MP JPEG

PREPARING TO BUY

In the compact-camera category there is a mind-boggling array of digital cameras to choose from. There's a seemingly constant supply of new models with more sophisticated features and boundary-pushing technology hitting the shelves weekly. It's easy to be overwhelmed with choice and to be confused by the new technology and jargon. If you're thinking about buying a digital camera consider:

▸ **how much you want to spend**
▸ **what you want to do with your pictures**
▸ **what kind of pictures you want to take.**

If you only require digital images for emails, web use or computer-based presentations, a simple compact camera with a sensor up to 1 MP will suffice. If you want postcard-size prints to put in an album, with the occasional shot enlarged up to 20cm x 25cm (8in x 10in), a 2 MP to 3 MP camera will do the job. If you take thousands of images and want to produce results that rival colour-transparency film and can be printed up to 40cm x 50cm (16in x 20in), you'll need to consider a professional DSLR with a 6 MP sensor. This is also what you'll need in order to have your pictures of a quality good enough to be reproduced in books and magazines.

There are two types of digital camera that are of most interest to travellers: compacts and DSLR. As with film cameras, higher prices should buy a camera with more features and better-quality components, construction and optics. In the digital world it also means more pixels, larger pixels, larger sensors, more in-camera computer memory and increasingly sophisticated and faster in-camera image-processing software. The quickest way to get a sense of what's out there and determine how much you'll need to spend to meet your photographic needs is to go online. The Internet is a great resource, especially once you're comfortable with the technology and terminology. There's a heap of information on every aspect of digital imaging, including test reports, camera comparisons, technical specifications, price guides, personal opinions, sample images, manufacturers' propaganda and lots of valuable and up-to-date information on buying and using digital cameras.

Visiting a large retailer is also a good idea. A good salesperson will quickly match your needs and budget and come up with a short list of possibilities. Spend time handling these cameras and take photos in and around the shop. It's the only way you'll discover which cameras fit comfortably in your hand, feel balanced, are easy to use, are too heavy or too light, or too big or too small. You'll also be able to determine if the controls and menus are easy for you to access and operate and if it feels comfortable to take, review and delete images. You should be able to access all key controls with fewer than three clicks of a button, or toggles of a switch.

Shopping around will also show you how much retail prices can vary, especially when a model is about to be superseded. Always check the warranty. This is particularly important if buying on the Internet or outside your own country. Make sure the warranty covers your home country and those you intend visiting. No matter how or where you buy your camera use it intensively in the first few days so that any problems are detected immediately. It's possible to buy a camera, take it out the box, set it on auto and get good pictures. But to ensure minimal problems, buy the camera far enough in advance to give yourself time to become totally familiar with all its functions and creative possibilities, especially if it's your first digital camera.

The prices given in this chapter are even more vulnerable to change than traditional photographic equipment. A year is a long time in the digital photography industry, and prices, features and performance of all products are changing rapidly. You should get opinions, quotes and advice from a number of places before you part with your hard-earned cash. The prices given should be regarded as a guide only and are not a substitute for your own careful, up-to-date research.

Compact Digital Cameras

Compact digital cameras are ideal for taking photos with a minimum of fuss – perfect if you want to travel light.

ADVANTAGES

- no accessories required
- easy to use
- good as second or backup camera for DSLR users
- image sensors range from 0.3 MP to 8 MP
- majority of cameras have a fully automatic mode and built-in flash and zoom lens
- models available to suit all budgets
- most cameras accept a removable and reusable memory card
- most models have at least three image-quality settings
- small, light and easily carried in a pocket or small bag
- underwater housing available for many models
- weatherproof models available
- wide range of sizes and styles

DISADVANTAGES

- battery power must be managed and batteries regularly charged to ensure the camera is always ready to go
- cannot change lenses
- cheaper models have low-quality lenses
- prices are higher than for film cameras offering comparable quality and features
- some cameras restrict file size when high ISO settings are selected
- lenses produce much greater depth of field compared to a 35mm film camera, which means selective focusing (throwing the background out of focus) can be very difficult to achieve
- accurate framing is limited when subjects are composed through an optical viewfinder (not the lens)
- battery power is consumed when subjects are viewed via an electronic viewfinder or LCD screen

Basic Compact Digital Cameras

The compact digital range starts with simple point-and-shoot cameras with a fixed lens, small LCD screen and low-power flash that fires automatically when the light is low (but can't be turned off). Resolution is low, with sensor sizes ranging from 0.3 MP to 1 MP. Memory is built-in and memory cards may not be accepted. Focus is fixed or has simple auto-focus controlled by one sensor in the middle of the frame. ISO is set automatically and can't be altered. White-balance adjustment is also not possible. Prices range from US$65 to US$199.

These cameras offer an inexpensive way to capture images to email, post on the web or use in computer-generated presentations, but are not suitable for printing. Often marketed towards children, they're not recommended for anyone interested in taking good pictures.

A little more money will buy a camera with a 2 MP sensor and removable memory card. These are still very simple to use but reasonable-quality prints up to 15cm x 20cm (6in x 8in) can be made from the better models in the range. Variation in image quality and price is due to the sensor technology used. The cheapest models often have cheap CMOS sensors that produce pretty awful colour and very granular looking images. Prices range from US$90 to US$300.

Standard Compact Digital Cameras

More highly recommended is the next level of compacts with 3 MP to 4 MP sensors. The 3 MP cameras in this category have led the way in making digital capture with impressive quality available at an affordable price. The result is that they've quickly become the first choice for family and holiday photography, just about pushing compact 35mm and APS film cameras out of the market. They offer similar results to film, if print size is restricted to less than 25cm x 20cm (10in x 8in). Prices range from US$200 to US$700. In automatic mode they're point-and-shoot cameras, but they have a number of features that give some control over composition and exposure. Cameras in this category often feature:

‣ 3x optical zoom lens
‣ auto-focus lens, often with manual focus pre-sets and macro capability to 10cm or less
‣ built-in flash with optional settings for red-eye reduction, fill-flash, night flash and flash off
‣ focus lock
‣ LCD screen
‣ moderate zoom lens range, around 6mm-18mm (36mm-108mm 35mm equivalent)
‣ optical viewfinder
‣ pre-set shooting modes for portrait, landscape, action and close-up pictures
‣ orientation sensor to rotate vertical images
‣ 'quick delete' button
‣ 'quick review' button
‣ slot for removable memory card
‣ three image-quality settings
‣ various review options
‣ varying levels of manual control.

Advanced Compact Digital Cameras

Advanced compact digital cameras offer another step up again in terms of functionality, features, performance and image quality. They're aimed at people who want more control over the picture-taking process but who don't want to carry the additional weight and size of a DSLR. Excellent print quality can be expected up to 40cm x 50cm (16in x 20in) with some manufacturers claiming film-quality 50cm x 76cm (20in x 30in) prints are possible. Some models offer powerful 6, 8, 10 or 12x optical zoom lenses. These cameras are physically bigger than traditional compact cameras to accommodate the lens; they look and feel like a cross between a compact and a DSLR camera. Cameras in this category have 4 MP to 8 MP sensors and range in price from US$600 to US$1500. If you want to capture your travels digitally and don't want to use a DSLR camera, an advanced compact is highly recommended. They offer everything that the standard compacts have plus many other features, such as:

- 4-5x optical zoom
- adjustable viewfinder diopter
- burst mode
- controls to adjust colour, contrast and sharpness
- digital zoom
- excellent build and component quality
- excellent-quality lens
- focus and exposure lock for accurate focussing and exposure of the main subject
- hot shoe for external flash
- image file data display
- increased ISO range
- increased white-balance options
- manual exposure modes
- multi-point auto-focus sensors to handle off-centre subjects
- self-timer
- clip-on conversion lenses and filters
- sound annotation
- video mode with sound capture.

DSLR Cameras

DSLR cameras look and feel like their film-based counterparts. As with film-based SLRs, you can't go past a DSLR for serious travel photography. In addition to weighing up the features unique to a DSLR, refer to p36 for general advice on buying SLR cameras.

DSLRs are available in a wide price range, with varying sensor sizes and build quality. Right now the entry price point is considerably higher than for equivalent 35mm film SLRs and the range of cameras is small, but the number of cameras in each category is bound to grow and prices will drop.

ADVANTAGES

- all DSLRs have a fully automatic setting making them easy to use even for the digitally challenged
- interchangeable lenses and accessories to suit every application
- large buffer memory to minimise delay between frames
- most models have built-in flash units
- most models have sophisticated light meters and auto-focus lens systems as standard features
- subject is viewed through the lens
- typically based on existing film camera systems, allowing the same lenses to be used

DISADVANTAGES

- heavier and bulkier than compact cameras
- investment in or upgrade of computer equipment and software may be required
- lens multiplier factor may require purchase of additional lenses
- more expensive than compact cameras with equivalent MP sensor
- more expensive than comparable film cameras

Standard DSLR Cameras

The standard DSLR category provides entry-level cameras aimed at the first-time SLR user.

They're compact, light and may be supplied with inexpensive, but slow, zoom lenses to allow attractive pricing. Most cameras are available as body-only purchases to allow consumers to buy a DSLR body to match their film SLR lenses. Most cameras have sensors with a minimum of 6 MP capable of producing excellent film-quality prints up to 33cm x 48cm (13in x 19in). Prices range from US$800 to US$1500 for a camera body and zoom lens. The list of features you can expect is long and will probably include:

‣ adjustable viewfinder diopter
‣ burst mode
‣ CompactFlash Type II slots that can accept high-speed cards and Microdrives
‣ controls for adjusting colour, contrast and sharpness
‣ focus and exposure lock
‣ histogram
‣ hot shoe for external flash
‣ image file data display
‣ manual exposure modes
‣ multi-point auto-focus sensors with selectable focus points
‣ orientation sensor to rotate vertical images
‣ RAW file capture
‣ self-timer
‣ wide range of file size and compression settings.

Professional DSLR Cameras

Aimed at the advanced amateur and professional photographer, cameras in this category have 4 MP to 14 MP sensors to suit the varying applications required by working photographers and are capable of producing excellent-quality prints up to 50cm x 40cm (20in x 16in). The high-end cameras in this range offer the ultimate in SLR digital capture and include models with full-frame sensors. Prices range from US$1300 to US$8000 (for camera body only). More robust than standard DSLRs they have all the features of the entry level DSLRs plus an expanded functionality list and more sophisticated image-processing controls including:

‣ advanced light-metering systems
‣ camera specifications tailored to suit specific professional applications
‣ colour-space options
‣ exceptional build quality
‣ extended ISO range
‣ extended white-balance options
‣ fast auto-focus
‣ fine adjustment controls for sharpness, contrast, saturation and colour tone
‣ high burst rates
‣ increased file size and compression options
‣ increased working-temperature range for reliability in extreme temperatures
‣ large memory buffer
‣ manual override of all automatic functions
‣ negligible lag time (mostly less than 0.3 sec)
‣ sensor-cleaning mode.

LENSES FOR DIGITAL CAMERAS

Lens quality is just as important in digital photography as it is in film-based photography (see p24). There are also some unique features and issues to understand about lenses for both compact and DSLR cameras.

Optical & Digital Zoom Lenses for Compact Digital Cameras

Zoom lenses are standard on most compact digital cameras and are available with either an optical or digital zoom, or both. The focal-length range of zooms varies from camera to camera, and manufacturers make the range a major selling point. It's also common to differentiate between the optical and digital zoom capability. The range, or power, of the zoom is expressed as a number followed by an x. A lens with a focal length range of 6.3–63.2 is described as a 10x zoom. If the camera also features a 3x digital zoom it would be described as having a 10x optical zoom with a 3x digital zoom and a 30x total zoom. Optical zooms are far superior, so be sure to clarify the type and respective range on every camera you consider.

Optical zoom works by physically moving the lens in and out of the camera body to vary the focal length and magnify the subject accordingly. Digital zoom uses the camera's image processor to enlarge a portion of the image by creating and adding pixels to the image using a process called interpolation, which gives the illusion of zooming in. It's similar to cropping an image and then enlarging it to the same size as the original. Digital zooms offer what may appear to be extreme zooming capability, but often the results are disappointing due to the fact that extra pixels have to be generated to maintain the set file sizes, resulting in loss of image sharpness and a fall-off in image contrast. Camera shake may also be a problem (see p96). The same effect can by achieved in a computer much more satisfactorily due to better and more controllable interpolation processing, and you'll be working with the superior file captured by the optical zoom lens.

If your camera has both optical and digital zoom capabilities you may have to activate the digital zoom function through the menu. Otherwise, it moves through the optical range first, then switches to digital for continuous zoom. Better cameras let you know that you've exceeded the optical zoom range and are composing with the digital zoom, usually via a line graph on the display. Be aware that the effect of digital zoom can't be seen through an optical viewfinder; you must compose with the LCD screen unless your camera has an electronic viewfinder.

Conversion Lenses for Compact Digital Cameras

Compact digital cameras do not have interchangeable lenses. However, some advanced compacts accept conversion, or auxiliary, lenses that clip or screw onto the front of the prime lens. These lenses are optical accessories. Wide-angle conversion lenses increase the viewable area; telephoto conversion lenses magnify the subject; and close-up conversion lenses allow macro photography. These accessories may provide an economical solution for people who want to increase their compositional options without the expense of a DSLR outfit. As with traditional optical accessories like teleconverters and filters, it's inadvisable to buy cheap conversion lenses. Inferior optics will degrade the image file. One major problem with wide conversion lenses is the very obvious distortion that is introduced to the image. Note also that lens speed, or light-gathering power, is reduced by up to two stops. They're also very heavy and can unbalance the camera. Additionally, they can only be used with the LCD screen or an electronic viewfinder and therefore demand greater battery power. Cameras with electronic viewfinders have special settings in the menu that must be activated when using conversion lenses.

Lenses for DSLR Cameras

Most DSLR camera bodies are based on film systems and accept lenses from camera manufacturers' existing lens range. This is great news for photographers with a bag full of lenses who can keep their investment in digital camera gear down by only having to buy a digital body. However, there is a catch! Except in the most expensive professional digital cameras that incorporate full-size image sensors, the area covered by all other sensors is somewhat smaller than the 24mm x 36mm area covered by a frame of 35mm film. Consequently, when lenses made for 35mm film SLRs are attached to a digital body the effective focal length is increased. This is known as the lens multiplier factor (LMF), or focal length conversion factor. The multiplier factor is determined by the sensor's size relative to a 35mm film frame. For example, if the sensor is two-thirds the area of a frame of 35mm film the camera has a LMF of 1.5x. A 100mm lens becomes a 150mm lens on the digital body; a 24mm–70mm zoom lens becomes a 36mm–105mm zoom. This can be a real bonus at the telephoto end of your zoom because an 80mm–200mm becomes a 120mm–300mm lens. However, if you take a lot of pictures with a 24mm wide-angle lens you'll be disappointed – suddenly it will become a not-so-wide 36mm. Be prepared to buy at least one new lens when you buy a DSLR. On the upside, the maximum aperture is not affected. Also, the smaller coverage required means that manufacturers have the opportunity to make lenses specifically for digital cameras that are smaller, lighter and, in the consumer range, cheaper than lenses made for film SLRs. Note that these purpose-designed lenses for DSLRs can't be used on film SLRs as they have a smaller imaging circle and will vignette the image.

Because many people already understand focal length and the relative angle of view (see p24 and p106) based on 35mm film cameras, manufacturers provide 35mm-equivalent focal lengths in their advertising and technical specifications for digital cameras and lenses.

IMAGE TRANSFER

One of the great attractions of the digital medium is the elimination of film and processing costs. To achieve this saving, the images on the camera's memory card must be transferred to a storage device. They can then be erased from the card and it can be reused. This process also provides an alternative to buying and carrying enough memory cards to cover all your expected requirements. Images can be transferred to various storage devices, typically computers, portable storage devices, CDs or DVDs.

All digital cameras have a socket for connecting, or interfacing, the camera directly into a computer, portable storage device or printer. If you own a computer ensure that it has cable ports compatible with the camera's cable. Most use fast Universal Serial Bus (USB) cables, or the even faster USB2.0. Some professional DSLRs and one or two advanced compacts use fast FireWire (IEEE 1394) connection cables.

Software

Cameras come with software programs aimed at making the transfer of images from the camera easy. The programs provide drivers to support the downloading of image files to a computer, plus tools for enhancing photos. The bundled software varies in functionality from simple to sophisticated, often related to the price of the camera. Even the most basic programs enable images to be viewed as thumbnails, enlarged through a zoom or magnification function, resized for sending via email, and printed easily on a desktop printer. Simple editing tools enable retouching, cropping, red-eye reduction and image rotation. Some cameras are bundled with panorama stitching and basic video-editing software. Additionally, file management functions allow images to be catalogued for quick access. This bundled software is great for people who want to keep digital imaging simple. For those who want to explore the opportunities and possibilities of the digital imaging world, investment in more advanced image-editing software will probably be required. Additionally, if you're shooting large quantities of images, serious consideration should be given to a cataloguing program right from the start. Cameras that can capture images in the RAW file format are supplied with proprietary software to process and convert the files so they can be opened in other photo-editing programs.

Transfer to Computer

Images can be transferred or downloaded to a computer by connecting the camera directly to the computer with a USB cable that is supplied with the camera. Alternatively, images can be transferred via a card reader or camera dock. Image transfer to the computer's hard drive is easy and no special software is required. Modern computer operating systems recognise the camera, reader or dock as an external disk drive and display a dialogue box with options allowing users to decide what they want to do with the files. Typically, you have the choice of copying or moving files once the camera is connected to the computer. 'Copying' duplicates the image files on the PC and does not delete the original files from the memory card. 'Moving' transfers the image files to the computer, emptying the card of images.

Card Readers

Card readers are compact devices that connect to a computer via a USB port. Cards are inserted into the card reader and images are transferred at the touch of a button. Available in single- or multi-format versions they can be left attached to a computer, which means less fiddling around with cables every time you want to transfer images. Multi-format card readers are particularly useful if you're using two or more cameras that use different memory cards.

Camera Docks

Camera docks, also known as cradles, power bases or docking stations, are a particularly useful accessory made for specific camera models. They make transferring images to a computer simple and simultaneously charge the battery. The dock is connected to the computer via a USB cable and can be left permanently attached.

TRANSFERRING IMAGES ON THE ROAD

Managing memory cards is a lot like managing film, the main aim being not to run out of space on either. If you intend to transfer images and reuse the card rather than carry enough cards to last your entire trip you need to have a plan. The choices are:

▸ CD, using retail services
▸ portable computer
▸ portable storage device.

Remember, when transferring RAW files you won't be able to see the actual images unless the device you're transferring to has your camera's propriety software loaded.

Compact Disks

An excellent option for the traveller who wants to keep equipment, cost, weight and bulk down is to use local CD transfer services, available in most cities (and more and more remote places). Always ask the operator to run the completed CD to verify the transfer has been successful before deleting the images from your memory card.

Portable Computers

Carrying a portable (laptop or notebook) computer gives you the ultimate flexibility for dealing with image files on the road. Assuming you've got access to power to recharge the battery, enough hard drive for storage and enough RAM for fast processing, you can review your pictures anytime. The large screen allows more accurate assessment of the images before deciding whether or not to delete them. You can also make copies, organise, email, caption and enhance the photographs using your preferred software as you go. However, portable computers are heavy and they make you a target for theft so they may not suit all travellers, especially those visiting out-of-the-way places.

Portable Storage Devices

A more practical alternative, especially if you're travelling for a while and intend shooting hundreds or thousands of images, is a portable storage device. They're compact, light, easy to use and use rechargeable batteries. They accept most memory cards either directly or via an adapter. Capacity ranges from 5 GB to 60 GB, allowing thousands of high-resolution images to be stored, ready to be transferred to a computer at a later date. The higher-priced units have LCD screens, so images can be reviewed anytime and, just as importantly, allowing visual verification of successful transfer. Portable CD readers and CD-RW units let you store images on a hard drive and make backup copies on CD, making you totally self-reliant.

PROTECTING YOUR IMAGES

Like exposed film, memory cards and portable storage devices soon fill up with precious photos that need to be guarded with your life. There are several things you can do to ensure minimal loss:

▸ Carry a portable storage device and transfer images each evening.
▸ Back-up images from the portable storage device to CD regularly.
▸ Don't plan to shoot your entire trip on one high-capacity card. Although very attractive in terms of convenience (especially if you're shooting large JPEG or RAW files) if the card is damaged, lost or stolen you lose all your pictures. Several 1 GB or 512 MB cards offer more peace of mind. Be sure to store them carefully, since some of them are very small and easily mislaid.
▸ Ideally, transfer images to two CDs and post one or both home (on different days).
▸ If you're not carrying a portable storage device, transfer images to CD regularly.
▸ Store (or hide) the storage device in your room in a separate place to your camera or place it in hotel safety deposit box.
▸ When home, copy image files to CD or DVD. The ideal solution is to make two copies and store one off-site. If your computer is stolen or the hard disk crashes it's then easy to restore your precious image collection to a new computer.

This last point cannot be emphasised enough. Storing the only version of your digital images on a computer hard drive is a very different proposition to throwing negatives or prints in a shoebox or drawer. Fewer things can go wrong with a shoebox or drawer!

PRINTING DIGITAL IMAGES

Printing digital images is easy. You can print them yourself or order them from a digital print service. Either way, one of the most significant cost savings gained by digital capture is the opportunity to review images before they're printed, allowing you to select only the images you want to print, instead of having to print an entire roll of film. Prints can be made from a digital camera's memory card in various ways:

▸ Transfer the images to a computer and then print on a desktop printer or via an Internet print service.
▸ Connect the camera directly to a desktop printer or insert the memory card directly into a printer.
▸ Take the memory card to a photo shop for printing.
▸ Visit a self-serve printing kiosk.

Printing your own photos has never been easier, with an ever-expanding range of desktop printers that produce photo-quality prints. You'll find a wide range of models to suit every budget and application. Some printers are so compact they're being promoted as an accessory to be carried around so you can print on location.

If the 'no computer' option interests you there are several choices. Some printers have cable ports that connect directly to the camera. Another range of printers has built-in slots that accept single- or multi-format memory cards for direct printing from the card. For future flexibility consider buying a camera and printer that are PictBridge compatible. PictBridge technology is an industry standard that allows devices made by different manufacturers to be connected. The main benefit is that you have a greater choice of camera and printer combinations and one component can be upgraded without having to replace the other.

Internet print services allow you to select the images in your image-editing software, enhance them if you want (for example remove red-eye or crop), and send your order via email. You then pick up your prints at a nominated local retailer or they're posted to your address. For most users Internet services are best used for postcard-size prints. If you think this is all too new then you're a bit behind. The IDC research company has calculated that in 2002 around 114 million prints were ordered in the USA from online suppliers. That figure jumped to 343 million in 2003 and is expected to reach a staggering two billion in 2007.

Some digital print retailers are tailoring services specifically to travellers. One of the most interesting possibilities is the ability to share your pictures with family and friends back at home long before you return yourself. A complete service includes printing directly from your memory card, copying the files to CD so you can reuse the card, and posting the images to a password-protected website. Family and friends are told the website address and password. They go online and view your photos in the comfort of their own home. Of course, if someone got hold of your camera and reeled off a few indiscreet shots at that great party that you really don't want your mum to see, you simply don't select them for posting to the website. Yes, they've thought of everything. Finally, the people who care about you can then order prints themselves, which are sent to their address within a couple of days. Apparently, business is booming.

Another variation on developing and printing is self-serve printing kiosks. Often located in photo shops (but expect to see them in more and more places), the kiosks are set up to receive digital files from most storage media. No computer knowledge is required and after inserting your memory card the software takes over and prompts you step by step. You select the images you want to print and the size required. You can also generally perform many of the standard image-editing functions found in basic image-editing software such as colour correction, cropping, red-eye removal and alterations to brightness, contrast and sharpness. When you've completed your order it's sent via the Internet to a minilab, which outputs the prints on standard photographic paper.

Finally, if you want to keep it really simple, take the memory card to a photo retailer for printing. This is just like taking a roll of film to a photo shop for developing and printing. However, if you want to reuse the memory card and want the option of making reprints or enlargements later, you also need to order a copy of the files before deleting them from the memory card. The photo shop will do this at the time of printing by transferring the files to CD. You'll then have the digital equivalent of negatives.

Print It or Risk Losing It

Even though manufacturers are doing everything they can to make printing as easy as possible it appears many people are storing digital images on hard drives and CDs with the idea of printing at a later date. This resulted in the photographic industry launching a media campaign in 2003 that carried the message 'print it or risk losing it'. The aim was to get people to make prints sooner rather than later. The concern is that delay in printing may mean that images are lost forever due to damaged CDs or DVDs, hardware failures and obsolete software.

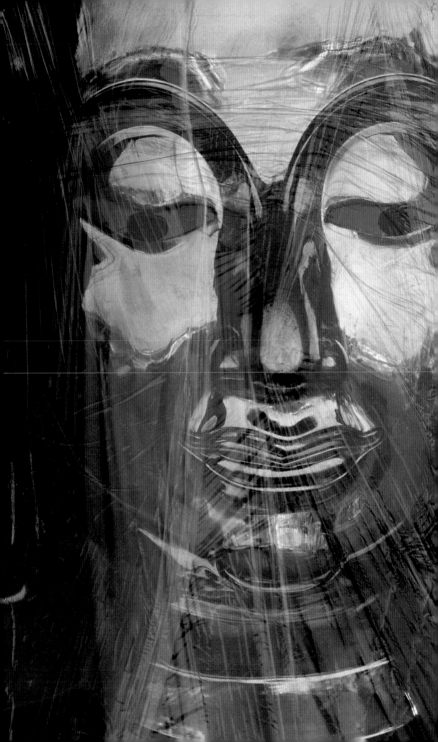

PART TWO:

For pictures to be more than simple snaps of a trip, it's important to understand some of the technical aspects of photography. Modern cameras have reduced the impact of common mistakes, like leaving the lens cap on, not putting film in the camera, setting the ISO incorrectly and inaccurate focussing, but no camera will make creative decisions for you, or get you to the right place at the right time. Time spent thinking about composition and the importance of light could make a dramatic difference to your photographs.

TAKING CONTROL

Buddha statue wrapped in plastic, Bangkok, Thailand
◄ 35mm SLR, 100mm lens, 1/125 f8, Ektachrome E100VS

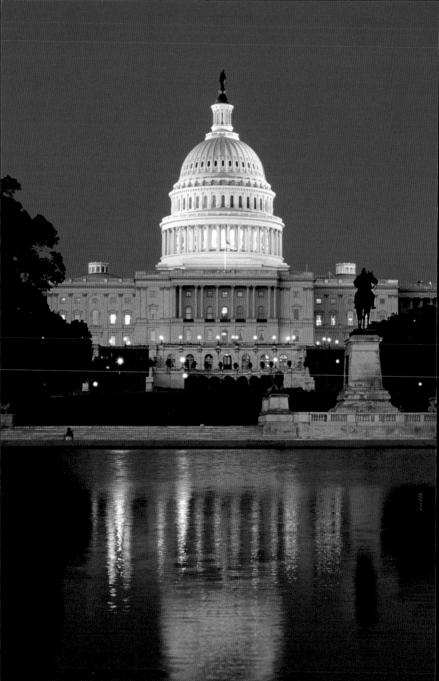

EXPOSURE

▶ **Setting the exposure is more than a technical necessity – it's a creative decision that controls the mood, quality and feel of the photograph.**

When you take a photograph you're translating what the eye sees, through the lens and onto the film or image sensor. The choices you make when setting the exposure play a big part in determining how well the translation happens.

Correct exposure means the film or sensor is exposed to just the right amount of light to record the intensity of colour and details in the scene that attracted you to take the photo in the first place. It's achieved through a combination of the film or sensor's ISO rating and the selection of the aperture and shutter speed.

SHUTTER SPEED

The shutter speed is the amount of time that the camera's shutter remains open to allow light onto the film or sensor. Shutter speeds are measured in seconds and fractions of seconds and run in a standard sequence: one second, and 1/2, 1/4, 1/8, 1/15, 1/30, 1/60, 1/125, 1/250, 1/500, 1/1000, 1/2000 and 1/4000 of a second. The higher the number, the faster the shutter speed and the less light allowed in. Many modern cameras allow intermediate settings such as a 1/90 of a second in automatic modes, but with manual cameras you can't set shutter speeds between these standard settings.

APERTURE

The aperture is the lens opening that lets light into the camera body. The aperture is variable in size and is measured in f-stops. The most familiar f-stop sequence, from the widest aperture to the smallest, is f1.4, f2, f2.8, f4, f5.6, f8, f11, f16 and f22. As you go up the scale to f22 you are 'stopping down', and with each stop you halve the amount of light that will reach the film. As you go down the scale to f1.4 each stop doubles the amount of light that will reach the film, and you are 'opening up' the lens until it's 'wide open' at its maximum aperture.

MEASURING LIGHT

Most modern cameras have built-in exposure meters that measure the amount of light reflected from the subject. All meters work on the principle that the subject is mid-tone; ie, not too light or too dark. In practice, most subjects are a mix of tones, but when the meter averages out the reflected light, a mid-tone reading results in a properly exposed image. When very light or very dark subjects dominate scenes, exposure compensation is required (see p92).

Capitol Building at dusk, Washington, DC, USA
◀ 35mm SLR, 35mm lens, 1/4 f11, Ektachrome E100VS, tripod

Centre-Weighted Meters These meters read the light reflected from the entire scene and provide an average exposure setting biased towards the centre section of the viewfinder. Generally, readings are accurate unless there are very large light or dark areas in the scene.

Multi-Zone Meters Now common in new mid-range SLRs, these sophisticated meters divide the scene into zones. They read the light in each zone and send the information to the camera's computer, which recognises the extreme tones and gives a reading based on what it evaluates as the most important parts of the scene. These are also called matrix, evaluative, multi-segment, multi-pattern and honeycomb-pattern meters.

Spot Meters These meters take a reading from a small defined area and are ideal for taking a reading of your main subject when it's part of an unevenly lit scene (backlit or spotlit).

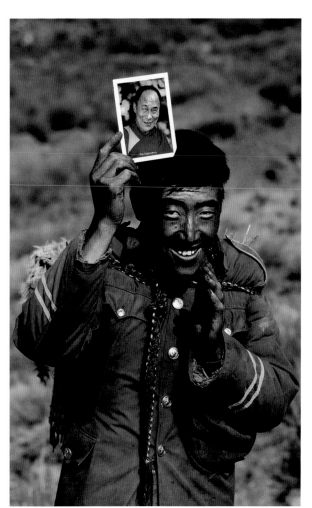

Man with Dalai Lama photo, Tibet, China

Built-in exposure meters set on automatic are perfect for when the lighting is even, the subject fills the frame and you've only got a split second to take the photo.

◄ 35mm SLR, 100mm, 1/125 f4, Kodachrome 64

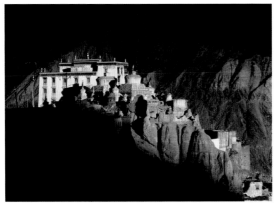

Lamayuru, Ladakh, India

As the last rays from the sun broke through the clouds the two elements that a travel photographer lives for came together: a great subject and great light. Because the scene contained very light and very dark areas, the camera's automatic meter reading averaged out the light levels. This resulted in some detail in the shadow area in the foreground, but the highlights in the monastery are washed out. The image lacks drama, colour and depth.

◄ 35mm SLR, 35mm lens, 1/30 f8, Kodachrome 64, tripod, average metering of scene

I used the camera's spot metering facility to take a reading from the building, choosing to retain the detail in the highlights, and allowing the darkest areas of the composition to go black. The result is a much stronger image with natural vignetting that takes the viewer's eye to the main subject.

◄ 35mm SLR, 35mm lens, 1/125 f8, Kodachrome 64, tripod, spot-metering on gompa

EXPOSURE MODES

Once the exposure meter has read the light, it recommends appropriate settings. Depending on your camera, you can prioritise the settings by selecting manual, semiautomatic or fully automatic exposure modes.

Manual Mode You set both the shutter speed and the aperture manually. Adjust either of the controls until the meter indicates correct exposure.

Shutter-Priority Auto Mode In this semiautomatic mode you select the shutter speed and the camera automatically selects an appropriate aperture.

Aperture-Priority Auto Mode In this semiautomatic mode you select the aperture and the camera automatically selects an appropriate shutter speed.

Program Auto Mode In this fully automatic mode the camera selects both the shutter speed and the aperture.

Subject Program Exposure Modes In these fully automatic modes you select a program mode to suit the subject (usually portrait, landscape, close-up, sport or night scene). The camera sets the appropriate shutter speed and aperture combination.

DETERMINING EXPOSURE

When you point your camera at a scene the meter recommends appropriate settings (depending on the exposure mode). You can accept the meter's recommendation or override it. One of the easiest and best methods of determining exposure is to expose for the main component of the image. In many cases the main component dominates the frame and exposure is straightforward. Difficulties arise when a scene contains large areas that are very light or dark, when shooting into the sun, when light sources are included in the frame, or when the subject is black or white. Try the following techniques when the lighting is difficult:

▸ Use the spot meter to take a reading off the subject.
▸ In manual mode, fill the frame with your subject, either by moving closer or zooming in, take a reading, then recompose ignoring the meter readout.
▸ In automatic mode, use the above technique but lock the exposure before you recompose or the meter will adjust the settings.
▸ On some fully automatic film SLRs, better compact digitals and all digital SLRs, override the meter settings using the exposure-compensation dial that allows over or underexposure of the film by third or half stops up to two or three stops. Turn the dial to +1 and you'll increase the amount of light reaching the film or sensor by one stop. Turn it to −1 and you'll decrease the amount of light by one stop. After ajusting the exposure-compensation dial remember to reset it.
▸ Manually adjust the film's ISO rating to trick the meter into allowing more or less light onto the film. This can only be done on automatic film cameras if you can override the film-speed setting automatically selected by the DX coding. To overexpose 100 ISO film by one stop, change the ISO setting to 50, doubling the amount of light that will reach the film. To underexpose by one stop, set the ISO to 200, and half the amount of light that will reach the film. This technique can't be used with digital cameras as the image sensor's sensitivity to light is varied electronically and will automatically compensate with a change in the shutter speed and aperture settings. After adjusting the ISO setting remember to reset it.

If the subject is black or white, the meter will average out the scene to a mid-tone. Your black or white subject will be rendered as a mid-grey if you don't compensate or override the meter's recommended settings. For white subjects take a reading off the subject and overexpose by one or two stops. For black subjects underexpose by one or two stops.

Colour Slide Film

Understanding the subtleties of exposure control is particularly important when using colour slide film. Slides can be unacceptable if they're overexposed (too light) or underexposed (too dark) by anything more than half a stop. However, as a general rule, colour slide film produces the best results when it's slightly underexposed. Slightly darker slides always look better than slides that are too light. This is easily achieved by exposing for the highlights, which ensures detail is retained in the lightest parts of the picture and produces more saturated, or stronger, colours. Many photographers also up-rate their colour slide film slightly by setting the ISO a quarter or a third of a stop above the actual film speed. Typically, 50 is rated at 64 ISO, 64 at 80 ISO and 100 at 125 ISO. Make sure you experiment with your own equipment and preferred film before shooting an entire trip worth of film at an up-rated ISO.

Colour Negative Film

In contrast, negative films are much more tolerant of exposure errors. It's possible for satisfactory prints to be made from negatives that are two stops over or underexposed. In fact, mistakes often go unnoticed because they're corrected automatically by the minilab when the prints are made. Although exposure latitude is greater with negative film, best results are produced when it's slightly overexposed. Expose for the shadows and the highlights will take care of themselves.

Image Sensors

Achieving correct exposure with digital cameras is essentially the same as with film cameras and just as important. Some cameras have a histogram function for analysing exposures (see p69).

The digital equivalent of the exposure-latitude variations between slide and negative film is the selection of file format. Shooting RAW files is comparable to exposing negative film. The unprocessed file allows images that were under or overexposed by up to two, or even three, stops to be successfully converted and printed. TIFF files also offer a fair bit of latitude, with over- or underexposure by up to 1½ stops not causing too many problems. Shooting JPEGs is more like exposing colour slide film. The processed file demands greater accuracy at the time of capture, but excellent results can still be achieved with files over or underexposed by one stop.

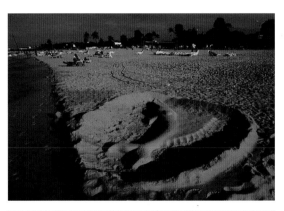

Sand dolphin, Veradero, Cuba

Veradero is Cuba's most popular international beach destination, attracting thousands of Canadians and Europeans who fly directly to the international airport. The beach and blue Caribbean sea are the main attractions. Bright sand, if it's dominating the scene, will cause the meter to underexpose the film. Compensate by increasing exposure by ½ to 1½ stops.

◀ 35mm SLR, 24mm lens, 1/125 f8, Ektachrome E100VS

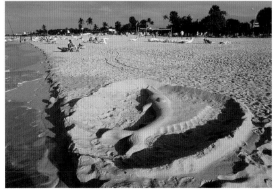

◀ 35mm SLR, 24mm lens, 1/125 f5.6, Ektachrome E100VS, one stop overexposed

SHUTTER SPEED/APERTURE COMBINATIONS

Film speed or image-sensor sensitivity, shutter speed and aperture are all closely interrelated.

▶ **The film or sensor's ISO rating is the foundation on which the variable settings of shutter speed and aperture are based.**

An understanding of the relationship between these variables, and the ability to quickly assess the best combination required for a particular result, is fundamental to creative photography. With 100 ISO film in your camera, or the image sensor set at 100 ISO, point your camera at a subject and your light meter may recommend an exposure of 1/125 at f4. But, for example, by decreasing shutter speed one stop to 1/60 and stopping down aperture by one stop to f5.6, you could still make a correct exposure (because the smaller aperture compensates for the longer time that the lens is open). Similarly, 1/30 at f8 or 1/15 at f11 would also be correct exposures. If you chose to use 400 ISO film or set the sensor to 400 ISO under exactly the same conditions, you could select 1/500 at f4, or 1/250 at f5.6, or 1/125 at f8, or 1/60 at f11. All of the above combinations will ensure the film or sensor is exposed to just the right amount of light. You have to decide which combination will give you the effect you want by giving priority to one element over the other. A photograph of a waterfall taken at 1/250 will look quite different to one taken at 1/2 (see p172 for an example). The combination you select is a creative decision.

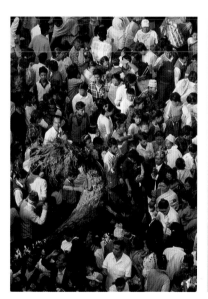 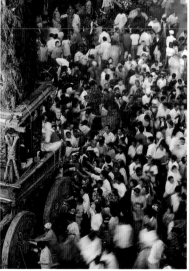

New Year's Festival, Asan Tole, Kathmandu, Nepal

By changing the combination of shutter speed and aperture the same scene can be interpreted quite differently. In the first photograph, to ensure a sharp image I used my standard settings. But I wanted to convey the feeling of movement as the people circled around the chariot, so in the second photograph I used a much slower shutter speed, which recorded movement as a blur. For this technique to work, something needs to be sharp to contrast with the blur, so it's still important to focus on the key element in the composition. At 1/15 sec, a tripod is essential.

▲ 35mm SLR, 100mm lens, 1/125 f4, Kodachrome 64   ▲ 35mm SLR, 50mm lens, 1/15 f11, tripod, Kodachrome 64

DEPTH OF FIELD

Aperture is also a key component in controlling the depth of field in a photograph. Depth of field is one of the least understood aspects of photography, but one of the most important creative controls available to the photographer.

▶ **Depth of field refers to the area of a photograph that is considered to be acceptably sharp.**

The smaller the aperture, the greater the depth of field, and vice versa. An aperture of f16 will give maximum depth of field, while f2 will give minimum depth of field. For general photography use f8 or f11 as your standard aperture setting. These apertures will generally allow you to use a shutter speed of 1/125, give enough depth of field for most shots and even give you some latitude against inaccurate focussing.

When you look through the viewfinder of a modern SLR you're viewing the scene through the lens at its widest aperture, or 'wide open'. This allows focussing and composing through a bright viewfinder. The lens doesn't 'stop down' to the selected aperture until the shutter is released. As a result, you'll be seeing your composition with very little depth of field. If your camera has a depth-of-field, or preview, button you can get an idea of what will be in focus at any chosen aperture by manually stopping down the lens before taking the shot. Select an element of your composition that appears out of focus and watch it come into focus as you stop down from f4 to f5.6 to f8. With each stop the viewfinder will get darker, but as you practice this technique the usefulness of controlling depth of field will soon become apparent.

Two other variables affect depth of field: the focal length of the lens and the distance between the camera and the subject. At the same f-stop, shorter focal length lenses, such as 24mm or 35mm, will give greater depth of field than telephoto lenses, such as 135mm or 200mm. The further away your subject is, the greater the depth of field. Move in close and you will reduce depth of field. So, maximum depth of field can be achieved by focussing on a subject over 50m away and using a wide-angle lens at an aperture of f16. Depth of field will be minimised by focussing on a subject under 5m away and using a telephoto lens at an aperture of f2.

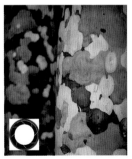
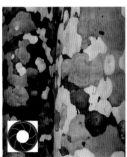
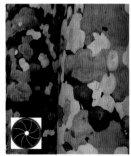

Tree detail sequence

This sequence clearly shows the dramatic effect the aperture has on the depth of field. Without changing the lens or point of focus, the tree on the left can be in or out of focus, creating quite a different image.

▲ 35mm SLR, 100mm lens f2   ▲ 35mm SLR, 100mm lens f8   ▲ 35mm SLR, 100mm lens f22

CAMERA SHAKE

A practical consideration when selecting shutter speeds is to ensure that your pictures don't suffer from camera shake as a result of the shutter speed dropping too low. This is a very common problem when cameras are used on automatic. If hand-holding the camera, a good standard shutter speed is 1/125 or 1/250. However, be prepared to vary your shutter speed depending on the lens you're using.

▶ **Avoid camera shake by selecting a shutter speed the same or higher than the focal length of the lens.**

With a 24mm lens, a shutter speed of 1/30 is recommended; with a 200mm lens, 1/250 is the desired minimum shutter speed. With zoom lenses the minimum shutter speed should vary as you zoom in and out. The longer the lens, or at the telephoto end of zoom lenses, the higher the minimum shutter speed required.

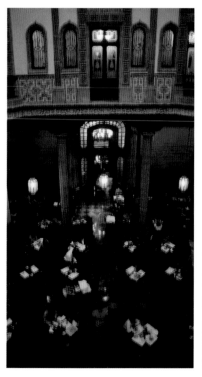 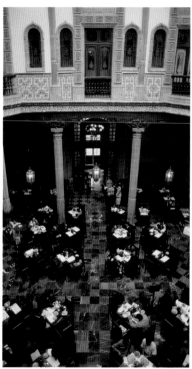

House of Tiles, Mexico City, Mexico

Late in the day the amount of available light in the restaurant was too low to hand-hold the camera and a bad case of camera shake was the result.

▲ 35mm SLR, 24mm lens, 1/8 f2 hand-held, Ektachrome E100VS

By returning the next morning when the light level was higher, I was able to shoot at a comfortable shutter speed for a 24mm lens.

▲ 35mm SLR, 24mm lens, 1/30 f2 hand-held, Ektachrome E100VS

BRACKETING

Bracketing is an important technique used to ensure that the best possible exposure is achieved. A standard bracket requires three frames of the same scene. The first is at the recommended exposure, say 1/125 at f11, the second generally at half a stop over (1/125 at f8.5) and the third at half a stop under the recommended exposure (1/125 at f11.5).

Bracketing, of course, increases film quantities and costs dramatically. Use it when the lighting is really difficult, or if you're photographing subjects you consider important enough to justify the extra film. For professional photographers bracketed film is not wasted film. As a backup against loss, damage or processing problems the extra frames can be invaluable.

Bracketing with digital cameras uses memory-card space. This can be recovered by deleting the less successful exposures. However, if you're bracketing a lot make sure you have enough memory-card capacity to cover your shooting requirements until you get a chance to review and delete, or transfer the images from the memory card.

If the shot really matters, then bracketing is the best way to guarantee that the image you see is the image you get.

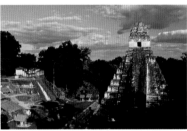

Temple of the Grand Jaguar, Tikal, Guatemala

A three-frame bracket shows the difference a full stop either side of the camera meter's recommendation makes.

The mix of dark and light areas has resulted in a good exposure.

◀ 35mm SLR, 24mm lens, 1/125 at f8, Ektachrome E100VS

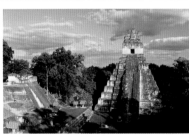

One stop over and the light areas have lost the depth of colour and the image looks weak, but there is detail and colour in the shadow.

◀ 35mm SLR, 24mm lens, 1/125 at f5.6, Ektachrome E100VS

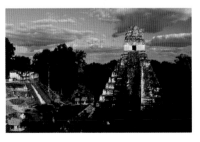

One stop under and the light areas still look good with lots of detail, but the dark areas have lost their colour and detail.

◀ 35mm SLR, 24mm lens, 1/125 at f11, Ektachrome E100VS

USING COMPACT CAMERAS

Compact, or point-and-shoot, 35mm film and digital cameras are extremely popular and the top-quality models are capable of producing good results. To get the most out of these cameras use the override features provided.

Focus & Exposure Lock

The auto-focus sensor is usually in the middle of the viewfinder, which tends to prompt people to put their subject in the middle of the frame. This isn't a recommended place for the majority of striking compositions (see the Composition chapter, p101). Unfortunately, when the main subject is not in the centre it's often out of focus. The focus sensor misses the subject and focusses on something in the background. Additionally, if the lighting is uneven the meter may take a reading from areas other than the main subject.

Most advanced 35mm compacts have a combined focus-and-exposure lock that can solve these problems and allow you to produce more creative and technically better pictures. Check your camera manual to learn how to engage the lock. Usually it involves selecting a 'spot mode', positioning the auto-focus mark on the subject, depressing the shutter button half-way and holding it there while you recompose. Press the button fully when you're happy with the composition. The camera will focus and set the exposure for the subject you spot-metered.

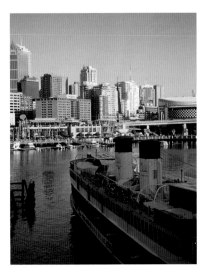

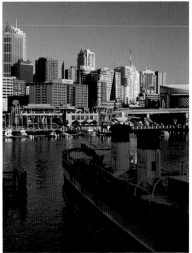

Darling Harbour, Sydney, Australia

The camera doesn't know if you're photographing the boat in the foreground or the city in the background, so it gives an average reading that has overexposed the skyline but stopped the boat going too dark. The image lacks colour and depth and isn't at all representative of how the scene looked to the eye.

▲ 35mm compact, fully automatic, Ektachrome E100VS

By overriding the meter with the focus-and-exposure lock, and exposing for the buildings, the photograph is much stronger.

▲ 35mm compact, exposure and focus lock on city buildings, Ektachrome E100VS

Flash Control

Most advanced compacts have five flash modes: auto, red-eye reduction, fill-in, night scene and flash off. The auto mode is always on and fires the flash automatically in low light and back-light situations. However, you can take control of the flash so that it only fires when you want it to. Too often the flash on compact cameras fires when it doesn't need to, overriding the available light to produce flat, brightly lit pictures that lack mood and render the background dark and uninteresting.

Most compacts have automatic shutter speeds from 1/500 down to at least one second. By turning the flash off, you can access these slower shutter speeds and take advantage of

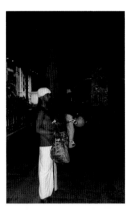

the available light. The camera probably won't tell you the shutter speed it's using, so in low light be aware of camera shake. Experiment in different conditions to learn how low the light has to be before needing a tripod or some other support. Further control can be achieved with the fill-in mode. (See p114 for techniques relevant to both compact and SLR users.)

Priests drumming, Temple of the Tooth, Kandy, Sri Lanka

This is the kind of picture most people are happy with from a compact camera. It's sharp and there's adequate light on the main subject. It isn't very creative though.

◀ Standard compact digital, 5.5-21.8mm lens at 5.5mm, 1/60 f2.8, 140 ISO, 1536 x 2304, 3.5 MP jpeg, automatic exposure, auto flash

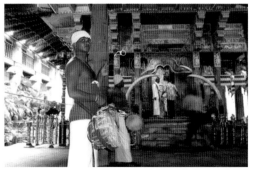

The second shot was recomposed to fill the frame with the interesting temple roof (not the uninteresting floor). Use of the focus lock allowed the subject to be framed off-centre. The night-scene mode allowed the warm ambient light and some movement to be recorded as well as preventing the ugly black shadow that straight flash throws directly behind the subject. The flash made sure the whole image didn't blur and the main subject was rendered sharp.

◀ Standard compact digital, 5.5-21.8mm lens at 5.5mm, 1/3 f2.8, 140 ISO, 2304 x 1536, 3.5 MP jpeg, automatic exposure, night-scene mode

The night-scene mode on compact cameras is also an excellent creative tool. Experiment with it in low-light conditions and you'll probably be pleasantly surprised. The shutter stays open longer to record the available light and the flash fires to add sharpness and ensure correct exposure of the subject, assuming the subject is within flash range. Static flash shots can be turned into images with mood and movement. The level of available light determines how long the shutter stays open, so it's hard to predict how much blur will be captured. It's worth a few frames just to see.

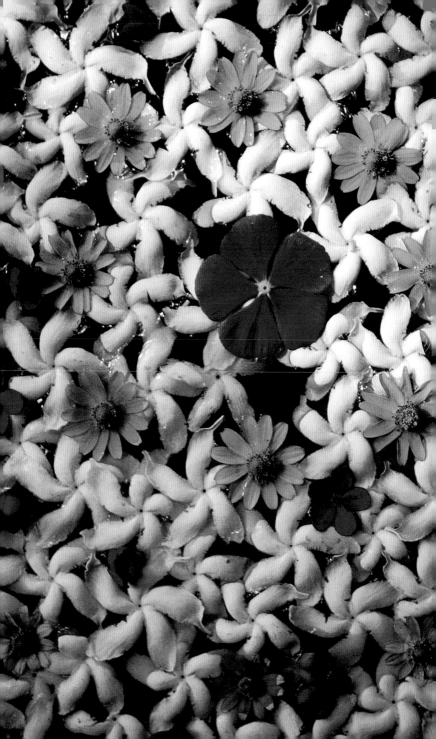

COMPOSITION

▸ **Good composition is a key element in creating striking photographs.**

Every time you take a photograph you'll have made a series of decisions resulting in a composition. You'll have selected a lens with a particular focal length, or zoomed in and out; decided where to take the photo from; included some elements and excluded others; and made a decision to take the photo vertically or horizontally. By considering these interrelated variables (which all defy automation) before you press the shutter, you can put your own interpretation on the subject.

For any given subject or scene there's never one correct composition and it's often worth taking several different compositions. Photographers regularly work the subject, exploring the different possibilities, all the time taking photos. Even at famous tourist sights where there's a certain place to stand to take 'the' photo, it's amazing how different people's photos can be.

▸ **Aim to have the main point of interest positioned away from the centre of the frame and avoid elements that conflict with the main subject.**

THE RULE OF THIRDS

As you work through the options keep in mind the rule that has traditionally been the starting point for successful composition:

▸ **The rule of thirds teaches that the main elements of a composition should be placed at points one-third of the way from the edges of the frame.**

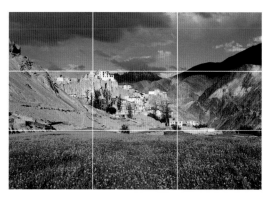

Village and mustard fields, Lamayuru, Ladakh, India

The mustard fields, the mountains and the sky form three distinct horizontal thirds. The monastery, at the high point of the village, is on a grid intersection. Most scenes can have different elements placed on the grid intersections. Try various options, especially those that feel right instinctively, and study the results at home.

◂ 35mm SLR, 24mm lens, 1/125 f11, Kodachrome 64

As you look through your viewfinder, imagine two vertical and two horizontal lines spaced evenly, creating a grid of nine rectangular boxes. Try placing the main elements, such as the horizon in a landscape or the eyes in a portrait, on or near the points where the lines intersect. Avoid placing the main element right in the centre of the frame – this can result in a very static image.

FRAMING

Framing Subjects

Framing subjects is a common practice, but if not executed well it can weaken a composition. The framing device must have some relevance to the subject. Very often it's just something at the edges of the picture that distracts the viewer's attention.

▶ **The frame shouldn't be so overpowering in colour or shape that it competes with the subject.**

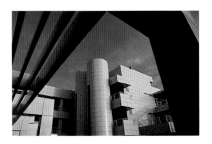

Getty Museum, Los Angeles, USA

This building is framed by another building. The framing device is relevant to the main subject, because it's part of it. It doesn't overpower the subject but, rather, leads the viewer's eye into the composition.

◀ 35mm SLR, 24mm lens, 1/60 f8, Ektachrome E100VS

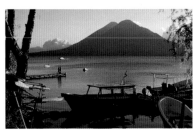

Lake Atitlan, Panahachal, Guatemala

The framing in this picture is quite ineffective, adding nothing to the image. There is no connection between the framing device and the scene in terms of colour or content. The trees simply clutter the edges of the frame.

◀ 35mm SLR, 24mm lens, 1/125 f5.6, Ektachrome E100VS

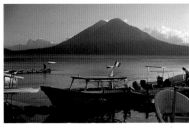

By taking a couple of steps forward down the bank I was able to avoid the trees and make a much cleaner picture with greater harmony between the elements and the colours.

◀ 35mm SLR, 24mm lens, 1/125 f5.6, Ektachrome E100VS

Filling the Frame

▶ **Once you've decided what you want to photograph try to fill the frame with it.**

A common mistake is to leave the subject too small and insignificant, in turn leaving the viewer wondering what the photograph is supposed to be of. Often just taking a few steps towards your subject will make an enormous difference.

VIEWPOINT

▸ **Don't assume that your eye level or the first place you see your subject from is the best viewpoint.**

A few steps left or right, going down on one knee or standing on a step, can make a lot of difference. Varying your viewpoint will also add variety to your overall collection.

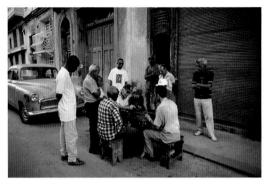

Playing dominoes, Havana, Cuba

All three photos are taken with the same lens, but with each shot I moved in a couple of paces. The first shot provides more information about where the game is being played, but the third gives a much greater sense of immediacy and shows clearly what the photograph is about.

◂ 35mm SLR, 24mm lens, 1/60 f5.6, Ektachrome E100VS

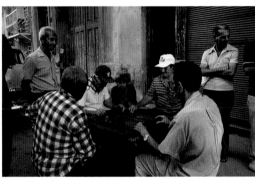

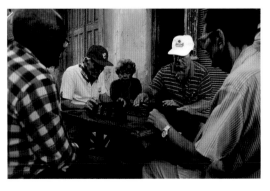

CONTENT SELECTION

▶ **What you leave out of the frame is just as important as what you leave in.**

Do you really want power lines running through the sky at the top of your picture? Get used to scanning the frame before pressing the shutter release, looking for distractions and unnecessary elements. Use the depth-of-field button (if you have one) to bring the background into focus, which will help you spot distractions behind the subject.

ORIENTATION

Horizontal or vertical? It feels much more natural to hold the camera horizontally, so it's not surprising that people forget to frame vertically. Start by framing vertical subjects vertically.

▶ **Consider the option of camera orientation as another tool for filling the frame and minimising wasted space around the subject.**

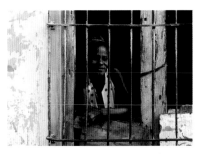

Woman from Trinidad, Cuba

The main subject is clearly taller than wider. Although the horizontal shows a little more of her surroundings, the lighter wall is a distraction from the main subject.

◀ 35mm SLR, 50mm lens, 1/125 f8, Ektachrome E100VS

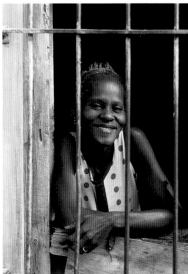

By taking a couple of steps towards the woman and framing vertically, the context is not only retained but also enhanced. The vertical bars and window frame are emphasised and the viewer is drawn to the expression on the woman's face.

◀ 35mm SLR, 50mm lens, 1/125 f8, Ektachrome E100VS

FOCUS

Take care when focussing.

▸ **If something other than the main subject is the sharpest part of the composition the viewer's eye will rest in the wrong place.**

There are five reasons why unsharp images are so common:

▸ Shutter speed is too slow for hand-holding, and camera shake results.
▸ The lens is focussed on the wrong part of the composition.
▸ The lens is not focussed accurately, particularly at wide apertures (f1.4-f4).
▸ The operator jabs the shutter release, wobbling the camera.
▸ The subject moves.

One of the traps with the rule of thirds for auto-focus cameras is that if the subject is not in the middle of the frame, it may not be in focus. Most auto-focus cameras have a focus-lock facility, which you should be confident using. This allows you to lock the focus on the main subject then recompose without the camera automatically refocussing.

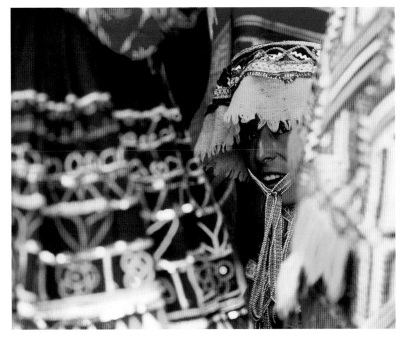

Inti Raymi (Festival of the Sun), Cuzco, Peru

No matter what kind of camera you use or whether you use manual or auto-focus lenses practice focussing fast and/or using the focus-lock facility until it becomes second nature. You'll get your reward when a great but challenging opportunity like this arises, where the subject gives you two seconds to take the shot, is a small part of the frame, is partially obscured and is off-centre.

▲ 35mm SLR, 100mm lens, 1/125 f5.6, Kodachrome 64

CHOICE OF LENS

Lens choice determines the angle or field of view, subject size, perspective and depth-of-field potential. See p24 for more information on the features of different types of lenses.

Angle of View

The focal length determines the angle of view and refers to the image area that the lens provides. On a 35mm camera a standard 50mm lens covers an angle of 46°, which gives about the same angle of view and subject size as the human eye. Wide-angle lenses provide a wider angle of view and smaller subject size than a standard lens. Telephoto lenses have a narrower angle of view and a larger image size than standard lenses. (See also, focal length conversion factor on p81).

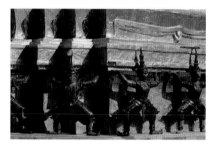

Statues at the Grand Palace, Bangkok, Thailand

Everyone takes this shot or something very similar. There's nothing wrong with that: it's a very attractive and interesting subject. But to find a new angle on an old subject is one of the great challenges for the travel photographer.

◀ 35mm SLR, 100mm lens, 1/125 f8, Ektachrome E100SW

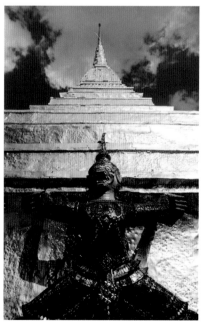

Not everyone takes this shot. A change of lens and a new camera angle is a quick and efficient way to create a completely new image from the same subject.

◀ 35mm SLR, 24mm lens, 1/250 f11, Ektachrome E100SW

Depth-of-Field Potential

The wider the angle of the lens, the greater its depth-of-field potential. The longer the focal length of the lens, the more its depth-of-field potential is reduced.

Perspective

Perspective refers to the relative size and depth of subjects within a picture. When the angle of view is wide (with wide-angle lenses), the perspective becomes more apparent because it's stretched. Close objects appear much larger than those in the background. With a narrower angle of view (with longer focal lengths), the perspective is foreshortened and becomes less apparent – far objects look like they're directly behind closer ones.

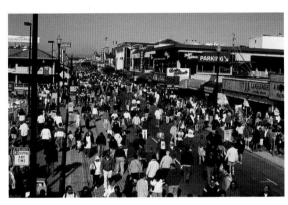

Fisherman's Wharf, San Francisco, USA

On the fourth of July Fisherman's Wharf is packed. The wide perspective of the 24mm lens gives a sense of place and the space between the people on the street is apparent.

◀ 35mm SLR, 24mm lens, 1/250 f11, Ektachrome

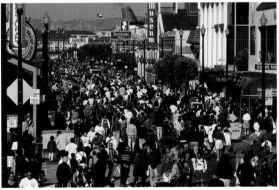

The 180mm lens shows only a small part of the scene. The foreshortened perspective brings the people on the street closer together, making it seem more crowded than it actually is.

◀ 35mm SLR, 180mm lens, 1/250 f8, Ektachrome E100SW

LIGHT

Once you're comfortable with the technical aspects of exposure and the various components of composition, you need to become familiar with the different aspects of lighting.

▶ **Light holds the key to the next level of creativity and personal expression.**

The majority of travel pictures are taken with the natural light of the sun, but you'll also use incandescent lighting indoors or at night, and flashlight when the available light is too low. There's light and there's the 'right light'. The key elements to the 'right light' are its colour, quality and direction. Once you understand these elements and the way they interrelate you can predict the effect they may have on a subject. This will help you decide what time of day to visit a place. The trick to shooting in the 'right light' is to find a viewpoint where you turn the conditions to your advantage, rather than struggle against them.

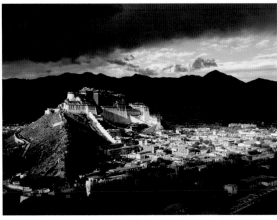

Potala Palace, Lhasa, Tibet, China

I was pleased to get a good standard shot of the Potala, but was keen to capture something a little different. The weather was changing away to the west, so I decided to stay and see what happened.

◀ 35mm SLR, 24mm lens, 1/60 f8 tripod, Kodachrome 64, 3pm

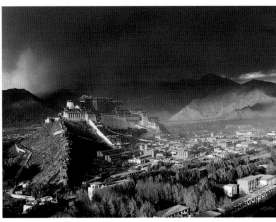

Two hours later I was rewarded with an unusual quality of light caused by the low angle of the sun and a dust storm.

◀ 35mm SLR, 24mm lens, 1/30 f8 tripod, Kodachrome 64, 5pm

Lake Pehoe at sunset, Torres del Paine National Park, Patagonia, Chile
◀ 35mm SLR, 24-70mm lens, 1/160 f5.6, Ektachrome E100VS

NATURAL LIGHT

Colour

The colour of the light changes as the sun follows its course through the day. On a clear day when the sun is low in the sky (just after sunrise or just before sunset), the colour of the light is warm and subjects can be transformed by a yellow-orange glow. This light enhances many subjects and it's worth making an effort to be at a predetermined place at the beginning and end of the day. As the sun gets higher in the sky, the colour of daylight becomes cooler, and more 'natural'. If heavy cloud is blocking the sun, the light will be even cooler and photographs can have a bluish cast. This will also happen on sunny days if your subject is in shade.

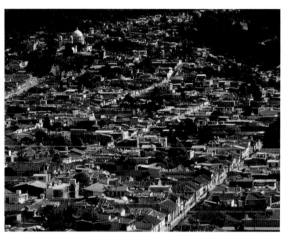

San Cristóbal cityscape, Mexico

The significance of photographing at different times of day can be clearly seen in these shots. By mid-morning the town was lit by the normal light of direct sun, fairly high in the sky. In the late afternoon, with the sun low in the sky, the city was bathed in a warm yellow light.

◀ 35mm SLR, 24mm lens, 1/125 f8, Ektachrome E100VS, mid-morning

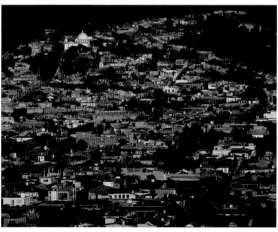

◀ 35mm SLR, 24mm lens, 1/125 f5.6, Ektachrome E100VS, late afternoon

Quality

The quality of natural light is determined by the position of the sun and the weather. Light quality can vary from one moment to the next. Direct sunlight becomes indirect as a cloud blocks its rays. A small break in heavy cloud just above the horizon can transform a scene from ordinary to spectacular in a split second.

Direct sunlight produces a harsh light, especially noticeable in the middle of the day. Shadows are short and deep and contrast will be high. Colours are strong and accurate, but can also be washed out by the intense, overhead sunlight.

In the two to three hours after sunrise and before sunset, direct sunlight is not quite as harsh and colours are still reproduced naturally. The lower angle of the sun gives shadows with some length, brings out textures and adds interest and depth to subjects.

At sunrise and sunset the very low angle of direct sunlight produces long shadows, and texture and shape become accentuated. Combined with the warm colour this is an attractive and often dramatic light.

Indirect sunlight produces a softer light. On overcast but bright days, or when the sun disappears behind a cloud, shadows become faint and contrast is reduced, making it possible to record details in all parts of the composition. Colours are saturated and rich, especially in subjects close to the camera. Rain, mist and fog produce an even softer light. Shadows disappear, contrast is very low and colours are muted. If the cloud cover is heavy, and light levels are low, the light will be dull and flat.

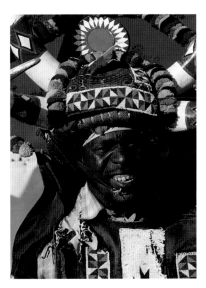 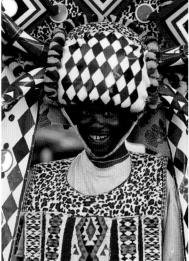

Rickshaw men, Durban, South Africa

Photographed within minutes of each other, one man was in direct sunlight, the other in indirect light. Direct sunlight has stronger, more natural colours, but the shadows on the face are harsh. The indirect light provides better lighting for a portrait, but the colour of the light has changed. There is excessive bluishness (common in open shade).

▲ 35mm SLR, 100mm lens, 1/125 f8 Ektachrome E100VS ▲ 35mm SLR, 50mm lens, 1/125 f5.6 Ektachrome E100VS

Direction

As the colour of light changes through the day, so too does the direction of light. Considering where light strikes your subject will improve your pictures significantly. Although the direction from which light strikes a subject is constantly changing, there are four main directions to consider: front, side, top and back. If the light is striking your subject in the wrong place you have several options: move the subject, move yourself, wait, or return at the appropriate time of day.

Back lighting This occurs when the sun is directly in front of your camera. Silhouettes at sunset are a classic use of back light. Back light has to be carefully managed or your subjects will lack colour and detail.

Front lighting This gives clear, colourful pictures. However, shadows fall directly behind the subject, causing photographs to look flat and lack depth.

Side lighting This brings out textures and emphasises shapes, introducing a third dimension to photographs.

Top lighting This occurs in the middle of the day and is rarely flattering, giving most subjects a flat, uninteresting look.

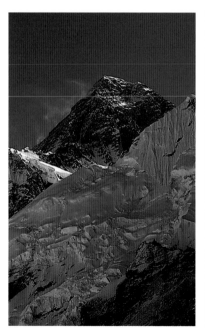
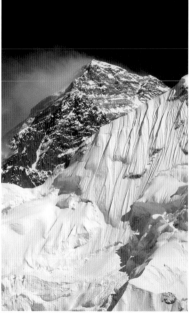

Mt Everest, Sagarmatha National Park, Nepal

The view is spectacular. However, the sun rises behind the mountain, so it's not until mid-afternoon that direct light strikes the mountain. The side lighting is worth waiting for because it brings out the colours of the rock and the texture in the snow. This increases the contrast between the snow, black rock and sky, so that the mountain stands out from the sky. To get both shots you have to wait for a few hours or return later in the day (or even eight years later, see image on p136)

▲ 35mm SLR, 180mm lens, 1/30 f8 tripod,
   Ektachrome E100SW, early morning, back lighting

▲ 35mm SLR, 180mm lens, 1/60 f8, Ektachrome E100SW,
   polarising filter, tripod, mid-afternoon, side lighting

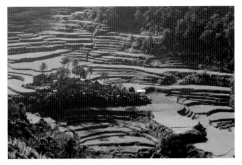

Bang'gann village, Philippines

In this instance I changed viewpoint to alter the direction of the light in the picture. A 200m walk along the road took me to the other side of the village – from shooting against the light to shooting with it. If you can visualise how changing your position will alter the light on the subject, you'll be able to decide if the walk is worth it (not so important for a flat 200m; very important if it's up the side of a hill for an hour).

◀ 35mm SLR, 100mm lens, 1/125 f5.6, Ektachrome E100VS, 9.15am, back lighting

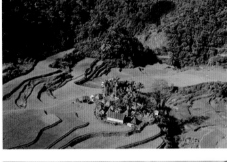

◀ 35mm SLR, 100mm lens, 1/125 f8, Ektachrome E100VS, 9.20am, front lighting

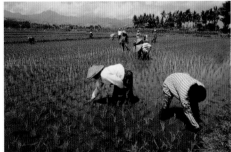

Planting rice, Lombok, Indonesia

Even though the light in the middle of the day isn't always ideal, for the traveller it's often a case of now or never. Except for when the sun is absolutely directly above your subject there will be a better side to photograph your subject from. Slight underexposure and a polarising filter help retain the colours in the scene.

◀ 35mm SLR, 24mm lens, 1/125 f11, Ektachrome E100SW, polarising filter

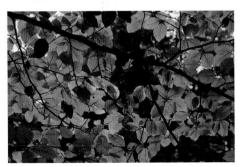

Autumn leaves, Australia

Back lighting has brought out the translucent nature of the leaves, and colours and details not normally seen.

◀ 6 x 7cm SLR, 105mm lens, 1/15 f11, Ektachrome 50STX, tripod

FLASHLIGHT

Flash provides a convenient light source that will let you take a photograph even in the darkest places without having to change films or use a tripod. Most modern compact cameras and SLRs have built-in flash units. Otherwise a separate flash unit can be mounted on the camera via the hot-shoe or off the camera on a flash bracket with a flash lead.

Pictures taken with flash from built-in or hot-shoe mounted units are usually unexceptional. The direct, frontal light is harsh and rarely flattering. It creates hard shadows on surfaces behind the subject and backgrounds are often too dark. To improve the look of your flash photographs get to know the features of your particular unit. If you have an SLR, explore the possibilities of off-camera flash, bounce flash and fill flash.

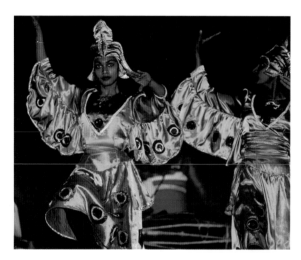

Dancers, Kandy, Sri Lanka

With modern cameras a hot-shoe mounted or built-in flash set on automatic is pretty well guaranteed to get you a sharp, well-exposed photo, as long as you stay within the output range of the flash. The subject will appear bright but the background fades to black very quickly.

◀ 35mm SLR, 24-70mm lens, 1/60 f5.6, Ektachrome E100VS, hot-shoe mounted flash

Technical Considerations

Built-in flashes and compact accessory units have limited power output. Subjects generally need to be between 1m and 5m from the camera for the flash to be effective (check your camera or flash manual for exact capabilities). Photographing an event in a big stadium at night with flash is pointless. If your picture comes out it will be because there was plenty of available light on the subject, not because your flash fired. Your flash will only have enough power to light up the four or five rows in front of you. Faster film will extend the effective range of your flash or let you work with smaller f-stops for greater depth of field.

Synchronisation (Sync) Speed

If you use an SLR on manual, or a non-dedicated flash unit, you must select a shutter speed that synchronises with the firing of the flash. This has traditionally been a maximum of 1/60. In recent times sync speeds have increased, but check your manual. If you select a shutter speed above the sync speed, part of your picture will be black. It's OK to select speeds slower than the designated maximum sync speed.

Red-Eye

If you use direct, on-camera flash when photographing people your portraits may suffer from red-eye. The flash is in line with the lens and the light reflects off the blood vessels of the retina straight back onto the film. Red-eye can be minimised with the following techniques:

▸ Ask your subject not to look directly into the lens.
▸ Bounce the flash off a reflective surface.
▸ Increase the light in the room, which causes the pupil to close down.
▸ Move the flash away from the camera lens.

Many modern cameras have a red-eye reduction feature, which triggers a short burst of pre-flashes just before the shutter opens. This causes the pupil to close down. It's a sophisticated way of increasing the light in the room.

Off-Camera Flash

Off-camera flash gives more pleasing results because the light is moved to the side and above the lens so that it's angled towards the subject. Red-eye is eliminated and shadows fall below the subject (rather than directly behind). A sync lead connects the flash to the camera, and although you can hold the flash and shoot one-handed, mounting the flash on a flash bracket makes life a lot easier. This will limit the angle you can use, but you'll soon be able to anticipate how the flash will light your subject.

Bounce Flash

Even more pleasing results are possible if bounce-flash techniques are employed. You need a flash unit with a tilt head or the ability to mount the flash off-camera on a flash bracket. The flash is aimed at the ceiling, wall or flash reflector, which bounces the light back at the subject. The light is indirect and soft and shadows are minimised. However, walls and ceilings come in varying heights and colours and this can present some problems. If ceilings are too high you won't be able to bounce the flash. Dark-coloured walls and ceilings will absorb too much of the light. The surface you bounce off should be white – coloured surfaces will give your picture a colour cast.

To overcome all these problems a bounce flash kit is worth the small investment. By using a flash with tilt head, the flash is bounced off a reflector attached to the flash head. The reflectors are interchangeable and available in different colours. A gold reflector will bounce warm light and a silver reflector will bounce cooler light.

Fill Flash

Fill flash is a technique used to add light to shadow areas containing important detail that would otherwise be rendered too dark. The flash provides a secondary source of light to complement the main light source, usually the sun. If executed well, the flashlight will be unnoticeable, but if it overpowers the main light the photo will look unnatural.

Fill flash techniques have long been the domain of professional photographers. Now most compact cameras, SLRs with built-in flash units, and advanced SLRs with dedicated flash systems, have a fill-flash feature. Some activate automatically; others require you to decide that fill flash is needed. Use the fill-flash feature when:

- The light on your subject is uneven, such as when a person's hat casts a shadow over their eyes but their nose and mouth are in full sun.
- Your subject is back lit and you don't want to record it as a silhouette.
- Your subject is in shade, but the background is bright.

Remember your subject must still be within the effective range of your particular flash unit.

If you're using a less sophisticated SLR and accessory flash, you'll need to override the flash so that it delivers less light than it would if it were the main light source (usually one to 1.5 stops less). Set your exposure for the brightest part of your composition, say 1/60 at f8, but set the flash on f5.6 or f4.5. Alternatively, you can change the ISO setting on the flash unit, from say 100 to 200. Both techniques trick the flash into thinking that the scene needs less light than it actually does. Output is reduced, which prevents it becoming the main light source while still giving enough light to fill in the dark areas.

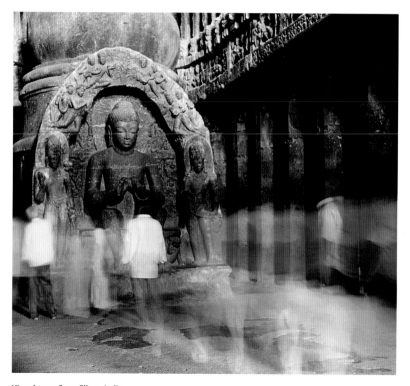

Viswakarma Cave, Ellora, India,

A straight flash exposure would not have worked here. The statue was out of range of the flash and the totally dark cave around it would have lacked any kind of interest. I could have gone closer (which I also did) but I wanted to capture the comings and goings of the local visitors. With the camera on a tripod, a long exposure picked up what little there was of the ambient light and recorded the movement of the people in the cave. The flash added the light required to emphasise the presence of people.

▲ 35mm SLR, 24mm lens, 10 secs f4, Ektachrome E100VS, hot-shoe mounted flash, tripod

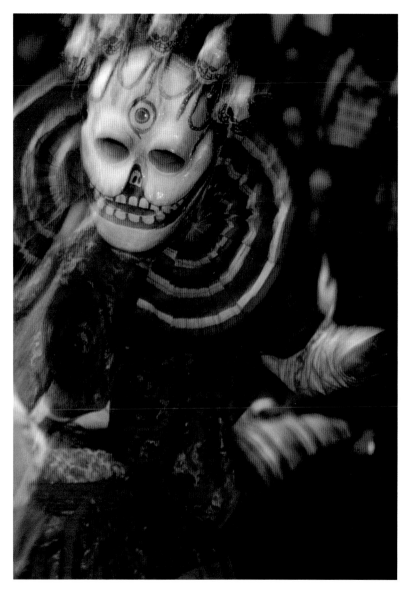

Masked lama dance at Mani Rimdu festival, Chiwang, Nepal

Much more interesting flash pictures result from experimenting with slow shutter speeds and flash. Many cameras have a night mode (see p99) or set a slow shutter speed as if exposing for the ambient light. The movement of the dance is captured through the blur allowed by the slow shutter speed, but the action is stopped and the subject rendered sharp at the moment the flash is fired. Until you've practiced a lot these kinds of shots have a high failure rate, so allow plenty of frames to experiment.

▲ 35mm SLR, 100mm lens, 1/15 f4, Ektachrome E100VS, hot-shoe mounted flash

INCANDESCENT LIGHT

When taking photographs indoors or after dark we often have to rely on incandescent, or artificial, light sources such as electric light bulbs, floodlights or candles. The concepts of colour, quality and direction discussed earlier are just as relevant to incandescent light – it's just that the light source is different.

When you find yourself in dimly lit locations don't assume you need a flash. As a rule, if you can see it you can photograph it. By using a tripod and a fine-grain film you will be able to shoot in low-light situations. Alternatively, fast film will allow you to hand-hold a camera in very low light.

There are good reasons for being prepared to work with the available light. Most importantly, you'll be able to take pictures in many places where the use of flash is impractical (floodlit buildings, displays behind glass), prohibited (churches, museums, concerts), intrusive (religious ceremonies) or would simply draw unwanted attention to your presence.

If you use daylight film in incandescent light your photos will have a yellow–orange cast. The strength of the cast varies, depending on the actual light source. The cast can be neutralised by using film (tungsten) balanced for incandescent light (see the Film chapter pp42-53), or light-balancing filters 82A, 82B or 82C (see p28). More often than not, the warm colours are appealing and help capture the mood of the location.

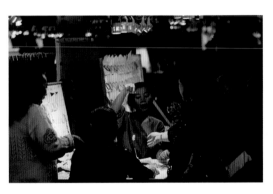

Jade market, Hong Kong, China

A mix of incandescent lights create a pleasing colour that retains the ambience of the place.

◀ 35mm SLR, 24mm lens, 1/30 f4, Kodachrome 200 rated at 400 ISO

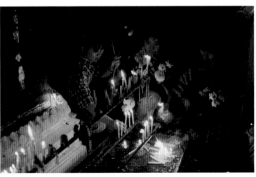

Magha Puja, Bangkok, Thailand

In this scene lit only by candlelight, the daylight film reproduces the light as a strong orange colour.

◀ 35mm SLR, 24mm lens, 1/30 f2, Ektachrome P1600

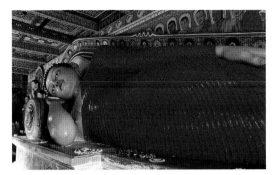

Reclining Buddha, Isurumuniya Vihara, Sri Lanka

Even when lit only by a single low-voltage light bulb it's often amazing how well some pictures turn out. Using flash on most subjects kills the atmosphere, reducing photos to simple record shots. With oblique views like this the flash fades away so only part of the subject is properly exposed. Making use of even the tiniest bit of ambient light will add life to your image collection. This can't be done without a tripod though!

◄ 35mm SLR, 24-70mm lens, 5 secs f16, Ektachrome E100VS, tripod

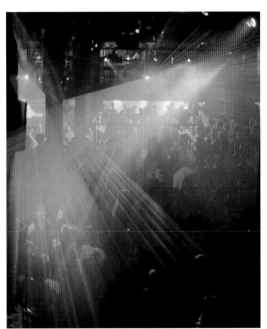

Nightclub laser show, Bangkok, Thailand

Photographing a laser show at 1am is not something I've done a lot of. It felt a bit hit-and-miss at the time, but fortunately the show went on long enough for a pattern to emerge and to get a sense of what my light meter was telling me. In order to remain inconspicuous, even though I had permission, I shot hand-held. I settled on 1/30 sec, varying the aperture to compensate for the dramatic swings in light intensity.

◄ 35mm SLR, 24mm lens, 1/30 f2, Ektachrome E100VS

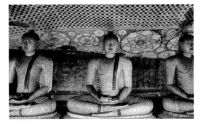

Buddha statues, Dambulla Cave Temples, Sri Lanka

Fluorescent light is the worst kind of incandescent light (unless you like your pictures to have a sickly green cast). The effect can be countered with a FL-W filter.

◄ 35mm SLR, 24-70mm lens, 10 secs f13, Ektachrome E100VS, tripod

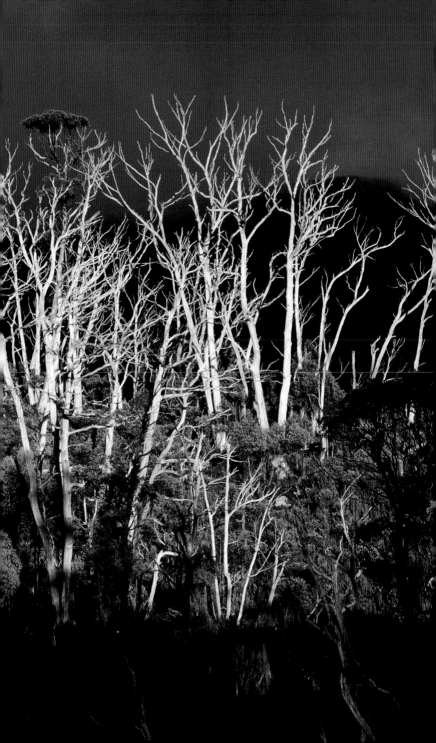

PART THREE:

Once you've got your equipment and film sorted, there are quite a few other things that you can do to make your trip photo-friendly. Time spent preparing and planning will be rewarded with increased photo opportunities and more pictures. Allow time to become thoroughly familiar with your equipment and film, practice your shooting techniques, research your destinations, prepare for the conditions you expect to take photos in, and make plans to ensure your equipment and images are kept as secure as possible.

BEING PREPARED

Bare trees, Cradle Mountain-Lake St Clair National Park, Australia
◀ 6 x 7cm rangefinder, 50mm lens, 1/4 f16, Ektachrome E100VS, tripod

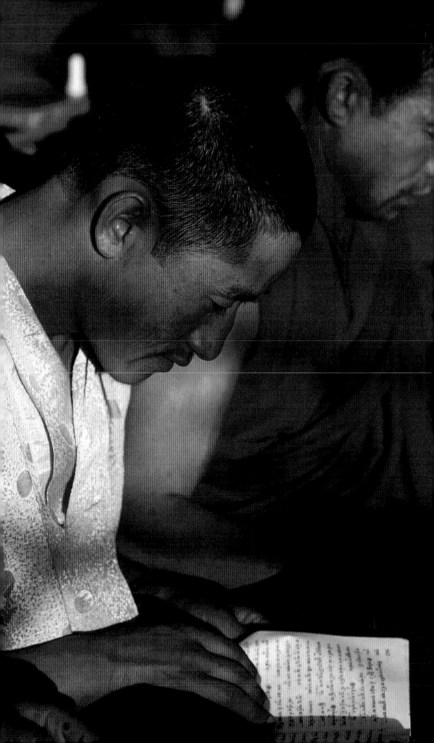

BEFORE YOU TRAVEL

If taking photos is an important part of your trip, it's worth planning your travels with your photographic goals in mind. Simply shooting as you go along will rarely provide enough opportunities to be in the right place at the right time. You might be lucky and stumble across a weekly market or an annual festival, but a little research can guarantee your presence at such events, which is much better than turning up the day after and being told how wonderful it was.

Often, even with thorough research, you'll still find yourself having to stand around in one spot for ages, or going away and returning. As most people travel with friends, family or partners the priority given to photography often has to be compromised, but with a little planning you can increase the amount of quality time available for taking pictures and still accommodate the needs of your travelling companions. If you're on a set schedule, on say a group tour, your options may be very limited, but that's even more reason to do some pre-planning with photography in mind.

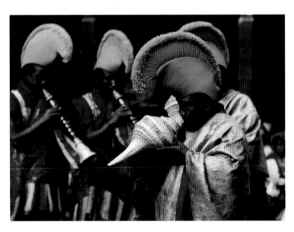

Monk sounding conch shell, Tengboche, Nepal

When the idea for a trip or the offer of an assignment first comes up the first thing I do is check the dates of festivals and the days of the week that markets are held. This information then forms the basis of my itinerary. In this case a 20-day trek to Gokyo and Everest Base Camp in Nepal was built around the annual Mani Rimdu festival at Tengboche Monastery.

◀ 35mm SLR, 70-200mm lens, 1/125 f2.8, Ektachrome E100VS, image stabiliser

RESEARCH

Most people do lots of research before travelling, but you can complement the obvious questions like how to get there, where to stay and what to see, with research into photo-friendly subjects, such as market days and festivals. Then add information gained from images in brochures, magazines and books and you'll be in a much better position to determine when to go, the order of your itinerary and how long you may need in each place to achieve your photographic ambitions. One day at the Pushkar Camel Fair in Rajasthan may be enough for the sightseer, but someone keen to take photographs could happily spend three days wandering around.

If you know people who have been to the same place, ask them what they did and look at their photos. This research will help you discover a great deal about your destination.

Monk reading prayers, Bodhgaya, India
◀ 35mm SLR, 100mm lens, 1/125 f5.6, Ektachrome E100VS

TRAVELLING WITH OTHERS

Trying to combine serious photography with a family holiday, or while on a group tour, can be a challenge. Group itineraries are rarely sympathetic to the needs of a keen photographer. The one exception to this is dedicated photo tours, often led by experienced travel photographers (I lead one every year myself). These trips are intended to put you in the right place at the right time and to give photography priority.

However, if you're not on a photo tour, with a little thought you can do many things within the normal parameters of a holiday with others and still maximise your time photographically. For example, many cities have observation decks at the top of buildings, or lookouts from nearby hills. A map will tell you if the direction of the sun will be best in the morning or afternoon. With this information you can suggest visiting the place at the best time for photos. Others won't care when they visit, as long as they visit, so take control of the timing. You can apply this tactic to the entire itinerary.

It's best to pick one or two themes to photograph comprehensively, and work on them within the framework of recording your trip. You could prioritise markets, allowing extra time and film for them and shooting the rest of your trip as it happens.

One of the easiest solutions to fitting in with others, but still giving photography some priority, is to get up and photograph before breakfast. The light is often at its best, the activity in towns and markets at its most intense and interesting, and you won't

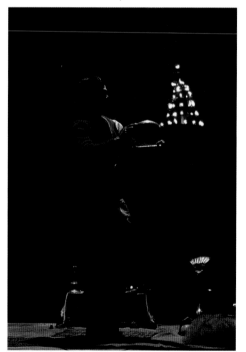

be inconveniencing anyone. The more thought you give to this possibility in the planning stage the more chance you've got of making it happen.

Use a guidebook to complement your group tour. There'll often be other attractions in the area that the tour won't visit, which you might be able to find time to get to alone.

Priest performing puja, Varanasi, India

Getting up early is one of the easiest and best ways to find time for photography when travelling with others. You'll often be rewarded with experiences and images that most people miss such as this priest performing a puja just before dawn.

◀ 35mm SLR, 50mm lens, 1/30 f1.4,
   Ektachrome E200 rated at 800ISO (2 stop push)

TIME

Allowing more time in any place to see the main sights has great benefits for photography. Sometimes just a few extra minutes can make all the difference. The sun may come out or go in, the right person may stop and stand in just the right place, the rubbish-collection truck that's parked in front of the city's most beautiful building may move on, the person buying the fruit may hand over their money. If you have days rather than minutes, you can look for new angles and viewpoints of well-known subjects, visit places at different times of the day, wait for the best light, and get better coverage.

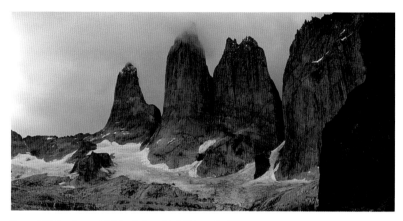

Torres del Paine, Torres del Paine National Park, Patagonia, Chile

Research and time made the difference between these two shots. Around 40 people made the two-hour climb up to the spectacular lookout to see the magnificent Torres del Paine. They did this in the afternoon in overcast weather and their pictures would look a lot like the first shot. Even if the weather had been fine, the light comes from the wrong direction in the afternoon. Four people walked up before sunrise the next day – the first hour in the dark. The reward for the photographer is obvious.

▲ 35mm SLR, 24-70mm lens, 1/30 f8, Ektachrome E100VS, tripod
▼ 35mm SLR, 24-70mm lens, 1/8 f16, Ektachrome E100VS, tripod

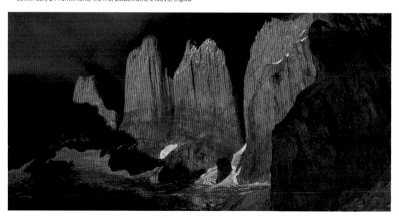

EQUIPMENT

Don't travel with equipment you've never used before. Organise it in plenty of time and use it for a while before you set off. If you don't have time to become familiar and confident with the gear, at least take the camera manual with you.

▶ **Check and clean gear at least six weeks before you travel.**

Allows plenty of time to have cameras serviced and repaired if necessary, or to buy new equipment. A basic check and clean for an SLR is quick and easy:

▶ Remove the lens and set the shutter speed on the 'B' setting.
▶ Hold the camera up against a plain light background.
▶ Release the shutter and keep you finger down so that the shutter stays open. You can now look right through the camera.
▶ Look for hairs intruding into the open shutter area, which leave an annoying black mark on every photo.
▶ Release the shutter.
▶ Hold the camera upside down and use a blower brush to clean dust off the mirror (don't touch the mirror with anything else) and out of the film-cassette space and the take-up spool (wind the film lever on a couple of times while you're doing this).
▶ Gently clean the pressure plate on the back of the camera. Be very careful when cleaning near the shutter curtain and ensure that hair from the blower brush doesn't get left in the camera.
▶ Put a lens on and, with the camera in manual mode, select the one-second shutter speed and the smallest aperture on the lens.
▶ Still with the back open, release the shutter. You will now see the shutter open and the aperture stop down. Repeat this at various shutter speed and aperture combinations with each lens.
▶ Clean all lenses and filters, preferably with a blower brush. If there's dirt or fingerprints that won't blow off, breathe on the lens or filter and then wipe the lens gently in a circular motion with lens tissue. If the marks are really stubborn you'll need lens-cleaning fluid. By always having skylight filters on your lenses you should rarely have to touch the lens.
▶ Blow dust off the rear lens element.
▶ Use lens tissue to clean the eye-piece.
▶ Check that all the screws on the camera and lenses are tight.
▶ Digital SLR users should check that the camera's image sensor is free from dirt and dust (see p60).

Confirm everything is OK by putting a roll of film through the camera or taking pictures on all the memory cards you intend travelling with. Take shots at various combinations of shutter speed and aperture. Test the self-timer and flash and use any other accessories you intend to take. Keep details of the shots so that if there's a problem you can easily identify which piece of equipment needs attention. This is also good practice immediately after your gear is serviced or repaired.

A compact camera or a second SLR camera body is great insurance against loss, damage and breakdown. A very basic model will do, but it must accept your system's lenses. And don't forget: it's no use having a second SLR body in your pack if all your lenses are stolen.

INSURANCE

Travel insurance is essential. Find a policy that includes coverage of your camera gear. If you're carrying anything more than a standard outfit it may be necessary to insure it separately with a specialist insurer. You'll need to list all the equipment with serial numbers and value. Carry two copies of this list on your travels. Keep one with your money and the other in your main bag. It will be very handy if your gear is stolen and you have to fill in a police report.

If you buy equipment on the road, make sure that your travel policy covers it. It's worth copying the receipts and sending one set home to prove ownership if everything is lost or stolen. If you have a dedicated policy make sure the new purchase is added immediately.

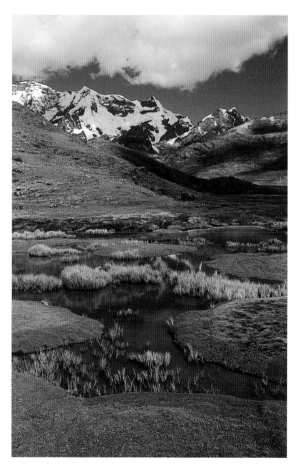

Mt Ausangate and the Upis plain, Vilcanota region, Peru

You'll often find yourself a long way from a camera repair shop, so even with your equipment properly insured, the last thing you need is a breakdown. You can't do much when you're in the middle of a two-week trek in the mountains of Peru, but a thorough check, clean and test of all your equipment before you leave home will help minimise the risk.

◄ 35mm SLR, 24mm lens, 1/15 f16, Kodachrome 64, tripod, polariser

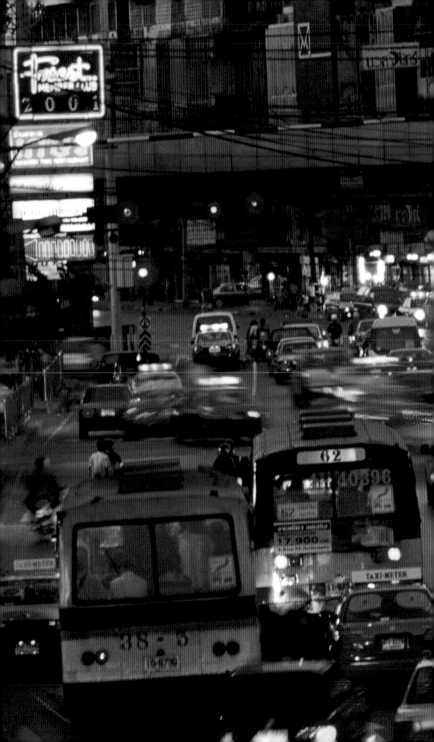

TRIP NOTES

When you finally hit the road and start taking pictures, new issues and challenges arise. If you've never been to the place before, study your guidebook maps to get a feel for where things are, the direction of the light in relation to the main sights, and the best ways to get around. When you're out and about there are ways of making every opportunity count. Security and camera care also need to be considered.

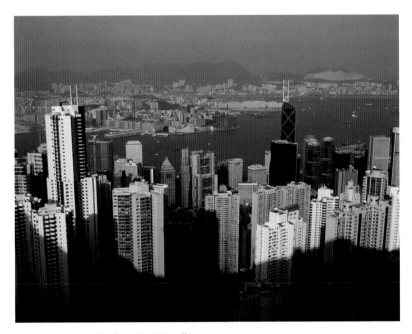

High-rise buildings and harbour, Hong Kong, China

You can go shopping in Hong Kong any time, but you can't always get a clear, smog-free view over the city from Victoria Peak. Your planning will have informed you that the view from Victoria Peak is a 'must see'. So if the weather is fine don't delay your photography.

▲ 35mm SLR, 180mm lens, 1/250 f5.6, Ektachrome 100STZ

AT CUSTOMS

Unless you have an unusual amount of equipment and film you should have no trouble clearing customs at your destination. Don't panic if you read that you're only allowed to take in 12 rolls of film – you'll rarely be questioned. If you are, three things can help: say you're carrying the film for a group (the size of which can vary, depending on how many rolls of film you have); tell them 'No video' (unless you have a video camera), as customs officers are much more interested in video cameras than still-camera equipment; finally, explain that you have so much film and camera gear because their country is so beautiful!

Evening traffic, Bangkok, Thailand

◀ 35mm SLR, 100mm lens, 1/4 f8, Ektachrome E100VS, tripod

AT YOUR DESTINATION

When you arrive at a new destination it's highly recommended you rush out and blaze away at everyone and everything that moves…while being culturally sensitive, of course. Once you've got over the initial rush of excitement, consider the following:

▸ Confirm the dates and times of events that your pre-trip research uncovered.

▸ Confirm opening hours of places of interest.

▸ Ask if anything interesting is happening in the area. There are far too many local festivals and events for guidebooks to list. Don't assume that people will spontaneously inform you of what's happening.

▸ If you know an event is going to take place, don't be put off by the fact that the tourist office may have no idea what you're talking about. Some local festivals are so local half the locals don't even know they're on.

▸ Ask the same questions of a variety of local people, not just the tourist office. The people at your hotel, taxi drivers, waiters – in fact, anyone who speaks your language (if you don't speak theirs) – can often give you new and useful information.

▸ Check out postcards, tourist publications, local magazines and books – they provide a good overview of the places of interest, as well as a guide to potential vantage points.

▸ Speak to other travellers and find out what they've seen and learnt.

▸ Make sure you're aware of any cultural restrictions or local sensitivities to photography. Borders are often sensitive areas, as are airports, bridges and anything that resembles a military checkpoint or installation.

If the weather is fine on the morning you arrive it's very easy to assume that it will still be fine in the afternoon. This is a big mistake. If you're clear about your priorities, start at the top of the list if conditions are good. If you arrive in unfavourable conditions you can start with lesser priorities that are more suited to the conditions.

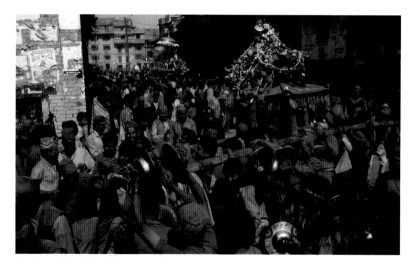

New Year's festival, Thimi, Kathmandu Valley, Nepal

Thimi is a small town only 15 minutes by car from Kathmandu, but no-one I spoke to knew anything about the New Year celebrations. I went anyway. In the centre of Thimi I was again told there was nothing happening. So I set off for the main temple and within two minutes walk I came upon the festival in full swing.

▲ 35mm SLR, 24mm lens, 1/250 f8, Kodachrome 64

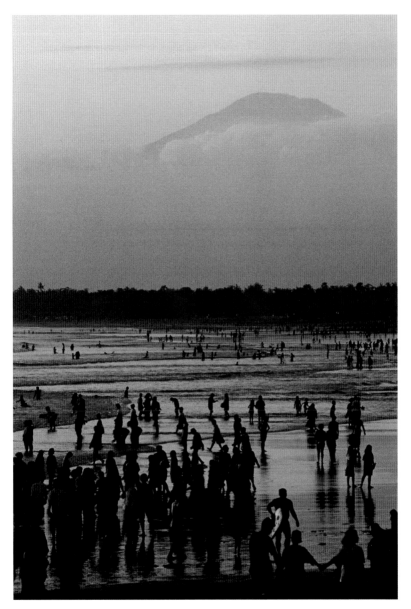

Volcano from Kuta Beach, Bali, Indonesia

There one day, gone the next. The first time I went to Kuta Beach I took one frame of the beach and distant volcano as I hurried to photograph the boats and the sunset…assuming I'd be able to do more shots the next day. I've been back to Kuta several times over several years and have never again seen the volcano from the beach.

▲ 35mm SLR, 180mm lens, 1/250 f5.6, Ektachrome 100STZ

ROUTINE & HABITS

Potential images come and go in front of your eyes in a matter of seconds and are easily missed. A good routine plays a big part in helping you react quickly to photo opportunities.

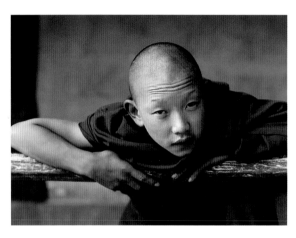

Novice monk at Drepung Monastery, Tibet, China

To improve the chances of a potential subject not changing their position when they realise you want to take their photo you need a plan. I never approach someone until I'm ready to shoot, which means choosing the right lens, checking the exposure settings, making sure I have enough frames left, confirming the direction of the light and selecting my viewpoint.

◀ 35mm SLR, 100mm lens, 1/125 f5.6, Kodachrome 64

▸ Have your camera around your neck, switched on and with the lens cap off. You can't take pictures quickly if you have to get the camera out of a bag, remove the case, turn it on and take off the lens cap.

▸ Always wind the film on so that the shutter is cocked.

▸ Be aware of existing light conditions and have your camera set accordingly. Change the settings as conditions change. If using manual settings, adjust the aperture and keep the shutter speed appropriate for the lens you're using.

▸ If your camera is set on auto, make sure the shutter speed doesn't drop too low for hand-held photography without you realising.

▸ Have the lens you're most likely to need on the camera. For example, if you're on a crowded street looking for environmental portrait opportunities, it might be a 24mm.

▸ Set zooms at the most likely focal length for the subject you're anticipating.

▸ Have a notebook and pen in your camera bag for recording important information quickly and accurately. Note-taking is an important part of the overall package for successful travel photography. Good notes are needed for correct labelling of the images, and as a reference for returning to the same spot at another time.

▸ Always change films as soon as a roll is finished, and memory cards when they're full, or even before. It's often worth changing film from frame 33, or memory cards when you only have a couple of shots left, if you think something could occur, rather than only having a couple of frames available when the action starts.

▸ Store full memory cards (in appropriately marked storage containers) separately from empty memory cards so you don't grab a full one when you're in a hurry (and have to spend precious time deleting images or finding another card before you can take photos).

▸ Always rewind the film completely into the canister so it can't be accidentally reused.

▸ Number each roll of film sequentially as you finish it.

CAMERA CARE

Unfortunately, things can go wrong. Problems are magnified in remote areas because camera repair shops and suppliers often don't exist. Problems with equipment can occur in all sorts of ways: it can get lost, dropped, stolen, or just stop working. Regular checks and cleaning help prevent some problems, but others will have to be dealt with along the way.

Do the basic check and clean described on p126 every couple of weeks while you're travelling. Check lenses and filters daily to prevent a build-up of dirt and fingerprints. These should be removed immediately, as they can cause flare and loss of definition, resulting in soft images. This is equally true for compact cameras as for SLRs.

On a long trip it's a good idea to get at least one roll of film processed occasionally, to make sure everything is working properly. If you're using slide film, it's usually easy enough to buy a 12-exposure roll of colour negative film. Just processing the negatives will confirm that everything is OK.

If your camera does break down while you're travelling there really isn't much you can do about it, except take it to the nearest camera shop. If it's a new camera, trying to fix it yourself by opening it up will void the warranty. If it has jammed, the first thing to do is to rescue the film. If you're in a town most camera shops will do it for you. If not, you can make a portable dark bag by putting the camera inside a zipped-up jacket and doubling over the neck and the bottom. Access the camera by putting your hands into the sleeves the wrong way (from the outside). Alternatively, go headfirst into a sleeping bag. When you're confident no light will reach the film, press the rewind button to release the take-up spool. Open the back, remove the film cassette from the camera and rewind the film manually. Once the film is safe, clean out the back of the camera in case bits of torn film have been left behind.

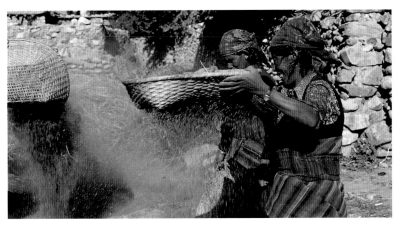

Villagers winnowing barley, Chhuksang , Mustang, Nepal

Mustang is a challenging environment for camera gear as strong winds blow daily down the barren Kali Gandaki valley. For a double dose of dirt and dust I spent some time up close to the village women as they furiously winnowed their grain, taking advantage of the strong winds. I was picking bits of barley out of my camera bag for the rest of the trek but made sure the camera was given a thorough clean that evening.

▲ 35mm SLR, 24mm lens, 1/125 f8, Ektachrome E100VS

PROTECTION FROM THE WEATHER

Weather conditions can change rapidly, so you have to be prepared. Just because it's a perfectly still, sunny day when you leave your hotel, doesn't mean that a dust storm won't engulf you an hour later. Unsettled or unusual weather often brings with it moments of spectacular light and a change in the daily activity of the locals. Get out there and you can be rewarded with fantastic photographic opportunities. To take advantage of changing, unusual or difficult situations, without putting your gear at risk, additional protection is needed.

Wet Weather

Just because it's raining, or snowing, doesn't mean you have to put your camera away. Most cameras can take a fair bit of rain, just wipe it dry as soon as you get inside. Unless someone is on hand to hold an umbrella for you, shooting with one hand from under an umbrella isn't easy – especially as the light is probably low. It's much easier to keep your camera under your jacket between shots. One quick and easy solution is the 'old plastic bag and rubber band' trick. Cut a hole in the bottom of a plastic bag just big enough for the lens to fit though and use a rubber band to secure it in place on or just behind the lens hood. You then access the viewfinder and shutter release through the bag's original opening. The lens hood will help protect the filter on the front of the lens from the rain or snow, but keep checking it and wiping it dry as necessary. Some camera bags have an outershell built in for protection against wet weather. If yours doesn't, a large plastic bag is easily carried and will do the job.

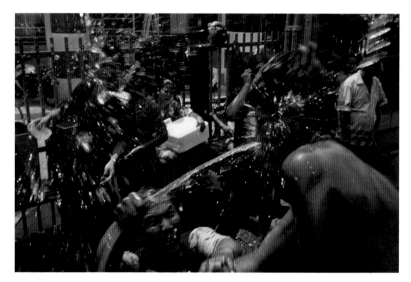

Songkran Festival, Bangkok, Thailand

Even on a perfectly fine day weatherproof, or even underwater, cameras come into their own when the event demands anyone in sight is drenched with water.

▲ 35mm underwater rangefinder, 35mm lens, 1/125 f8, Ektachrome E100VS

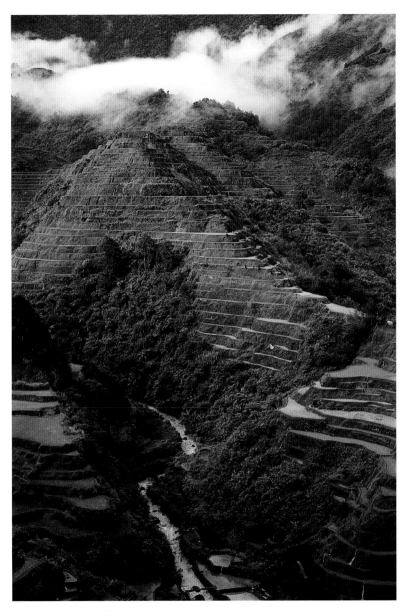

Rice terraces, Banaue, Philippines

Often after heavy rain there will be a period of beautiful light. If you and your equipment are well protected you can remain in the right place to take pictures rather than taking shelter elsewhere. This shot of the rice terraces of Banaue was taken in that fleeting moment between downpours.

▲ 35mm SLR, 50mm lens, 1/125 f5.6, Ektachrome E100VS, polariser

Extreme Cold Weather

Most modern cameras will function properly down to 0°C. Mechanical gear will operate adequately around –10°C to –15°C. The biggest problem in very cold temperatures is that batteries will fail. You can often fix this problem by removing the batteries from the camera and warming them in your hands. To minimise battery problems, keep your camera and the batteries in the camera warm until you start shooting. If you're going out at first light, sleep with your camera; ie, keep it in your sleeping bag during the night. When you head out into the cold morning have the camera under your jacket until you need it; shoot quickly, then tuck it back into your jacket as soon as you've taken your shots.

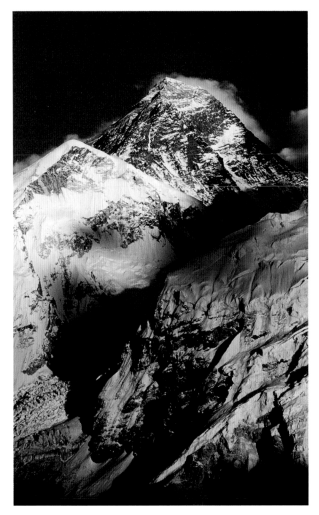

Mt Everest from Kala Pattar, Sagarmatha National Park, Nepal

When it's really cold and the wind is so strong that it's a challenge just holding the camera to your eye, it's not only the camera equipment that needs to cope – it's you. The right clothing and other personal equipment will keep you in the right place at the right time, no matter how cold it is.

◀ 35mm SLR, 24-70mm lens, 1/125 f8, Ektachrome E100VS

In very cold weather film can become brittle and snap if not handled carefully. Turn off the film winder and advance and rewind the film slowly to prevent tearing it. Winding on and off too quickly can also result in static discharges that appear as clear blue specks or streaks on the film.

Condensation can also be a problem. When changing film and lenses outdoors don't breathe into the back of your camera or onto the lens, and ensure snow doesn't get into the camera. Entering a warm room causes the water vapour on the cold metal and glass surfaces to condense rapidly and mist up with tiny water droplets. When you go out again this water will freeze. To prevent this, wipe off as much moisture as possible, and don't open the camera back or change lenses until the camera has warmed up.

In extreme cold, don't touch the camera's metal parts with bare skin because it will stick. These problems don't usually arise above −10°C. Make sure you've got a large eye-cup on and tape over the metal parts to help prevent your face coming into contact with them. Otherwise you could find your camera stuck to your face (which would be rather unpleasant, but could make a great shot for some other photographer).

Hot & Humid Weather

Extreme heat can melt the glues holding the lens elements in place, but the biggest problem is the damage it can cause to film. Film is not only light sensitive, but heat sensitive, and cooking it will result in very pink photos. Film can actually withstand much more heat than you might think, but it's still best to be on the cautious side. It's recommended that you:

▸ Be aware that the floors of buses and cars can get very hot on long journeys, especially around the engine.
▸ Don't leave film in rooms in cheap hotels that become ovens around midday.
▸ Never leave equipment or film in direct sunlight.
▸ Never leave gear or film in a car, especially in the glove box. On a hot day, say 37°C, temperatures in cars can range from 64°C to 107°C.

High humidity also speeds up the natural deterioration of film, and can lead to fungus growth on equipment and film. Packets of silica gel (available from camera shops), which absorb moisture, should always be in your bag when travelling in humid climates.

Moving from an air-conditioned room to warm temperatures outdoors causes condensation on lenses and viewfinders that can take up to 10 minutes to clear. As soon as you get outside take your camera and each lens out of your bag and remove the front and rear lens caps, so that the condensation can clear naturally. Don't wait until your first photo opportunity comes along or you'll spend precious minutes wiping the lens, including the rear lens element, which is best not touched.

Salt Water

Salt water and sea spray can cause irreparable damage to your camera. When photographing by the sea, protect your camera with a plastic bag (see p134) and keep your bag closed. Cameras can also be protected against sea spray by wiping with a cloth lightly soaked in WD40 (or any substance that displaces moisture).

When travelling by small boat, place equipment and film in strong, sealable plastic bags. If you drop a camera in the sea, the only thing you can do is wash it under fresh water as quickly as possible, to remove the salt. The camera's chances of survival aren't good.

Sand & Dust

Sand and dust are deadly enemies of photographic equipment. If you find yourself in sandy or dusty conditions when the wind is blowing, be especially protective of your equipment and film. A single grain of sand in just the right (or wrong) place can cause a lens to seize up. If any sand gets caught in the film cassette's light seal it can scratch a straight line along the entire film.

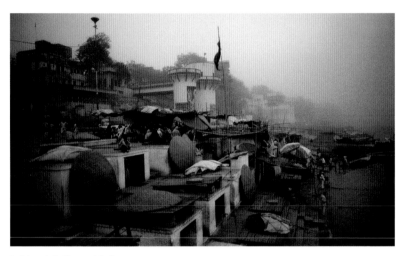

Bathing ghats, Varanasi, India

This sandstorm swept down the Ganges River from out of nowhere and the colour and quality of the light changed dramatically. It just goes to show that even on seemingly perfect days you should be prepared to be covered in sand, sea spray or rain.

▲ 35mm SLR, 24mm lens, 1/125 f5.6, Kodachrome 200

To prevent damage from sand and dust:

▸ Avoid opening the camera back or changing lenses if sand and dust are in the air.
▸ Blow and wipe off dust and sand as soon as possible, and again before opening the camera back.
▸ Don't put your camera bag down on the sand.
▸ If conditions are really severe put your camera bag inside a large plastic bag or place equipment in plastic bags inside your camera bag. Don't leave equipment in plastic bags for more than a couple of hours when the humidity levels are high.
▸ Keep your camera bag well sealed.
▸ Use the camera-in-the-plastic-bag technique for shooting and changing films (see p134).

SECURITY

Tourists and their cameras are particularly attractive targets for thieves just about everywhere. Being overly concerned about the security of your equipment doesn't only take the fun out of photography; it can prevent you from taking photos at all. A camera is no good at home, or in the hotel, or at the bottom of the day-pack on your back. By taking sensible precautions and staying alert you should be able to access your camera quickly and easily and still retain possession:

- Cameras, film and memory cards should be carried onto the plane as hand luggage on the way to your destination. Even if your clothes don't make it, at least you can take photos. You may choose to pack some equipment in your check-in luggage on the way home.
- Carry the camera bag across your body, not on your shoulder – it's harder to snatch.
- Carry your camera around your neck, not on your shoulder.
- Don't put your gear in an expensive-looking bag with 'Nikon' emblazoned on the side.
- If travelling on overnight sleeper trains use the bag as a pillow, perhaps under a jacket.
- If you go out without your camera it's best locked in your main pack or suitcase, rather than a portable camera bag. If you have more than one camera, separate them.
- If you have a top-opening bag, close it between shots.
- Never leave equipment, and especially exposed film or memory cards, in an unattended car.
- Never place your gear on overhead racks on trains, boats or buses. In other words, never let it out of your sight.
- Never put film in your check-in luggage.
- Put your film and memory cards with your money in the hotel's safety deposit box.
- When you put your bag down, put your foot through the strap.

PROCESSING FILM

Colour print film can be conveniently and cheaply developed and printed in most towns. A good lab will be well patronised by locals (like a restaurant), so if it's busy it's probably doing a good job.

Most big cities have professional labs that process colour slide film. If you're in doubt about the lab doing a decent job, don't leave your film. Process one roll as a test before committing the film from your entire trip. Unless you're carrying a loupe (magnifier), use a lens with the front element to your eye to magnify the slides for easier viewing. A 100mm lens is ideal.

SHIPPING FILM

If you're travelling for an extended period (over three months) you may want to consider sending film home for security and practical reasons. If you've processed it, you'll soon find that packets of prints and boxes of mounted slides take up a lot more space and are heavier than unexposed film cassettes.

If you do ship processed film, send the negatives and prints separately, and post them a week apart from different post offices. If you've numbered your films sequentially, split them into odds and evens and ship them separately, again on separate days from separate places. If the worst happens, you won't lose a big chunk of images from one part of your trip.

Ship unprocessed film with one of the main air-courier services, rather than through the post. The extra expense is well justified. Shipping unprocessed film raises the issue of x-rays again. Parcels may be x-rayed. Depending on the company, and the countries you're shipping between, you may be able to get an assurance from the agent that parcels won't be x-rayed, but there's some risk. Identify your parcels as having undeveloped film inside: *not to be x-rayed*.

Let someone know the film is on its way. They can take it to your lab of choice for processing or store it in a cool, dry and dark place. The refrigerator is a good place for this.

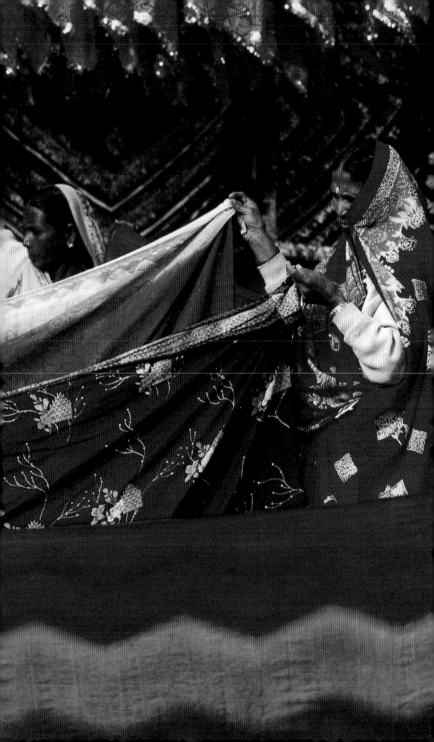

PART FOUR:

There are countless subjects to photograph when travelling. On the Road illustrates and considers specific issues related to successfully photographing the most popular travel subjects.

ON THE ROAD

Women drying saris, Varanasi, India
◄ 35mm SLR, 24mm lens, 1/60 f8, Ektachrome E100VS

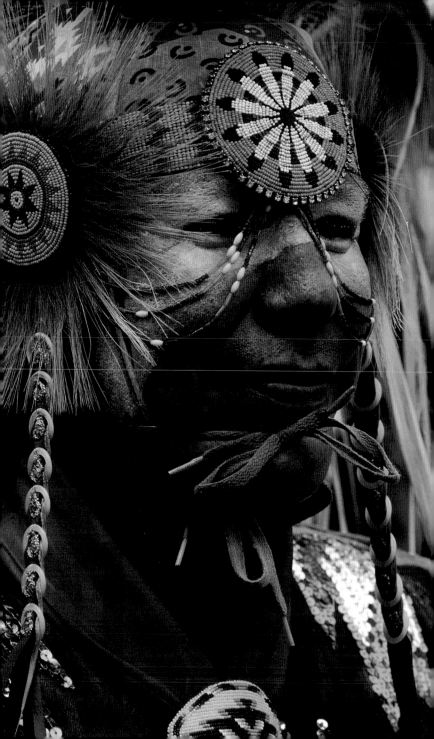

PEOPLE

Photographing people well is one of the most difficult tasks faced by any traveller. Hundreds of potential subjects surround you daily, yet the step from seeing a potential photograph to actually capturing it on film doesn't come easily to many people. Often travellers are reluctant to photograph people because they're too shy or self-conscious to ask permission, or fear they won't be understood, or that they're invading people's privacy. They sometimes feel guilty, especially when the people being photographed are living in poverty.

Photographs of people can be simply categorised into two groups: portraits and environmental portraits. Portraits are close-up studies of a subject's face. Environmental portraits include the subject's surroundings as an integral part of the image, providing a context for the portrait.

There are two ways to go about photographing people. One is to get to know the people by spending time with them, or at least spending time in the locality. In theory, this should lead to better access and more relaxed, natural photos. The other is to jump straight in, get the pictures, and get out. Travellers will find themselves in the second category most of the time, whether they like it or not.

▸ **You'll become more comfortable photographing people, and enjoy better results, if you're able to compose and make technical decisions quickly.**

Ensure you're completely comfortable with your equipment. A good way to miss people photos is to start messing around with gear and settings in front of them. People quickly become self-conscious and often stop what they're doing and go into their 'camera pose'. It's important to develop techniques that make photographing people easier and minimise the intrusion into your subject's day.

Plan the shot before you approach your subject. Should it be portrait or environmental, horizontal or vertical? Have an idea of the viewpoint you intend to use. Study the light on the person's face and check where it's coming from; this will allow you to position yourself correctly in the first instance. Once you have permission to take a photo the person will follow you with their eyes if you move. The slightest change of camera angle can make all the difference. If your subject is wearing a hat in a sunny location half of their face will be in heavy shadow. Overcome this by asking them to look up slightly or to push the hat back a bit.

Lots of things can go wrong with people pictures, including unsharp photos due to inaccurate focussing or subject movement; closed eyes if your subject blinks; an unflattering expression, especially if the person is talking; and loss of eye contact if your subject is distracted or shy. People often relax a little after they hear the click of the camera, thinking you've finished; a second frame may capture a more natural pose.

Native American, Washington, DC, USA

As he waited for his group's turn to join the Independence Day Parade, this man was happy to be photographed but wouldn't look at the lens. The way people respond to the presence of a camera is always interesting. Some pose, some turn away, some just carry on. It's the varied responses that give character and personality to a collection of people pictures.

◂ 35mm SLR, 100mm lens, 1/125 f5.6, Ektachrome E100VS

COMMUNICATION

Some photographers ask before shooting, others don't. It really is a personal decision and often decided on a case by case basis. Asking permission allows you to use the ideal lens, get close enough to fill the frame, provides the opportunity to take several shots, as well as to communicate with your subject if necessary. Relatively speaking, very few people refuse to be photographed when asked.

Even if you are refused, which can be very discouraging, it's a mistake to assume that everyone will refuse to be photographed. Of course, you should make sure there aren't any religious or cultural reasons that discourage or prohibit photography. If in doubt ask a local.

How you approach people will affect the outcome of your request for a photo. Simply smiling and holding your camera up is usually sufficient to get your intention across. You may choose to learn the phrase for asking permission in the local language, which is the polite thing to do, but it can be less effective than sign language. Trying to speak the language has its own complications, like having to repeat the sentence 10 times to make yourself understood.

Approach the person with confidence and shoot quickly. By working quickly you'll increase the possibility of capturing more spontaneous and natural images. There's nothing more frustrating than seeing someone you think would make a great photograph, only for them to change position when they realise you want to photograph them. If people stiffen up in front of the camera it's up to you to get them to relax. Often it's a good idea to take one frame however they have posed themselves, then put your camera down and wait or talk to them before trying again. Demonstrate the pose you want by doing it yourself.

The direct approach of asking permission results in more satisfactory images than trying to sneak them from a distance. People will be more suspicious of your intentions and less cooperative if they spot you pointing a long lens at them from the shadows. The reality is you still have to be fairly close, even with a 200mm lens, to get a frame-filling portrait. It's best to be open about what you're doing.

A good way to get started with portraits is to photograph people who provide goods or services to you. After a rickshaw ride, or buying something from a market stall, ask the person if you can take their photo. Very rarely will they refuse.

PAYING FOR PHOTOS

In popular destinations you could be asked for money in return for taking a photo. This may be considered a fair and reasonable exchange, but it can become tiresome and discourage you from photographing people. Certainly don't hand out money if it's not requested, but if it is be prepared to pay or walk away. It really comes down to how important or unique the potential image is. I don't give money to children, but I do make donations to the sadhus, or holy men, of the Subcontinent. I also give to beggars and people in poverty when asked, and wherever there's an official donation box.

Agree on the price beforehand to avoid problems afterwards (and make sure you're working in their economy, not yours). Always have coins and small denomination notes with you in an easily accessible pocket (a different pocket from where you carry the rest of your money).

People often ask you to send them a photo. If you take people's names and addresses with the promise of sending a photo, make sure you do. If you don't, it makes it harder for the next traveller, and gives tourists a bad name. Just remember that when you get home, organising photos for a dozen strangers in distant lands is much more of a chore than it appears when you're having fun collecting names and addresses.

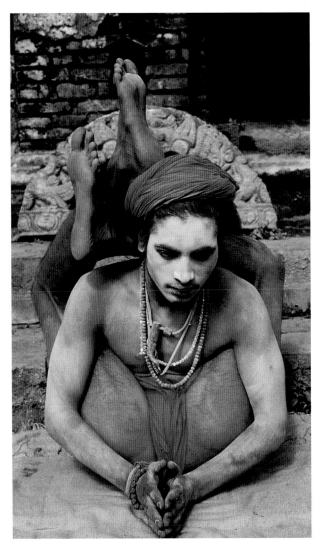

Sadhu, Pashupatinath, Nepal

There are some subjects where it's just best to be upfront and ask how much taking pictures will cost. This young sadhu (holy man) was happy to go through a series of yoga positions for my camera, at 10 rupees a pose. I had to put an end to the session myself when it became apparent he wasn't going to run out of new postures quickly.

◄ 35mm SLR, 50mm lens, 1/125 f8, Ektachrome E100VS

PORTRAITS

Capturing close-ups of people is a challenging and sometimes daunting proposition, but if done successfully it will add a great deal of depth, interest and personal satisfaction to your travel pictures.

▶ **Concentrate on filling the frame with your subject and you'll be rewarded with a stronger image.**

Avoid backgrounds that are too busy or have very light or very dark patches of colour. Your eyes should not be distracted from the subject's face. Always focus on the eyes. It doesn't matter if other features are out of focus: if the eyes aren't sharp the image will fail.

Expose for your subject's face: it's the most important part of the composition. The ideal focal-length lens for shooting portraits is between 80mm and 105mm. Lenses in this range are often called portrait lenses because of the flattering perspective they give to the face. They also allow you to fill the frame with a head-and-shoulder composition while working at a comfortable distance from your subject. If using a zoom lens on an SLR or compact camera, preset it to 100mm, then position yourself to suit – this will guarantee

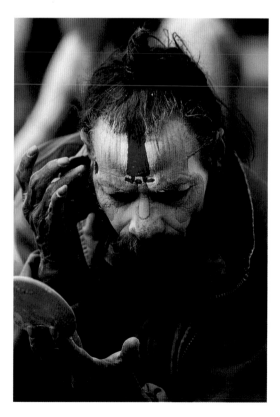

Sadhu, Pashupatinath, Nepal

Generally I like my portrait subjects to make eye contact with the viewer by looking straight into the lens. However, if they're engaged in something I prefer them to look at what they're doing for a more natural, candid shot. Here a sadhu (holy man) is applying sandalwood paste to his face.

◀ 35mm SLR, 70-200mm lens, 1/200 f8, Ektachrome E100VS

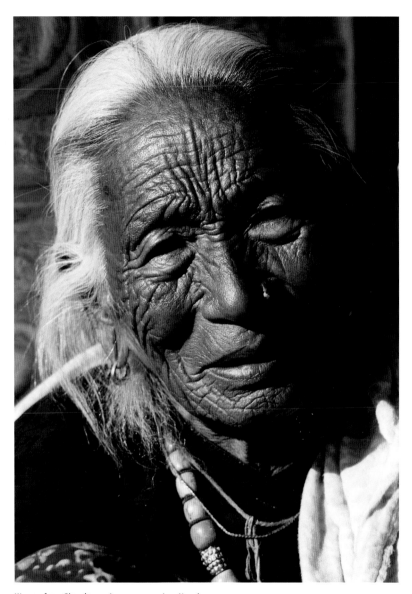

Woman from Ghandrung, Annapurna region, Nepal

Watching the world (and Western trekkers) go by from her veranda, this woman portrayed to me the spirit of the people of the Himalaya: her face is weathered, warm and dignified. I was staying in the village and first saw her sitting with her back to the sun. I returned later in the day to find her back on the veranda, only now the sun had come just far enough round to light her face evenly. There was just enough side light to emphasise the lines on her face.

▲ 35mm SLR, 100mm lens, 1/125 f8, Kodachrome 64

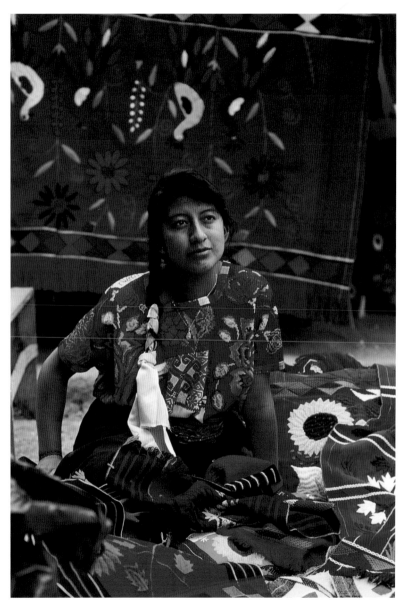

Woman from Zinacantán, Mexico

I had read that the Tzotzil Indian village of Zinacantán had banned photography. Local inquires suggested this wasn't the case, but there were some restrictions and extra sensitivity was called for. To avoid potential problems I chose to visit with a local guide. He introduced me to a family who were quite happy to be photographed.

▲ 35mm SLR, 100mm lens, 1/125 f4, Ektachrome E100VS

a pleasing perspective. Set your shutter speed to at least 1/125 to prevent movement by the subject resulting in a blurry photo. A wide aperture (f2–f5.6) will ensure that the background is out of focus and help minimise any distracting elements. Compose the photo vertically, which will minimise empty, distracting space around your subject. In low-light situations when it's not possible to hand-hold your camera consider using a faster film rather than flash.

If you're using a compact camera remember not to get closer than the minimum focussing distance (usually 1m).

Overcast weather is ideal for portraits. It provides even, soft light that eliminates heavy shadows and is usually quite flattering to the subject. It allows you to take pictures of people in all locations and to work on auto to shoot quickly.

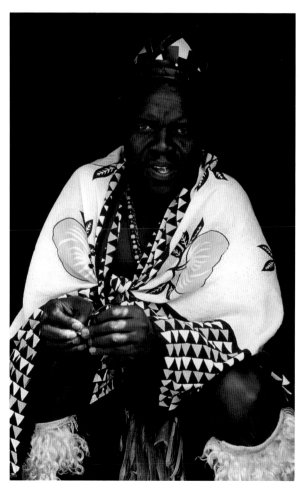

African chief, Phe Zulu, Umgeni Valley, South Africa

On a visit to the village of Phe Zulu we were invited to the chief's hut. He sat at the back in almost total darkness explaining what his role in the village was. In the darkness a built-in flash would have used its maximum output to light the scene and caused badly overexposed photos. On request, the chief was perfectly happy to move to the entrance of his hut for a photograph.

◄ 35mm SLR, 100mm lens, 1/125 f8, Ektachrome E100VS

ENVIRONMENTAL PORTRAITS

Environmental portraits add context and allow the viewer to learn something about the person. This kind of portrait lends itself to the use of wide-angle lenses. The wider field of view offered by 24mm, 28mm or 35mm lenses allows you to get close but still include plenty of information about where the subject is. Slower shutter speeds can be employed to maximise depth of field. This is important because the location is an integral part of the picture. Get close so that nothing comes between the camera and the subject. This technique is great for crowded situations such as markets and busy streets.

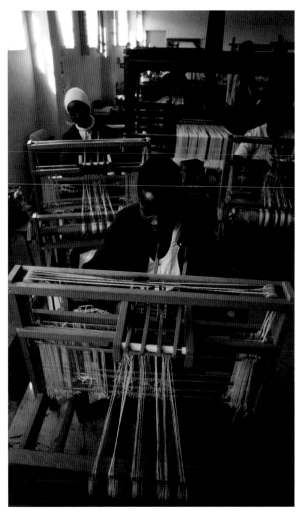

Weavers, Bulawayo, Zimbabwe

At Bulawayo Home Industries, the weavers were working on looms. I chose to photograph this weaver because she was working by a window. The available light ensured natural-looking colours and retained the atmosphere of the environment.

◄ 35mm SLR, 24mm lens, 1/125 f5.6, Ektachrome E100VS

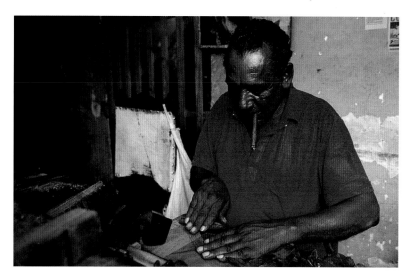

Cigar maker, Trinidad, Cuba

People at work make excellent subjects for environmental portraits. They're often less self-conscious in front of the camera because they're occupied. This cigar maker was working in a dim room, but by opening the window shutters on one side of the room I had just enough light to hand-hold the camera and use standard 100 ISO film.

▲ 35mm SLR, 24mm lens, 1/60 f4, Ektachrome E100VS

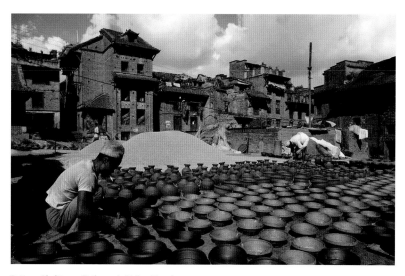

Potters, Bhaktapur, Kathmandu Valley, Nepal

Newly made pottery is placed in the sun to dry in the Potters' Quarter of Bhaktapur, the third major town of the Kathmandu Valley. This portrait clearly shows what these men do and where they do it. The 24mm wide-angle lens allowed me to get close enough to show the detail of the work and still include background for context.

▲ 35mm SLR, 24mm lens, 1/60 f8, Kodachrome 64

GROUPS

People gather in groups large and small for all sorts of reasons: to wait for a bus, watch a street performance, make a purchase at a market stall, even just to stand around and watch the foreigner take photos. Unlike the formal groups we like to pose at home, groups encountered on the road are best treated as informal; photograph them how you find them. The larger the group the less chance you have of getting a shot where everyone looks good, so take as many frames as you can.

When you've taken the group shot consider moving, or zooming in on, individuals for portrait shots.

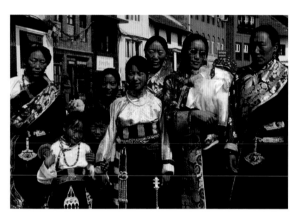

Family at Bodhnath, Kathmandu Valley, Nepal

Sometimes you have to organise people into a group photo. This family, dressed in their finest clothes, were walking around Bodhnath Stupa celebrating Losar (Tibetan New Year) but were quite spread out. I sought permission to take the photograph from one of the women who then chased the rest of the family down. All I had to do was get them all to look at the camera.

◀ 35mm SLR, 24-70mm lens, 1/160 f8, Ektachrome E100VS

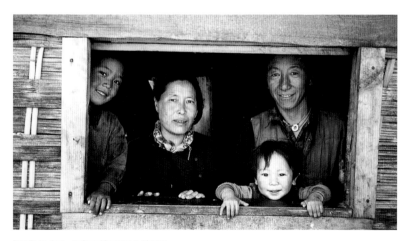

Family in shop window, Bhumtang, Bhutan

This family appeared at the window of their shop upon hearing English spoken outside. I had the compact camera in my hand and quickly took a frame rather than risk losing the shot while I changed cameras.

▲ 35mm compact, Kodacolor 100

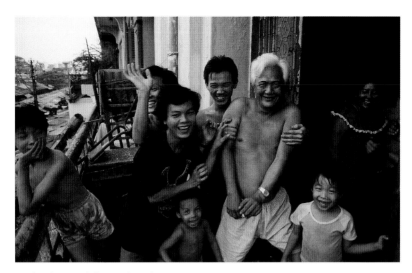

Family at home in Cholon, Ho Chi Minh City, Vietnam

In my search for a viewpoint over Cholon Market, I was invited into a house overlooking the street. The whole family joined me on the balcony. Before asking for permission to photograph, I put a 24mm lens on and set the shutter speed and aperture. My suggestion to photograph them resulted in great hilarity and while they organised themselves I was able to shoot a group shot with lots of life and a spontaneous sense of fun. You can't ask people to pose like this.

▲ 35mm SLR, 24mm lens, 1/125 f8, Kodachrome 64

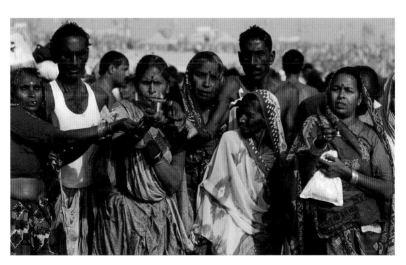

Family making offering, Allahabad, India

The chance of getting a great shot of a group diminishes in direct proportion to how many people are in the group. With this many people I always aim to shoot seven or eight frames to hedge against the inevitable closed eyes and weird facial expressions that are so easy to capture.

▲ 35mm SLR, 100mm lens, 1/125 f8, Ektachrome E100VS

CHILDREN

Many people feel more comfortable taking pictures of children than adults. They're usually very enthusiastic about being photographed and will often give you the time to take several frames.

A great way to break the ice with children, and to give them something in return, is to let them look through the viewfinder. This is especially exciting for them if you have a telephoto lens on. It's a good idea, if you can, to turn the camera off – some children are very quick to figure out how to press the shutter! If you're shooting digitally, showing them the result on the LCD screen is even better.

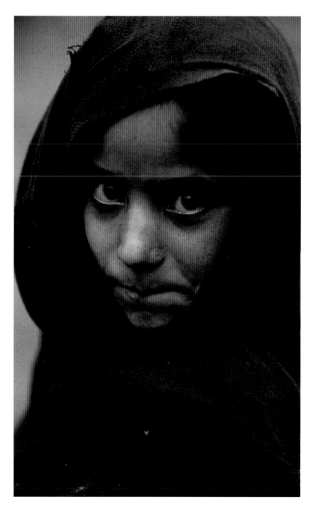

Girl from Sonamarg, Kashmir, India

This image has all the elements I aim for in a portrait. An interesting face, a natural pose, a unique expression, eye contact, no distracting elements and a background that complements the colours of the subject. She gave me one frame before running off to join her friends.

◄ 35mm SLR, 100mm lens, 1/125 f5.6, Kodachrome 64

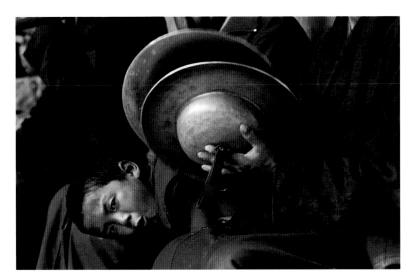

Novice monk, Tengboche Monastery, Khumbu Himal, Nepal

During preparation for the annual monastery festival, this novice monk was quite happy to play peek-a-boo with the tourist, disappearing between his friends every time the camera went to my eye. Fortunately, he peeked once too often and lost.

▲ 35mm SLR, 100mm lens, 1/125 f4, Ektachrome E100SW

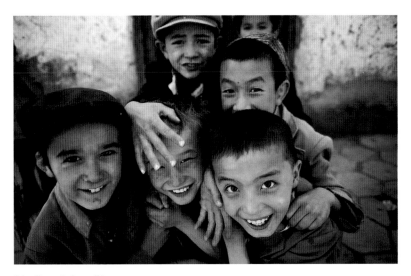

Schoolboys, Kashgar, China

On their way home from school these young Uiyger boys were only too willing to pose for the camera – in fact, it was their idea! If you're walking the streets hoping to take photos it's much better to have your camera out – they only asked because they saw the camera.

▲ 35mm SLR, 24mm lens, 1/125 f5.6, Kodachrome 64

TRAVEL COMPANIONS

Treat taking pictures of your friends and family as seriously as the other people pictures you take. A great way to get good shots of your companions on the road is to look out for situations where they are interacting with the locals or are occupied with something of interest. This will create much more rewarding shots than by getting them to look at the camera. Look for instances where your friends are bargaining for a souvenir, loading packs on the bus roof or looking at temple statues. Your photos will capture the travel experience in an active rather than passive way.

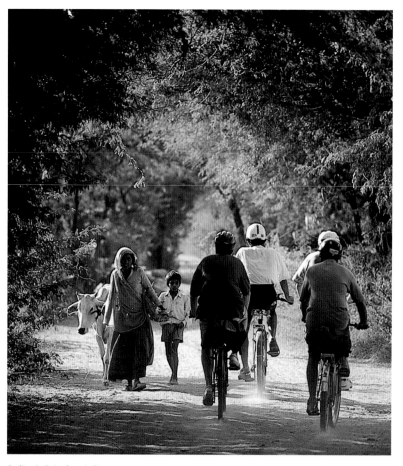

Cycling in Rajasthan, India

To contrast the crowds of the town a peaceful, rural image was required. Anticipating the place where the cyclists and the woman would meet I composed the shot and waited for the subjects to pass each other.

▲ 35mm SLR, 100mm lens, 1/250 f5.6, Ektachrome E100SW

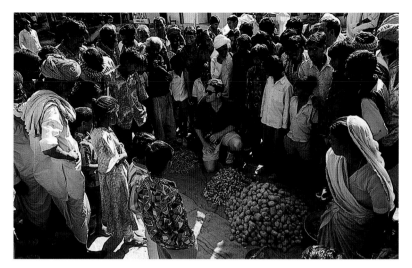

Street market, India

Every village we stopped at while cycling in Rajasthan brought crowds out. To capture this I looked for a suitable location where I could get a viewpoint without being engulfed in the crowd myself. I asked a fellow traveller to look at the goods for sale. Within a minute a crowd had gathered.

▲ 35mm SLR, 24mm lens, 1/125 f11, Kodachrome 64

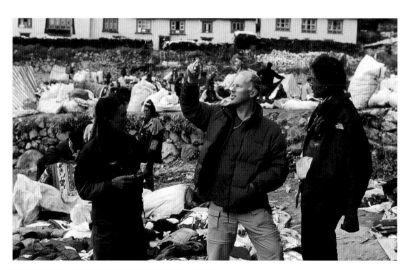

Shopping at the Tibetan Market, Namche Bazaar, Nepal

Natural-looking shots of your friends should be easy. If you don't manage to catch them in the right place at the right time, organise the elements yourself. The hardest thing is remembering to take these shots as seriously as other subjects.

▲ 35mm SLR, 24-70mm lens, 1/125 f6.3, Ektachrome E100VS

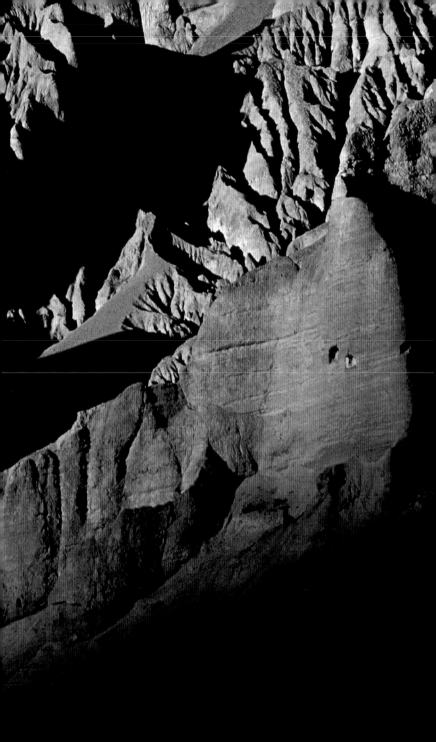

LANDSCAPES

When we look at a scene we scan a wide area, noting the colour, beauty, scale and main features – we see straight through power lines and rubbish bins and create in our mind's eye a perfect impression of the scene. The camera sees everything; it doesn't know you didn't mean to include the toilet block on the left or the 'Keep Out' sign on the right.

When you're confronted with a beautiful scene it's very tempting to put on the widest lens to try and get everything into your composition. Remember that landscapes don't have to always take in the big scene. Isolate elements that say something about the environment and complement the panoramic views. As with all good compositions, there needs to be a point of interest in the landscape, a main feature that can hold the viewer's attention. Choice of an appropriate lens plays a major part in achieving this.

Wide-angle lenses increase the foreground and sky content, exaggerate sweeping lines and make the subjects in a landscape smaller. Make sure that the foreground and sky are interesting and relevant to the composition. Telephoto lenses allow you to select a part of a scene and to flatten the perspective, making the foreground and background elements appear closer to each other. What you focus on will become larger.

Generally, the aperture is given priority when shooting landscapes, to ensure sharpness from front to back. For maximum depth of field, focus on a point one-third into the scene, just beyond the foreground subject, and stop down to f16. Use the depth-of-field button to confirm visually what you're hoping to achieve. At this aperture, with 100 ISO film, shutter speeds will drop below 1/15. A tripod and cable release are essential equipment for the serious landscape photographer. On windy days slow shutter speeds will record movement in the landscape. Swaying branches will blur at 1/15 or slower, depending on how strong the wind is. This can be very effective if desired. Clouds may also blur if exposures are longer than half a second, which isn't so effective. As you compose landscapes pay particular attention to the horizon and check the elements in the frame.

▸ Place horizons carefully. Start with the rule of thirds to ensure the horizon is placed away from the middle of the frame. If the sky is dull and lacking detail it will look flat. Place the horizon in the top third of the frame. If the foreground is uninteresting place the horizon on the bottom third. If both do nothing for the photograph, eliminate them by moving closer or zooming in.

▸ Horizons should be straight.

▸ Scan your viewfinder before you release the shutter to check for unwanted elements, particularly at the edges of the frame.

▸ Don't accidentally photograph your shadow in the landscape. You have to be especially careful when shooting very early or very late in the day with wide-angle lenses. Shoot from a low angle or position your shadow in a natural shadow area of the composition.

Because landscapes don't walk off like other subjects you can spend time experimenting with composition and exposure, and you can return to the same place at a different time to experiment with light. Professional landscape photographers habitually rise early for first light and return two or three hours before sunset to make the most of the warm, low-angle light. This light is available to everyone. You don't need expensive equipment to get up early…just a good alarm clock and a lot of will power.

Drakmar landscape, Mustang, Nepal

The red colour of the earth and the deep gullies that are a feature of the dramatic, barren landscape around the village of Drakmar are emphasised by the warm colour and low angle of the light just before sunset.

◂ 35mm SLR, 180mm lens, 1/30 f11, Ektachrome E100VS, tripod

MOUNTAINS

There's nothing quite like being in the right place to photograph the first and last rays of warm light on snow-capped mountains.

Big mountains always look impressive, but when they're lit by the early-morning or late-afternoon sun and they glow pink or gold you'll be glad you packed that extra film. These colours don't last long and frequently occur at the same time as a build up of clouds, particularly in the evening. Rapidly changing and unpredictable weather is standard issue in the mountains and demands that photographers are patient, organised and fully prepared before the light show begins.

- Be in position at least half an hour before sunrise and an hour before sunset.
- Mount your camera on a tripod.
- Spend time, while you're waiting, experimenting with different compositions and lenses and decide which composition you'll start with. You may only get one chance, so make the first shot count.
- If cloud is threatening to engulf the mountain take a photograph every couple of minutes in case it disappears completely before the light peaks.
- Ensure you have plenty of frames left. The mountain can disappear in cloud in the time it takes to change films.

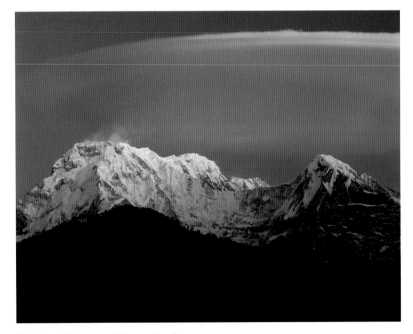

Sunrise in the Annapurnas, Dhampus, Nepal
One of the great advantages of trekking in the mountains is that you often don't have far to go, after you've dragged yourself out of bed, to catch the sunrise. I shot this from outside my tent (I wish it were always that easy). Mountains are more likely to be clear in the mornings and the intense colours don't last long.
▲ 35mm SLR, 100mm lens, 1/8 f11, Ektachrome 50STX, tripod

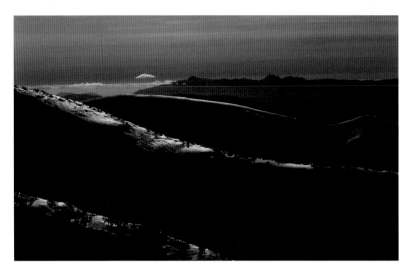

Ranges to Mt Buffalo, Victorian Alps, Australia

Back lighting has highlighted the tops of the snow-covered ridges, emphasising their shape and separating one from the next. The exposure difference between the highlights and shadows was too great to even think about retaining detail in the shadows. By exposing for the highlights (with slide film), the detail in the snow and the colour in the sky were retained. The shadows were allowed to go black to create a dramatic image.

▲ 6 x 7cm SLR camera, 105mm lens, Ektachrome 50STX, tripod

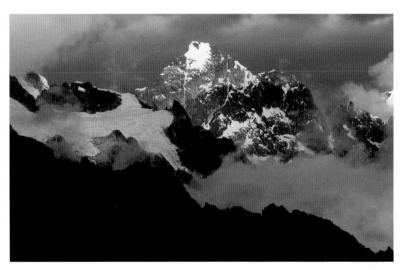

Inca Trail peaks, Peru

Each frame brings something different when photographing mountains – shadows, light and cloud come and go. Patience will be rewarded with a photograph that captures just the right mix of mountain, cloud, shadows and highlights.

▲ 35mm SLR camera, 180mm lens, 1/60 f11, Fujichrome 100RDP, tripod

SNOW SCENES

Snow causes a high level of reflection when it's the dominant element in a shot. The camera meter will underexpose the film, particularly on sunny days. To compensate, override the meter. Older cameras may require you to overexpose by one or two stops. Modern cameras with advanced metering systems cope much better, but it's still worth overexposing by a half stop and one stop until you learn how your camera's meter performs in different situations. Bracketing in half-stop increments is recommended to guarantee an accurate exposure, as is shooting early or late in the day. The lower angle of the sun brings out detail and texture in the snow and the contrast levels are more manageable.

In overcast conditions snow will record with a bluish cast. An 81B warming filter eliminates this colour shift and helps keep the snow white. Be careful using polariser filters for snow scenes. Often blue skies are already very dark and can go almost black.

When shooting landscapes in snow be aware of where you're walking – you could leave your own footprints in an area you want to photograph. (See p135 for information on photography in the cold.)

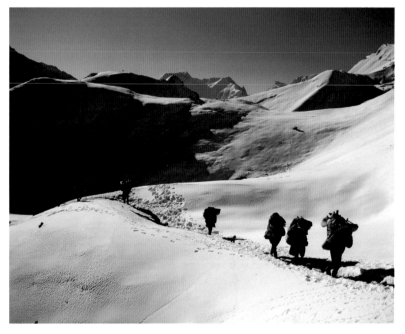

Porters on Thorung La, Annapurna region, Nepal

Crossing Thorung La is the high point of the Annapurna Circuit, one of the most popular treks in Nepal. I slept with my camera in my sleeping bag and then walked with it under my jacket in the freezing cold at 4.30am. By the time I was on the pass the sun was up. The side lighting has retained some texture in the snow but with such a large expanse of bright snow filling the frame it was necessary to overexpose the camera's recommended setting by 1½ stops. This retained the whiteness of the snow and the little colour that there was in the porters' clothing.

▲ 35mm SLR, 28-90mm lens, Kodachrome 64

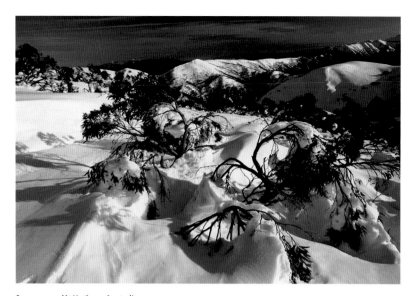

Snow gums, Mt Hotham, Australia

Bright snow will usually cause the meter to underexpose the scene. The snow gums in the foreground helped balance out the meter reading and I overexposed the meter reading by one stop. Even with the latest multi-zone metering systems, it's always wise to bracket in difficult lighting conditions, particularly with slide film.

▲ 6 x 7cm SLR, 45mm lens, Ektachrome 50STX, tripod

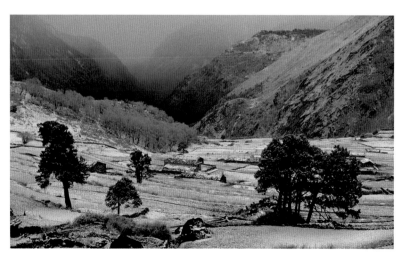

Phortse after snowfall, Khumbu Himal, Nepal

A very cold Himalayan morning, just after a snowfall, is accentuated by the way film records colour in open shade. The blueness could have been reduced with an 81C warming filter, but I wanted the photograph to show just how cold it was.

▲ 35mm SLR, 24mm lens, 1/8 f11, Kodachrome 200, tripod

DESERTS

Photographing deserts is a little like photographing snow, except you'll probably be too hot instead of too cold. If conditions are really bright, bracket exposures, favouring over-exposure up to one stop. As usual, early-morning and late-afternoon sun will make desert landscapes much more interesting. The low angle of the sun's rays will emphasise the contours of the dunes and bring out the details and textures in the sand. Remember to watch where your own shadow is falling and not to leave footprints in areas you want to portray as pristine. Look for a vantage point to survey the area and walk around the edges of potential picture subjects. Climb dunes on the shadow side, as you're less likely to make it a feature of the landscape. Extra attention must be paid to camera care (see p138).

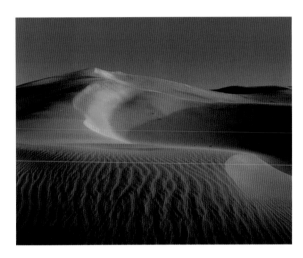

Sand dunes, Eucla, Australia

The small town of Eucla, on the Nullarbor Plain, is surrounded by a stunning expanse of sand dunes. It can be hard work shooting in this environment especially on windy days.

◀ 6 x 7cm SLR, 45mm lens, 1/4 f16, Ektachrome 50STX, polarising filter, tripod

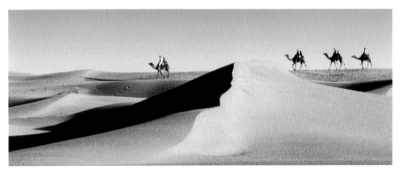

Camels on dunes, Jaisalmer, India

Riding camels in the Thar Desert is a popular activity for travellers visiting Jaisalmer. If you go, take a sunset trip – the weather will be more pleasant and the light is ideal for photography. Protect your camera equipment before you start walking on the dunes. The day after I took this shot my auto-focus lens was made unworkable by a single grain of sand.

▲ 35mm SLR, 28mm-90mm lens, Kodachrome 64

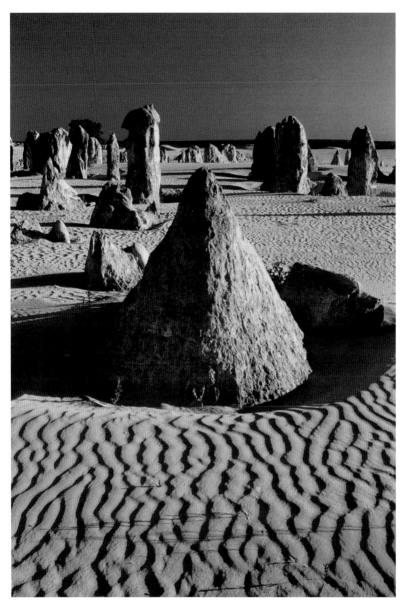

Pinnacles Desert, Nambung National Park, Australia

Limestone pillars are a feature of this coastal desert national park and many people come to photograph them. It can get crowded during the day and it's hard to avoid other people in the background and footsteps in the sand. The only way to get pristine-looking images is to get there before everyone else, or walk a lot further from the road.

▲ 6 x 7cm SLR, 45mm lens, 1/8 f16, Ektachrome 50STX, polarising filter, tripod

THE COAST

High cliffs, rugged coastlines, pounding seas, still rock pools, beaches, boat harbours and lighthouses…the coast has enough photographic possibilities to give you no time to lie around on the beach all day. The sea adds an intriguing new element to landscapes. Unlike the rock-solid landforms it meets at the shoreline, the sea is in a constant state of change. Not only does the light change throughout the day, so does the subject. Fast shutter speeds (higher than 1/250) will stop the motion of the waves and freeze sea spray. Slow shutter speeds (less than half a second) will blur the waves and soften the seascape. A polarising filter will often improve the colour and contrast in photographs taken around water by reducing the glare of the light reflecting off the water. (See p136 for information about protecting your equipment around salt water.)

To get the most out of a trip to the coast, try some of the following:

▸ Head down to the waterfront in the morning to catch the colourful and interesting fishing boats.
▸ Explore fish markets and shops until lunchtime.
▸ Walk along the beach in the afternoon and then head out to photograph the natural beauty of the coast a couple of hours before sunset.

Before you know it another day in paradise has whizzed by.

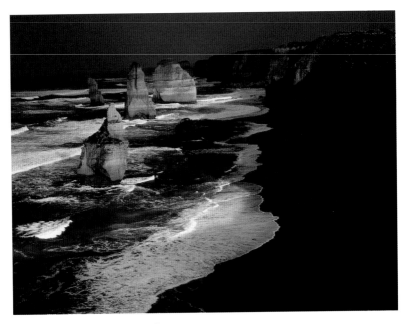

Twelve Apostles, Port Campbell, Australia

The natural rock formations known as the Twelve Apostles are a major attraction, but few people see them in great light. This shot was taken in the early morning with a storm threatening. Getting up early may not be the thing to do on holiday, but it's the thing to do when you're chasing great landscapes.

▲ 6 x 7cm SLR, 105mm lens, 1/30 f11, Ektachrome 50STX, polarising filter, tripod

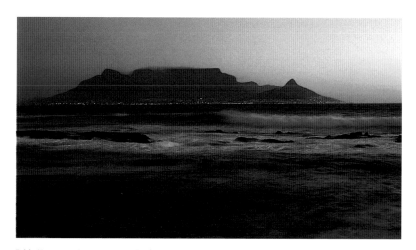

Table Mountain, Cape Town, South Africa

It took three trips out to Blouberg beach to get a view of Table Mountain unobscured by cloud. A slow shutter speed has recorded movement in the waves and softened the foreground, which has been emphasised by placing the horizon high in the frame.

▲ 35mm SLR, 100mm lens, 1 sec f11, Ektachrome E100VS, polarising filter, tripod

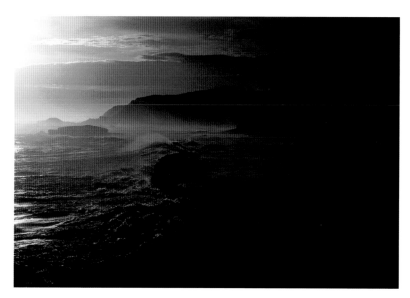

Sunset at Portsea, Point Nepean National Park, Australia

The dynamic nature of coastal landscapes is clear in this image. All the things that make it work are moving, never to be repeated in exactly the same way: the setting sun, the wispy waves behind the seabirds, and the thundering breakers in the foreground. It is this moment of absolute harmony that makes standing around on cold, windy cliffs so attractive.

▲ 6 x 7cm SLR, 200mm lens, 1/250 f11, Fujichrome Velvia, tripod

RAINFORESTS

Rainforests are one of the most difficult landscapes to photograph well. Often the light is too low to hand-hold the camera and causes automatic flashes to fire. If the sun is shining strongly enough to break through the canopy, the trees become speckled with uneven light and pictures will look colourless and messy. The best time to take pictures in a rainforest is after it has rained, or in light drizzle. The cloudy skies guarantee an even light and the water on the leaves adds life and emphasises the colour. With fine-grain film, a polariser and low light, shutter speeds will be too low to hand-hold. Use a tripod to get maximum depth of field. The polariser will cut down the reflection off the wet leaves, increasing the intensity of the colours.

Without a tripod, or with compact cameras, look for brighter areas of the rainforest where hand-held photography may be possible. You'll find these around the edges of the forest or in clearings near streams, rivers and waterfalls.

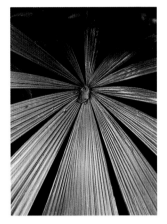

Palm leaf, Daintree, Australia
If the lighting is patchy or you can't find a suitable viewpoint for a scenic shot, look for details that are evenly lit.
▲ 6 x 7cm SLR, 105mm lens, 1/30 f11, Ektachrome 50STX, tripod

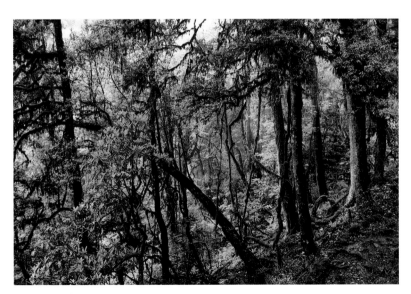

Rainforest above Bakkhim, Sikkim, India
In a more open patch of rainforest like this it's possible to hand-hold the camera.
▲ 35mm SLR, 35mm lens, 1/60 f5.6, Kodachrome 25, polarising filter

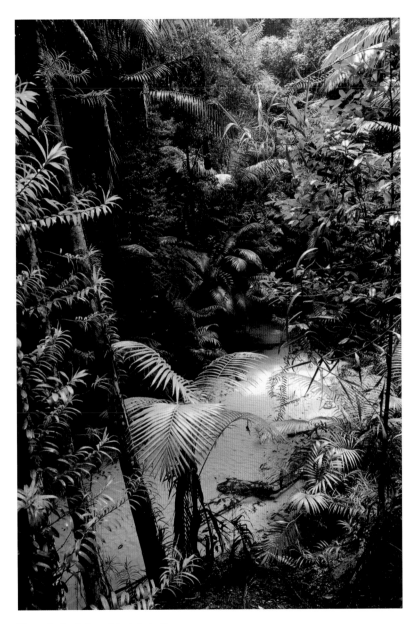

Wangoolba Creek, Fraser Island, Australia

Wangoolba Creek on Fraser Island is one of the most beautiful and atmospheric patches of rainforest in Australia. In the soft light of a rainy day the colours are intense and detail is easily recorded in all parts of the scene.

▲ 6 x 7cm SLR, 45mm lens, 1/8 f16, Ektachrome 50STX, polarising filter, tripod

UNDERWATER

At many coast and beach destinations you'll find that some of the attractions are under the water. Serious underwater photography requires specialist photographic equipment such as Nikonos cameras or underwater housings for conventional cameras; macro lenses; sports finders; and bulky flash equipment. It also helps if you're a good diver.

Those who don't want to buy expensive equipment can use underwater APS or 35mm compact auto-focus cameras or single-use, or disposable cameras (the cheapest option). Underwater housings are also available for many compact digital cameras. These cameras are capable of acceptable results on sunny, calm days at depths of 2m to 3m, making them suitable for recording your snorkelling or shallow dive experience. Even with these cameras, it's worth remembering that water acts as a filter on sunlight, reducing its intensity and changing its colour. The deeper you go the more light is absorbed and the bluer your pictures will become. Colours should record naturally down to 2m or 3m, but in deeper water a flash is essential to capture the natural colours of marine life. To increase the number of successful shots without diving and underwater photography experience, aim to:

- Shoot in the middle of the day, between 10am and 2pm, when the sun is at its brightest and the maximum amount of sunlight penetrates the water.
- Look for subjects in shallow areas.
- Get as close as you can to your subjects. Colours will be stronger, contrast higher and pictures sharper if you keep subjects within 3m or 4m.
- Use fast 200 ISO or 400 ISO film and fast shutter speeds to prevent camera shake and subject movement.
- Rinse your camera in fresh water as soon as possible when back on dry land.

If you're keen to experiment and learn more about underwater photography, some dive destinations hire out underwater camera equipment and offer introductory lessons. This is an excellent way to use professional equipment without the expense of buying it.

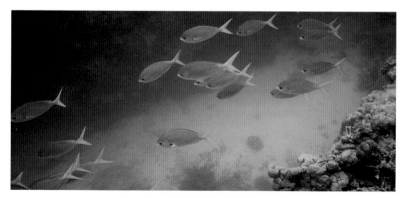

Yellow-tailed fusiliers, Great Barrier Reef, Australia

Snorkelling provides the traveller with an accessible window into the world of underwater photography. I don't shoot underwater regularly, but when you're somewhere such as the Great Barrier Reef it's hard to resist. Be patient – let the fish come to you and you'll get much better results than chasing them around.

▲ 35mm underwater compact, Ektachrome 100STZ

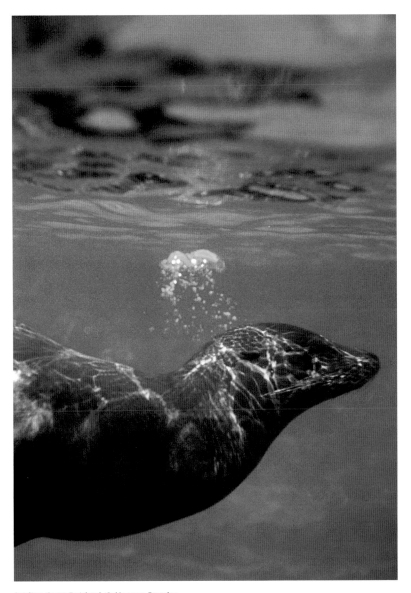

Sea lion, Santa Fe Island, Galápagos, Ecuador

A trip to the Galápagos meant that I had to go underwater twice a day for eight days; I still don't really like it. Without flash equipment I stayed in the shallows or waited for the marine life to come up to me to maximise the strength of the sun. The pictures still had a strong blue cast, which is OK in this instance because it's countered by the speckled sunlight. My underwater pictures are getting better, but I suppose I need to change my attitude and use flash to take the next step.

▲ 35mm underwater rangefinder, 35mm lens, 1/250 f8, Ektachrome E100VS rated at 200 ISO (one-stop push)

RIVERS & WATERFALLS

The flowing water of rivers and waterfalls can be interpreted in different ways through shutter-speed selection. To give the impression of running water, experiment with shutter speeds from 1/30 to one second. If the flow is fast 1/30 will do and you may be able to hand-hold the camera using a wide-angle lens. For best results and maximum depth of field, use a tripod. Start at 1/15 and go down to one second depending on the rate the water is flowing and the amount of blur you're after. Quite a different effect is achieved with fast shutter speeds (1/250 and higher), which 'freeze' the water in mid-flow, bringing out colour and detail. Like rainforests, waterfalls photograph best in the even light of a bright overcast day. Contrast between the water and the surroundings is often naturally high, and the soft, indirect light allows detail to be recorded in the highlights and the shadows. A polarising filter can improve the image by cutting out reflections from the wet rock and surrounding vegetation.

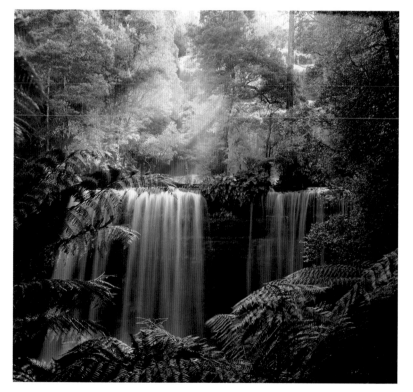

Russell Falls, Mount Field National Park, Australia

The shutter speed and the speed the water is flowing control the amount of blur. Longer exposures provide a softer, milkier effect than short exposures.

▲ 6 x 7cm SLR, 45mm lens, 1/2 f11, Ektachrome 50STX, polarising filter, tripod

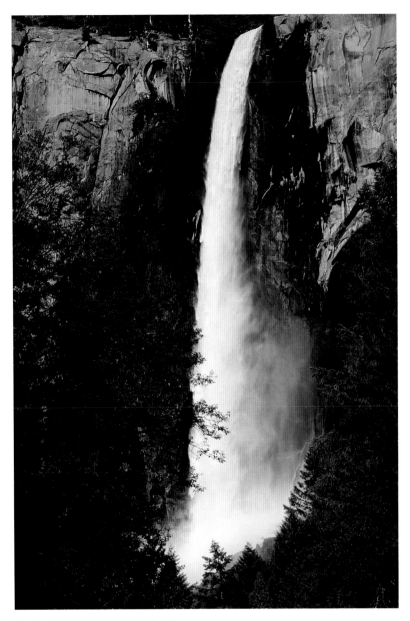

Bridal Veil Falls, Yosemite National Park, USA

When a high waterfall is flowing fast even fast shutter speeds don't completely freeze the water. The tight vertical framing of this waterfall isolates it from its environment and emphasises its height.

▲ 35mm SLR, 180mm lens, 1/250 f8, Ektachrome E100SW, polarising filter

LAKES & REFLECTIONS

Lakes add a dynamic element to a landscape. Be aware that a gust of wind can change the look of a lake significantly – a mirrored landscape can quickly become an abstract interpretation of the same scene. Reflections can't be guaranteed, but are more likely early in the day. See what effect a polarising filter has on the reflection as you rotate it. You can sometimes get two different-looking photos by changing the position of the filter. The reflected part of the landscape is often darker than the actual subject. Take your meter reading from, and focus on, the landform rather than the reflection so that the landform is sharp and correctly exposed. If there's more than two stops difference between the two parts of the composition a graduated neutral density filter will even out the lighting.

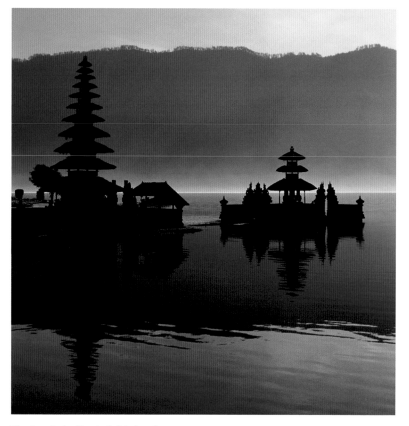

Ulun Danu Bratan Temple, Bali, Indonesia

In the early morning this beautiful Hindu–Buddhist temple is reflected in the waters of Lake Bratan. Sometimes placing the horizon in the centre of the frame does work, especially with reflections because it emphasises the symmetry of the scene.

▲ 6 x 7cm SLR, 105mm lens, Ektachrome 100STS, tripod

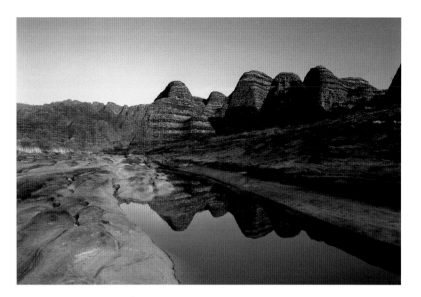

Bungle Bungles, Purnululu National Park, Australia

Wherever there is water lying around there is the possibility of a reflection. A reflection in the little water left in the essentially dry riverbed adds a surprising element to the landscape.

▲ 6 x 7cm SLR, 45mm lens, 1/15 f11, Ektachrome 50STX, polarising filter, tripod

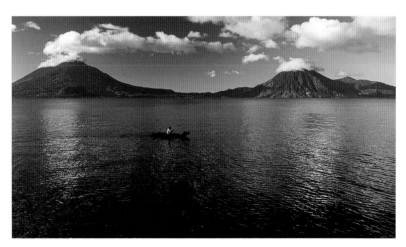

Lake Atitlan, Panahachal, Guatemala

The choppy waters of Lake Atitlan denied me a reflection of the volcanoes. It wasn't until the fourth morning and the appearance of clouds that I was able to take a photograph with added interest in the water. Although the sky was also interesting, I placed the horizon in the top part of the frame to emphasis the size of the lake. I used a polariser at half strength to increase the contrast between the clouds and the sky, while still retaining some reflection off the water.

▲ 35mm SLR, 24mm lens, 1/250 f8, Ektachrome E100VS, polarising filter

RAINBOWS

Fleeting and colourful, rainbows add a surprising element to a landscape. Like colourful skies, a rainbow in your composition doesn't automatically make a good photo. The landscape itself should be interesting, and then enhanced by the inclusion and careful placement of the rainbow. Use a polarising filter to increase the contrast between the rainbow, clouds and sky. It will strengthen the colours of the rainbow and cut down distracting reflections in the landscape. In some cases rainbows will not record on film without the aid of a polariser. Rainbows will really test your ability to work quickly, as they rarely last more than a few minutes – and be prepared to get wet.

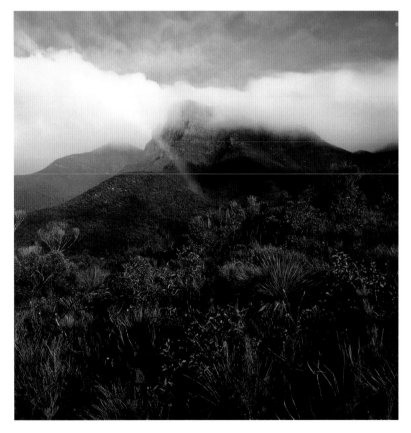

Bluff Knoll, Stirling Ranges, Australia

The up side of a rainstorm is that when it ends there's often a period of wonderful light as the sun breaks through the clouds. When it does, the chance of rainbows is high, but the trick is to find a landscape to include with the rainbow. A rainbow alone won't make any photograph worth looking at. A polarising filter will intensify the colours of a rainbow, but in this landscape it also cut out the reflection from the wet vegetation.

▲ 6 x 7cm SLR, 45mm lens, 1/30 f11, Ektachrome 50STX, polarising filter, tripod

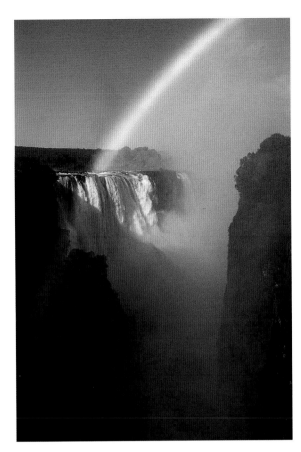

Victoria Falls, Zimbabwe

Rainbows also appear on waterfalls if the sun strikes the rising spray at just the right angle. Around mid-afternoon is a good time to see the dramatic rainbows that form on Victoria Falls.

◀ 35mm SLR, 24mm lens, 1/250 f8, Ektachrome E100VS, polarising filter

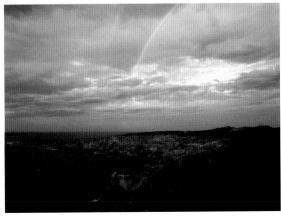

Cape du Couedic, Kangaroo Island, Australia

The double arch of a rainbow above the lighthouse lasted about one minute. When the sky is interesting, emphasise it by placing the horizon in the bottom third of the frame.

◀ 6 x 7cm SLR, 45mm lens, 1/15 f16, Ektachrome 50STX, polarising filter, tripod

FLOWERS

Flowers are a common travel subject that require close focussing for impact. Flower studies require macro equipment if you want to fill the frame with a single flower. If you're using the macro facility on a zoom lens and can't fill the frame, treat the flower as one element of the picture. Alternatively, fill the frame with the colour of many flowers. If there is the slightest breeze, flowers move and blur, which can look great if it's what you want. Shutter speeds over 1/125 will stop most movement except on very windy days, but if using speeds slower than 1/60 wait for a still moment. Light-coloured flowers against dark backgrounds can fool light meters, so meter for the flower to maintain detail and colour.

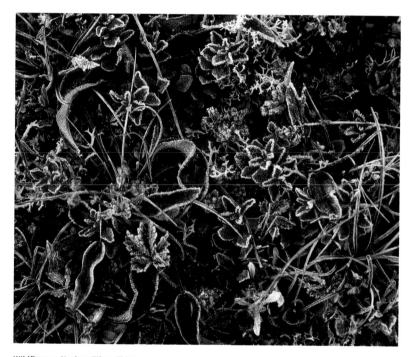

Wildflowers, Nyalam, Tibet, China

It's so easy to miss subjects like this when you've got a clear objective in mind. I was up in the hills behind the village of Nyalam photographing the mountains when the flowers caught my eye. I changed my focus from 6000m peaks to 6mm flowers (using the same lens). I spent the next few minutes quickly photographing the flowers before the sun reached this part of the hillside and the frost disappeared.

▲ 35mm SLR, 100mm lens, ½ sec f11, Ektachrome 50STX, tripod

Cosmos, Morioka, Japan

If your equipment doesn't let you get close, look for expanses of flowers and go for a more scenic approach. By eliminating other elements from your composition you'll still have a flower photo. I use a 50mm standard lens and 100mm lens for taking close-ups. The 100mm only focuses down to 0.7m, but its magnification increases the size of the subject sufficiently for the kind of general close-ups I take.

▶ 35mm SLR, 50mm lens, 1/125 f8, Ektachrome E100VS

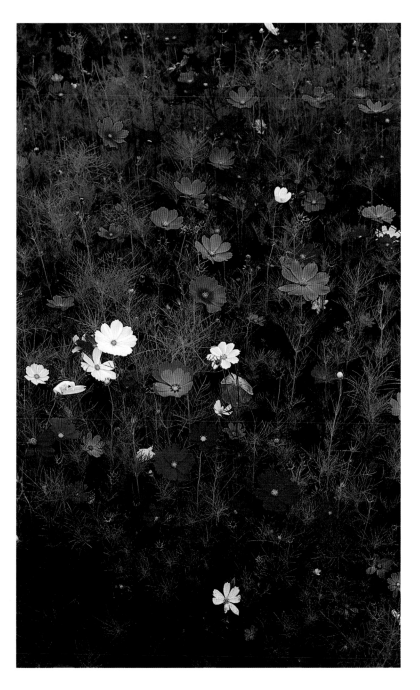

HUMAN SCALE

Include a human element in a landscape and you add a sense of scale that is clearly understood. Place the element in the middle distance and use a standard to telephoto lens for best effect. If the subject is too close to the camera and you use a wide-angle lens, perspective will be exaggerated. The subject will appear far bigger than the background elements, and all sense of scale will be lost. If you are using people to show scale, ensure that they're looking into the scene. This will lead the viewer's eye to the main subject rather than to the edges of the composition.

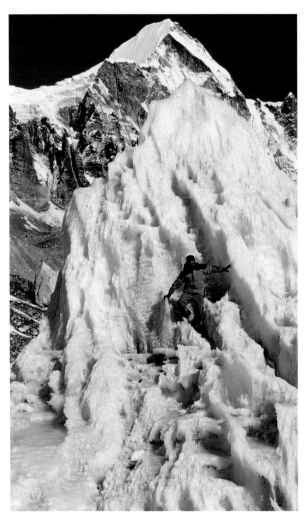

Trekker on ice pinnacles, Sagarmatha National Park, Nepal

Without the human element the size of the ice pinnacles in the Khumbu Glacier that comes off Mt Everest would remain a mystery to the viewer. By including a person, obviously having fun, the geological feature is given some relativity and the experience of being there is captured.

◀ 35mm SLR, 24-70mm lens, 1/250 f6.3 (+½ stop), Ektachrome E100VS

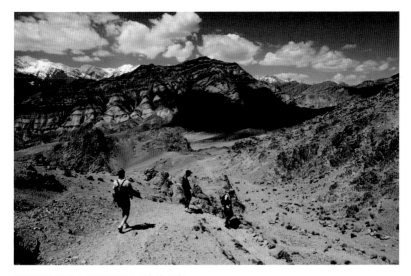

Trekking from Chiling to Sumdoo, Ladakh, India

The inclusion of the trekkers emphasises how vast the landscape is in this remote part of the Indian Himalaya.

▲ 35mm SLR, 24mm lens, 1/250 f11, Kodachrome 64, polarising filter

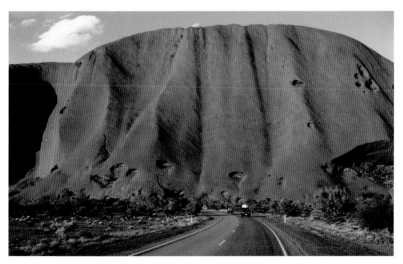

Road to Uluru, Australia

Uluru is big, but until you've been there you don't realise exactly how big it is. The road and the car provide familiar reference points to help establish a sense of size. If the sky had been eliminated the sense of scale wouldn't be quite so clear.

▲ 35mm SLR, 35mm lens, 1/125 f8, Fujichrome 100

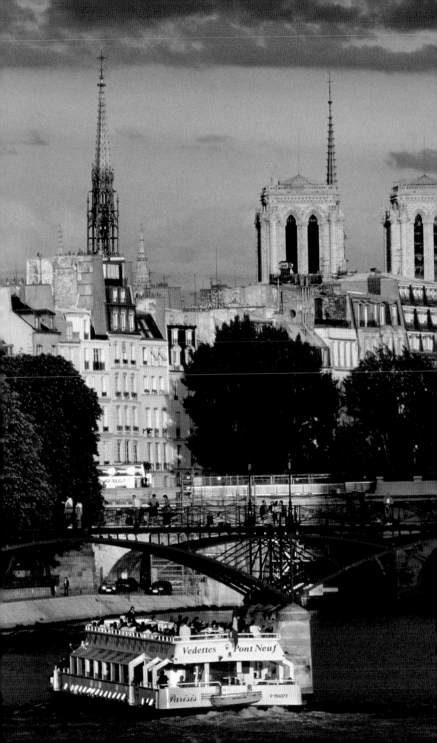

CITIES

Cities offer enormous photographic opportunities. Within all cities you'll find focal points that present scenes, buildings and activity that typify the country and go way beyond the glossy brochures. After you've seen the famous places, spend some time wandering the streets; observe daily life and delve deeper into the city's atmosphere.

▶ **The key to photographing a city is to walk, walk, and walk.**

When you've walked everywhere: do it again in a different direction, at a different time of day, in different weather, on a different day of the week. Venture away from the regularly visited areas and you'll discover lots of people who aren't tired of having their photo taken.

City tours are offered everywhere and are useful to get a quick overview of a new city and its main sights. However, they have limited use for good photography as they're usually run in the middle of the day and give very little time at each destination. If your budget isn't too tight forget the bus and do the same thing in a taxi.

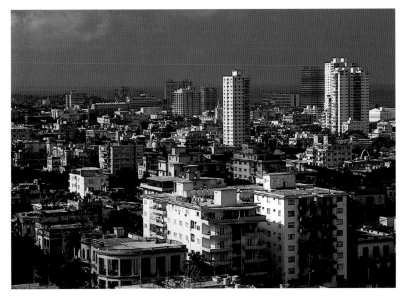

Havana, Cuba
My guidebook listed the hotels in Central and Old Havana with rooftop bars. I picked three that were located centrally and did the rounds late one afternoon. You can try going up other tall buildings, but hotels are accustomed to foreigners and rarely ask questions.
▲ 35mm SLR, 50mm lens, 1/125 f8, Ektachrome E100VS, polarising filter

River boat on the Seine at dusk, Paris, France
I had almost given up – the wind was cold, the light was dull and I'd been standing around for over an hour, hoping the sun would break through the clouds. Fortunately, when it did the colour of the light was beautiful and I had the Paris view I had envisaged earlier in the day.
◀ 35mm SLR, 180mm lens, 1/60 f8, Ektachrome E100SW, tripod

CITYSCAPES

Skylines and city views are wonderful scene setters for your album or slide show, providing a context for the photos that follow. Big cities often have official vantage points on nearby hills or at the top of tall buildings that provide great views of the city. These places are easily accessible and you know what you'll be seeing. After taking in the official views seek out different vantage points to create unique photos. Smaller places may not advertise a lookout, but most taxi drivers will know where you can look over their town. Hotels, of all standards, sometimes have rooftop bars and restaurants, which are easily accessed. Check out a few during the day noting where the sun will set and rise, and return later to the best placed viewpoint.

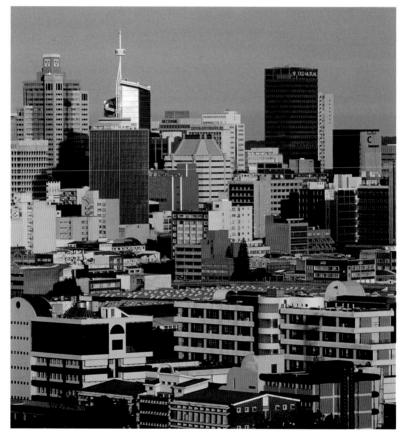

Durban, South Africa

When there are hills near a city there has to be a good view of the skyline from somewhere. With no previously published pictures as a guide I hired a taxi and explained what I was after. It took a while but eventually we found a piece of open ground with a clear view of the city. The driver had never been there before.

▲ 35mm SLR, 180mm lens, 1/30 f11, Ektachrome E100VS, tripod

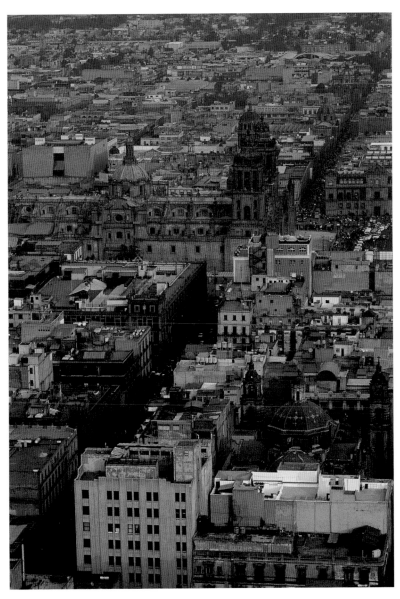

View to the Zócalo, Mexico City, Mexico

I always take the opportunity to photograph cities from their designated lookouts. The view from the Latin American Tower in Mexico City is a must for any tourist. The city disappears into the haze in all directions but the tower is close enough to the historic centre, known as the Zócalo, on one side, and the high-rise towers on the other, for a good selection of shots.

▲ 35mm SLR, 100mm lens, 1/125 f5.6, Ektachrome E100VS

BUILDINGS

Tilt your camera up to photograph a building and it will appear to be falling backwards. Converging verticals or linear distortion can be effective when the composition exaggerates the distortion. Looking up at skyscrapers is a good example of this technique. To record buildings faithfully the camera must be level. Photographers specialising in architectural work achieve this with perspective correction (PC) or shift lenses that allow control of the angle of the plane of focus through tilt and shift movements. Perspective correction is also possible without specialist lenses by:

▸ Finding a viewpoint that is half the height of the building you're photographing.
▸ Finding an interesting foreground to fill the bottom half of the frame.
▸ Moving away from the building and using a telephoto lens.

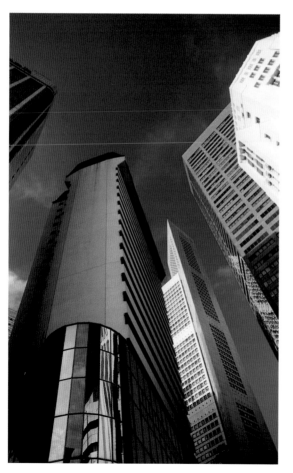

Skyscrapers, Singapore

Converging verticals can be used to good effect by exaggerating them.

◂ 35mm SLR, 24mm lens, 1/125 f11, Ektachrome E100SW, polarising filter

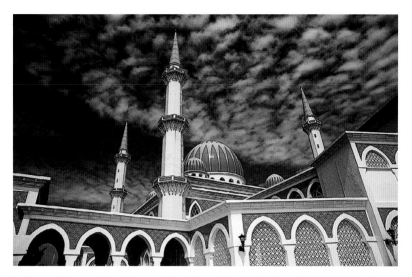

Looking up at the mosque from close range with a wide-angle lens has tilted the vertical walls and minarets backwards and inwards.

▲ 35mm SLR, 24mm lens, 1/125 f11, Ektachrome E100SW, polarising filter

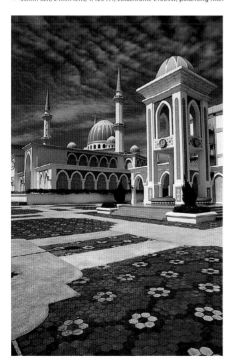

Sultan Ahmed Mosque, Kuantan, Malaysia

By including an interesting foreground the film plane can be kept reasonably parallel to the building and the verticals kept straight.

◀ 35mm SLR, 24mm lens, 1/125 f8, Ektachrome E100SW, polarising filter

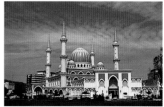

Alternatively, move back and use a telephoto lens to fill the frame with the building to keep the verticals straight.

▲ 35mm SLR, 100mm lens, 1/125 f8, Ektachrome E100SW, polarising filter

FAMOUS PLACES

Every country has buildings on its 'must see' list. The Taj Mahal, Machu Picchu, the Great Wall, the Pyramids, the Eiffel Tower…places whose image is already deeply etched in our mind's eye years before we visit them. These sites are photographed millions of times a year by visitors from all over the globe and printed in books, magazines and brochures, on postcards, tea towels, cups and place mats. If you want a real challenge, set yourself the double task of taking pictures of famous places that are as good as the published images, and then create a different photograph to those you've seen before.

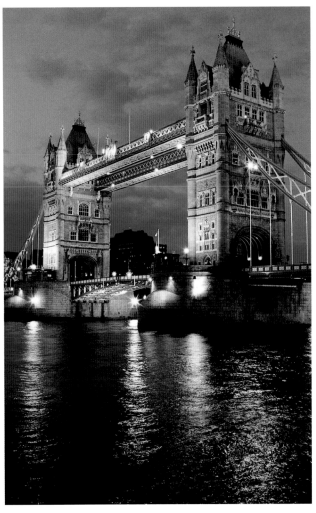

Tower Bridge, London, England

Famous places always deserve more than one visit. On your first visit you'll probably be inclined to blaze away at the subject from all angles. Great, but a second visit can be approached more calmly and deliberately. A review of published material (postcards, etc) after your first visit will make a lot more sense. You'll know where things are and where the light will be. Revisiting places, especially after you've seen the results from your first attempt, is one of the best ways to improve your travel photographs.

◀ 35mm SLR, 50mm lens, 2 secs f11, Ektachrome E100SW, tripod

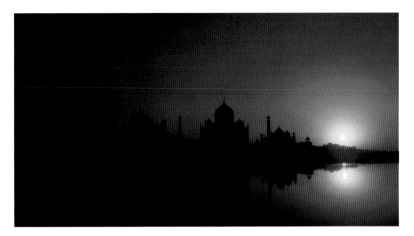

Taj Mahal, Agra, India

I got the standard shots: morning, noon and evening. Now I wanted a different view. Not many visitors cross the river behind the Taj, but it's the only place to be if you want to see the sun set behind India's most famous building. The price was a very uncomfortable 26km auto-rickshaw ride. Take a taxi.

▲ 35mm SLR, 35mm lens, 1/4 f11, Kodachrome 64, tripod

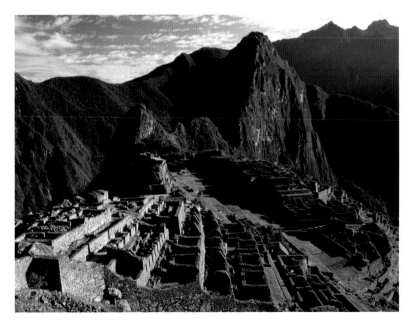

Machu Picchu, Peru

Sometimes you have to plan ahead even for straightforward shots. I got up to the ruins two hours before they opened by organising a ride with the workers.

▲ 35mm SLR, 35mm lens, 1/15 f11, Kodachrome 25, polarising filter, tripod

SACRED PLACES

Monasteries, temples, churches, mosques and shrines are a focus of day-to-day activity in many places, from the smallest village to the biggest city. They are great places to hang around, camera at the ready. Places of worship attract a steady stream of pilgrims and devotees. At the entrances and in the surrounding streets, vendors selling religious paraphernalia, souvenirs and flowers contrast with the usually quiet, calm interiors. Around the buildings look for detail images that have relevance to the religion. Incense sticks and coils, texts and motifs on the walls all make interesting subjects and say something about the place and religion.

Visitors are generally welcome to enter and observe the activity in places of worship, and, in return, sensitivity and respect are expected. Find out if certain days or times of day are busier than others because you'll be far less conspicuous in a crowd. Always ask before shooting if there's any doubt as to whether photography is allowed. Religious ceremonies are not put on for the benefit of tourists and you really should take a step back and consider the situation before jumping in with all flashes blazing. It's possible to be respectful and still come away with a rewarding experience and images to match.

During ceremonies, especially those indoors, turn off the camera's flash and film winder if you can or, if your camera allows, switch to the slower but quieter silent-advance mode. Take up a position where you can come and go without disturbing others and that makes the most of any available natural or incandescent light.

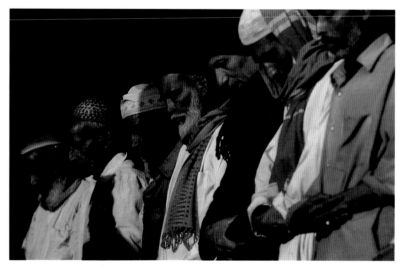

Evening prayers, Kolkata, India

When I enter places of worship I always have my cameras out so I can shoot quickly and don't give the impression I'm trying to sneak pictures. At Tippu Sultan mosque I checked that it was OK to take pictures, took up a position on the west side and waited for the prayers to start. By arriving early I had the chance to talk to some of the men and tell them what I was doing so that when prayers began no-one gave me a second glance.

▲ 35mm SLR, 100mm lens, 1/125 f8, Ektachrome E100SW

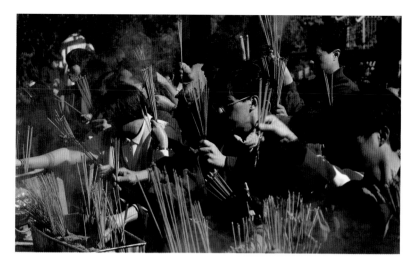

Wong Sin Temple, Hong Kong, China

When it's really busy at Wong Sin Temple it gets noisy and very crowded around the altar. Take advantage of these circumstances to get in close to the action and your pictures will have an intimacy about them. With this many arms and hands flying about, extra frames are well justified to ensure you get the shot.

▲ 35mm SLR, 24mm lens, 1/250 f8, Ektachrome E100SW

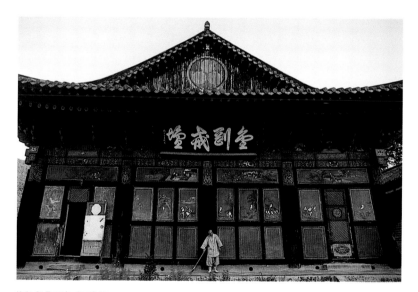

Hain Sa Temple, South Korea

Early morning at Hain Sa Temple and there wasn't much going on. A solitary monk was sweeping around the temples, so I followed him at a distance until he moved in front of one of the several impressive buildings in the temple grounds.

▲ 35mm SLR, 24mm lens, 1/60 f5.6, Kodachrome 200

INTERIORS

Photographing interiors requires the ability to switch from one technique to another, depending on the amount of available light. Individual displays are sometimes lit with spotlights intense enough to allow the camera to be hand-held. Generally, though, light levels are too low to photograph interiors with 100 ISO film hand-held. If this is the case, switch to a faster film, use flash or mount your camera on a tripod. Be prepared for all three situations. In many places flash and tripods are prohibited, so there's no choice but to use fast film or put your camera away. If flash is permitted remember to keep your subject within the range of your unit. The main advantage of a tripod is that you can use your standard fine-grain film and get lots of depth of field.

Most interiors are lit predominantly with incandescent light, which records as a yellow–orange colour cast on standard film balanced for daylight. The actual colour and strength of the cast depends on the type and mix of artificial lights (see p118 for more information). This caste creates ambience and shows that it was taken indoors. If you want to record the colours more faithfully use an 82 series colour-conversion filter or tungsten film. Unless you plan to take a lot of pictures with tungsten film it's impractical to carry on your travels. Digital cameras solve the problem electronically through the white-balance function (see p72).

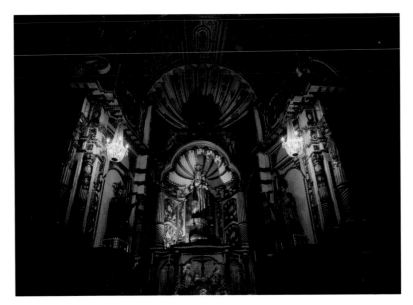

Lima Cathedral, Lima, Peru

Interiors are rarely lit brightly enough to allow hand-held photography with slow- or medium-speed films. To photograph the interior of Lima Cathedral with a compact or built-in flash would be ineffective: the subject is too far away. With a tripod the amount of light available can be very low and your standard film can be used. The colour is different to the other interiors because of the varying mix of incandescent light sources.

▲ 35mm SLR, 24mm lens, 1/8 f11, Kodachrome 64, tripod

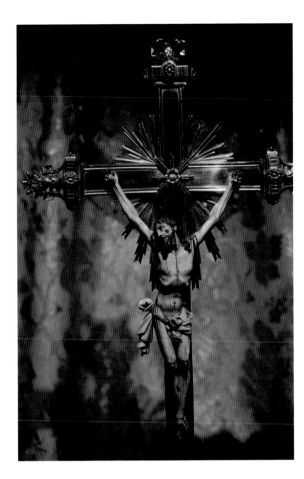

Statue of Jesus on cross, Porto, Portugal

In the museum at Porto Cathedral this statue was displayed behind glass. By placing the lens firmly against the glass, reflections are cut out and slower shutter speeds can be used. Turn the camera's built-in flash off to prevent it bouncing light off the display cabinet.

◄ 35mm SLR, 50mm lens, 1/15 f1.4, Ektachrome 50STX

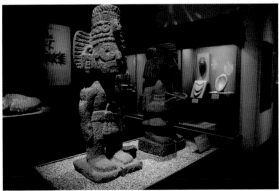

Museum of Anthropology, Mexico City, Mexico

No flash, no tripod, no problem if you've got fast film on hand. If you haven't, look around for displays that are near windows or get close to individual displays that are lit with intense spotlights.

◄ 35mm SLR, 24mm lens, 1/60 f2, Ektachrome E200 rated at 800 ISO (2 stop push)

LIFE ON THE STREETS

An itinerary that only takes in a country's main sights will leave you with a limited experience and equally limited photo opportunities. Wandering the streets of a new city is one of the great pleasures of travel. In many countries life is lived on the street. Meals are cooked and eaten; clothes, bodies and teeth are washed; games are played and business is transacted; all in full view of the passing public. As with all people photography you'll have to develop your own approach to taking pictures of people on the street, but the opportunities are many and varied.

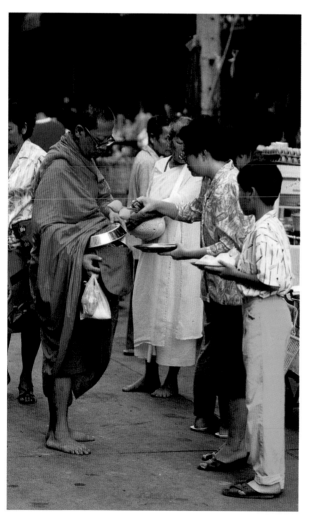

Monk collecting alms, Bangkok, Thailand

Every morning around 280,000 monks hit the streets of Thailand to collect alms. It's a scene that says a lot about the country and its people. Just when you thought you could sleep in, there are 280,000 more reasons to be up early.

◀ 35mm SLR, 100mm lens, 1/125 f4, Kodachrome 200

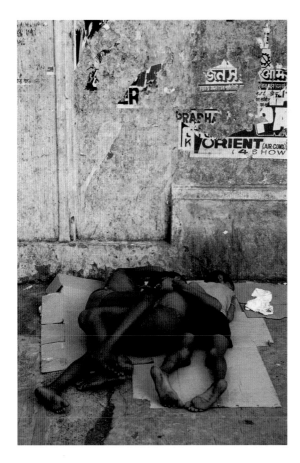

Street sleepers, Kolkata, India

It's much harder to photograph the poor than the Palaces of Rajasthan, but both say something about India.

◀ 35mm SLR, 24mm lens, 1/125 f4, Kodachrome 200

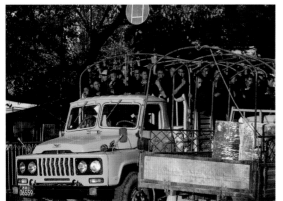

Monks in truck, Lhasa, Tibet, China

You never know what you'll stumble across while walking the streets. You can be nowhere near a major tourist sight and something unique about the country will pass right in front of you. That's why your camera shouldn't be in the bottom of your day-pack.

◀ 35mm SLR, 100mm lens, 1/250 f8, Kodachrome 64

AFTER DARK

Cities and buildings take on a completely different look and feel after dark, and the images will add an extra dimension to your collection. The best time to photograph is around 10 to 20 minutes after sunset. By then the incandescent lighting provided by interior, spot and streetlights will be the dominant light source, but there'll still be some light and colour in the sky. When it's completely dark, concentrate on filling the frame with well-lit subjects and avoid large areas of unlit space. Night photography requires a tripod and cable release, as exposures are generally long. To record detail, overexpose by one and two stops – otherwise the only thing that will come out will be the lights themselves. As with all difficult lighting situations, bracketing is recommended.

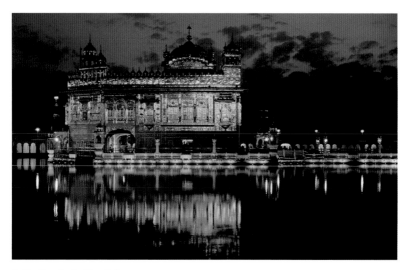

Golden Temple, Amritsar, India

The Golden Temple really lives up to its name when photographed at night. If you're going to the trouble of carrying a tripod use it for some night shots of key cityscapes and buildings. When you see the results you'll be pleased you went to the extra trouble.

▲ 35mm SLR, 50mm lens, 1 sec f8, Ektachrome E100SW, tripod

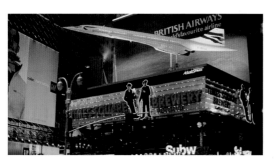

Times Square neon lights, New York, USA

Fill the frame with neon lights and there'll be enough light to hand-hold the camera and automatic meter readings will usually be accurate. If you're using a fully automatic camera turn the flash off. Scan the frame to make sure you haven't left large areas of black space.

◄ 35mm SLR, 50mm lens, 1/125 f2, Ektachrome E100VS

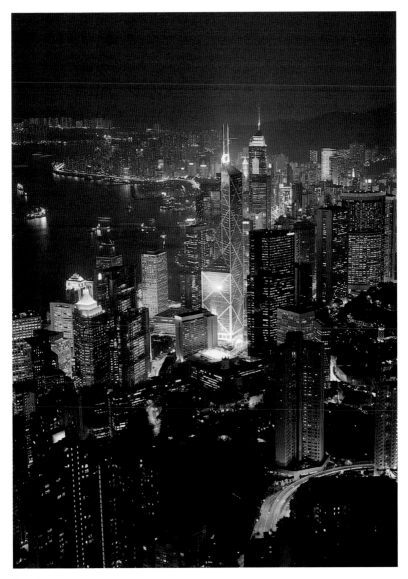

Central district from Victoria Peak, Hong Kong, China

The view from Victoria Peak of the Central district of Hong Kong is spectacular anytime. At night it's quite magical. Usually skylines work best when there's still light in the sky, rather than late in the night. However, the best shot from the series of skylines I took was from the end of the session, when the light had almost faded and the city lights were at their brightest.

▲ 6 x 7cm SLR, 105mm lens, 20 secs f8, Ektachrome 100STZ, tripod

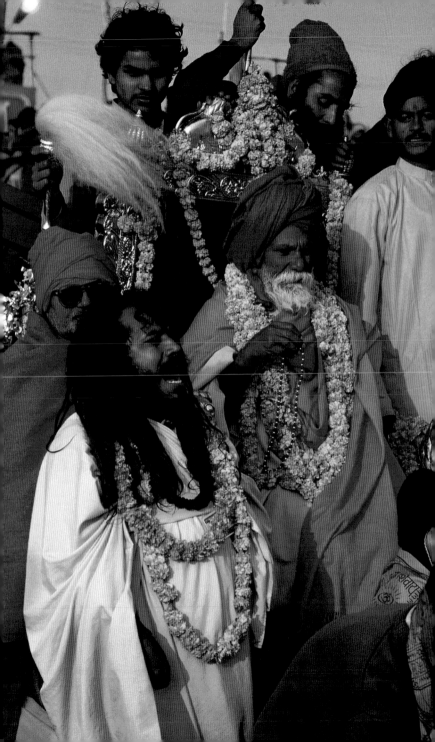

SPECIAL EVENTS

The spectacle, colour and crowds that are the hallmarks of special events around the world make them a great subject for travel photography. Research and planning will get you there on the right day and give you an idea of what you can expect to see. It's easy to be overwhelmed by the crowds and the uncertainty of not knowing exactly what, when and where things are going to happen. Early arrival at scheduled events gives you time to look around for good viewpoints, secure a seat and ask questions of local people and event organisers. Less organised events require more patience and flexibility, as it's often more difficult to find anyone who knows what's going on. Remember also that special events in urban areas can cause traffic chaos and that crowd-control measures may close roads around the focus of activity. It's better to be in position a little early than too late, so allow extra time to get to the event.

At seated events, getting close to the action can be difficult and a telephoto lens is essential. If you're stuck in one place or the participants are moving around a stage, wait for the action to come to you. Change lenses, zoom in and out, frame vertically and horizontally to get variety into your shots. Remember to turn your lens on the spectators who also make great subjects as they watch and react to the event.

If your trip does coincide with special events you'll probably want to at least double your film quota for those days.

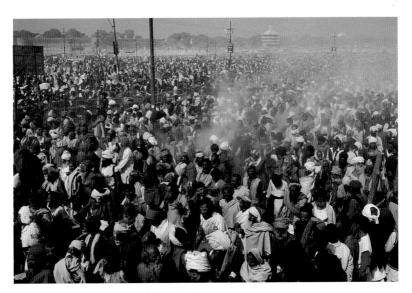

Procession at Khumb Mela festival, Allahabad, India

The 2001 Khumb Mela was the biggest gathering of humanity ever. On the main day around 30 million people bathed in the holy waters at the junction of the Ganges, Yamuna and the mythical Saraswati rivers. It was the ultimate special event. When there are this many people around, just getting into position, and holding it, is as much a challenge as hitting the shutter at the right moment.

◀ ▲ 35mm SLR, 100mm lens, 1/125 f5.6, Ektachrome E100VS

FESTIVALS

Festivals are fantastic events to photograph. They often occur as part of a holiday and attract local people from outlying areas. People dress up and are relaxed and in high sprits. Take advantage of the crowds and festive atmosphere to mingle with the locals and get in close to the action. There's often a lot going on, so be prepared for long days and lots of walking.

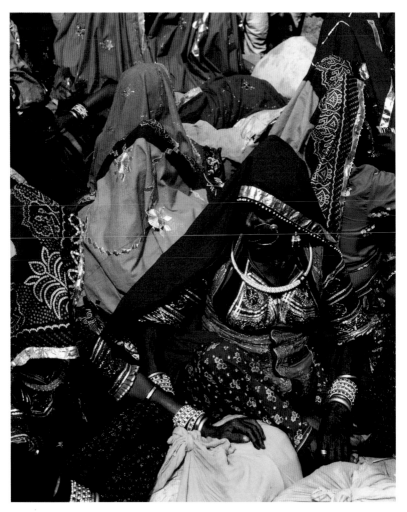

Woman at Pushkar, India

The annual Pushkar Fair is one of India's most colourful events. By filling the frame with the bright colours of sari clad women, the colour and crowds are emphasised.

▲ 35mm SLR, 24mm lens, 1/250 f11, Kodachrome 64

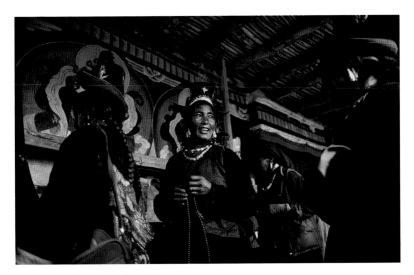

Gompa festival, Timosgan, Ladakh, India

On arrival at the *gompa* (monastery) the local people walk clockwise around the main building three times. I took up a position where the light was at its brightest and I wasn't in the way. I photographed the people as they passed. By kneeling I was not in the people's immediate line of vision, which reduced the number of people looking straight into the camera.

▲ 35mm SLR, 24mm lens, 1/125 f8, Kodachrome 200

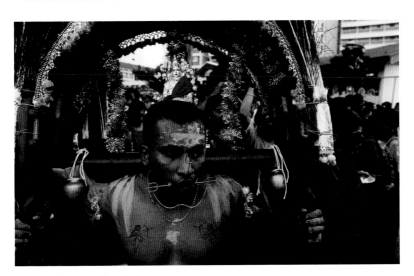

Devotee at Thaipussam festival, Singapore

If you're into body piercing, Thaipussam is the festival for you. Singapore's Indian Hindu community honour Lord Subramaniam by piecing their cheeks and tongues with metal skewers and carrying large metal and wooden frames, decorated with feathers, fruit and flowers, attached to their body with metal hooks.

▲ 35mm SLR, 24mm lens, 1/125 f5.6, Kodachrome 200

PARADES & PROCESSIONS

Parades and processions are demanding subjects. By their very nature (they're moving) you don't get a lot of time to think, compose and shoot. Big, organised parades attract big crowds and routes are often roped off, making it difficult to move around quickly. You may also prefer to remain in one place if you're with family or friends. If so, choose your position carefully in relation to the direction of light and the background of the parade. You don't want to find yourself looking into the sun or at a jumble of power lines, unable to move. If you do have the freedom to move, try walking with the parade. This will give you the opportunity to concentrate on the elements you find most interesting and to try various viewpoints. Excellent photo opportunities are also to be found where people gather before and after the parade. This is a great time to take portraits of people in costume, which is difficult while the parade is moving.

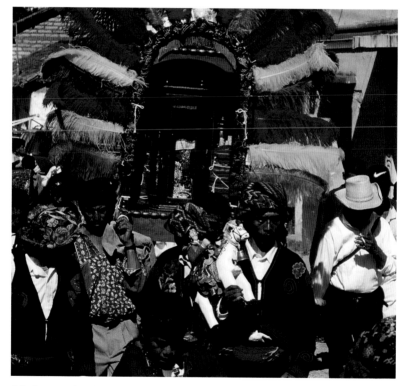

Cofradias procession, Chichicastenango, Guatemala

The ringing of bells alerted me to this small parade of Cofradias, a traditional religious brotherhood. Whenever I hear bells ringing I drop everything and investigate. The group was moving quickly along a small street with lots of obstacles, so I decided to run ahead and let them come to me rather than walk with them. On a bright day such as this, fast shutter speeds and small apertures are ideal because there's little time to think or focus.

▲ 35mm SLR, 100mm lens, 1/250 f11, Ektachrome E100VS

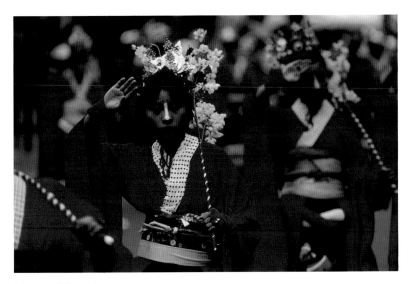

Tono matsuri, Tono, Japan

If the parade isn't moving too quickly, or at moments when it comes to a standstill, look for opportunities to make portraits of the participants. In the low light of a rainy day I concentrated on the groups wearing the brightest costumes. I also narrowed my view to just one of the participants because I was working with little depth of field.

▲ 35mm SLR, 100mm lens, 1/125 f2.8, Ektachrome E100VS

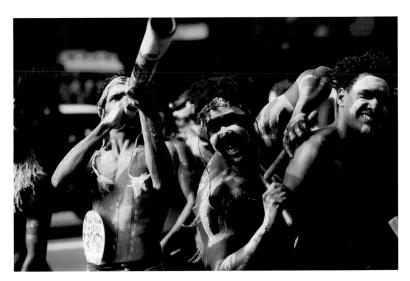

Nanoo group, Sydney, Australia

If you're close to the action have your widest lens on. People will often play up for the camera when they see you're interested in them.

▲ 35mm SLR, 24mm lens, 1/250 f8, Ektachrome E100SW

PERFORMANCES

You'll come across theatre and dance indoors and out, in venues large and small, on the street in impromptu shows and in hotels accompanied by dinner. For performances indoors or at night, successful pictures are difficult to achieve unless you override the light meter. Stages and performers are rarely lit evenly. Usually the performer is lit by a spotlight and is much brighter than the background. Fast film is best for capturing the mood and colour of the event. You can use 400 ISO film, or an equivalent setting on a digital camera, but 800 ISO will give you extra latitude to increase shutter speeds or give extra depth of field. Unless the performer fills the frame, automatic meters will overexpose the subject. This is the ideal situation to use your camera's spot metering system. Alternatively, zoom in and fill the frame with the spotlit performer, lock the exposure and recompose, or underexpose the meter's recommendation by one and two stops. Using flash will at least guarantee a record shot of the performance, but experiment with the slow shutter speeds on SLRs and night mode on compact cameras for more interesting shots (see p99 and p114).

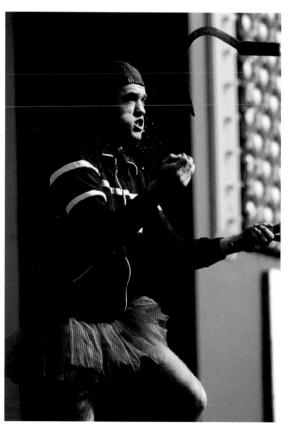

Busker, Melbourne, Australia

A guy wearing a pink tutu, eating an apple, and juggling knives atop a 3m mono bike deserves to be photographed. Performance photography will test your stamina unless you know exactly what's going to happen and when. If you don't you'll find that you have to watch the event through the viewfinder to catch the most theatrical moments. You can't pick the camera up when something interesting happens, it'll be over by the time it reaches your eye.

◀ 35mm SLR, 180mm lens, 1/250 f5.6, Ektachrome E100SW

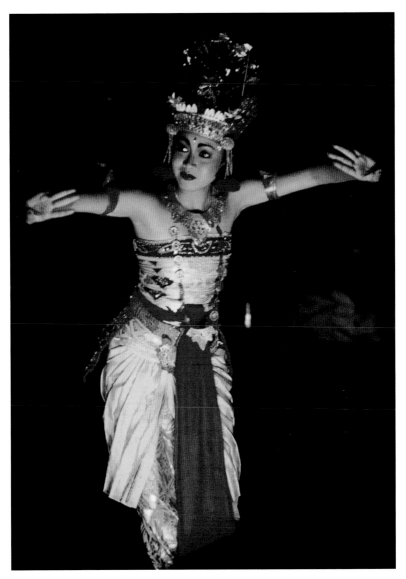

Dancer, Ubud, Bali, Indonesia

Every night in and around the village of Ubud, Balinese dances are performed. They're extremely popular and a central, clear view of the stage can only be guaranteed by arriving 45 minutes before performance time. Very weak spotlights light the front of the outdoor stage. I waited until the dancer moved close to the lights and took a spot-meter reading, eliminating the dark background from the equation.

▲ 35mm SLR, 180mm lens, 1/125 f2.8, Kodachrome 200 rated at 400 ISO (one-stop push)

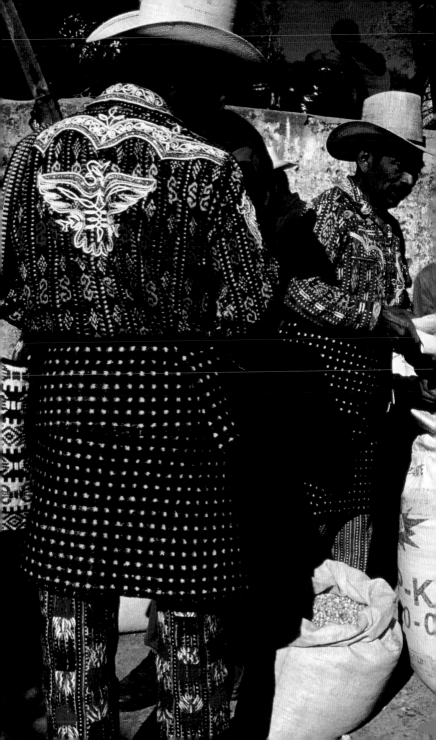

MARKETS

Markets are wonderful places to visit and photograph. There are lots of subjects, and lots of people who are too busy to notice you. Look for a vantage point for an overview of the market; move closer for shots of people at work, portraits of the vendors and close-ups of the products for sale. Wait for goods to be weighed and anticipate when money will change hands.

Markets are at their busiest and most interesting early in the morning when the produce arrives and stalls are set up. As soon as you arrive have a quick walk around and note the things that are different to what you've seen at other markets, the areas that look most interesting, and the areas that have the best light.

In cities the big markets are open daily, but in smaller towns and villages time your visit to coincide with market days. Weekly markets have a festive atmosphere as people from the surrounding areas travel into town to trade and socialise. Lighting can be difficult in markets but careful observation of where the light is falling will prevent wasting film or time. Umbrellas or sheets of plastic cast heavy shadows. Concentrate on finding subjects that are either in full shade or full sun. If the produce is in full sun but the vendor is in shade the photo will be unsatisfactory, unless you use flash to brighten the area in shadow.

Covered markets pose a particular problem. The light is usually very low and often comes from fluorescent tubes that turn daylight film a horrible blue–green. Digital photographers will again benefit from the white-balance function that corrects colour casts automatically. For film photographers, flash is one option or use fast film and search out areas where there is a mix of lighting. Better still, concentrate your efforts on the stalls near the entrances and around the edges of the market. These areas are usually the brightest and the quality of light is better.

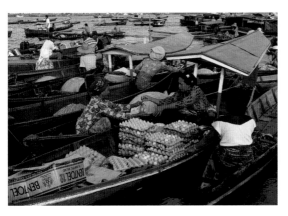

Pasar Kuin floating market, Kalimantan, Indonesia

The floating market at the junction of Kuin and Barito Rivers attracts hundreds of boats. Boat-to-boat trade is a fascinating sight. To show the buying and selling of eggs in the context of the market a high viewpoint was needed. Standing up in a little boat that's rocking about can be tricky. If you include the horizon make sure it's straight and use a fast shutter speed to prevent camera (or boat) shake.

◄ 35mm SLR, 24mm lens, 1/250 f5.6, Kodachrome 64

Market day, Solola, Guatemala

Market days in Guatemala's towns and villages are as colourful as you could hope for. Often spread out over quite a large area they offer lots of stalls in varying light conditions and a variety of viewpoint possibilities. Devote some of your photography time to markets anywhere and you'll rarely be disappointed with the photo opportunities you uncover.

◄ 35mm SLR, 24mm lens, 1/250 f8, Ektachrome E100VS

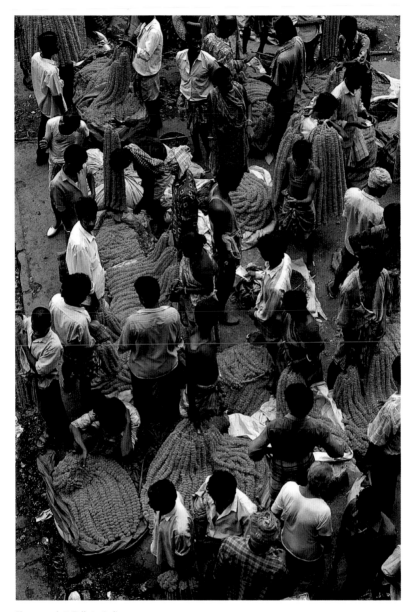

Flower market, Kolkata, India

The flower market under the Howrah Bridge is one of Kolkata's most intriguing sights. Lots of stalls, under cover and in the open, and a variety of viewpoint possibilities make it a good place to spend some of your photography time.

▲ 35mm SLR, 100mm lens, 1/125 f8, Ektachrome E100SW

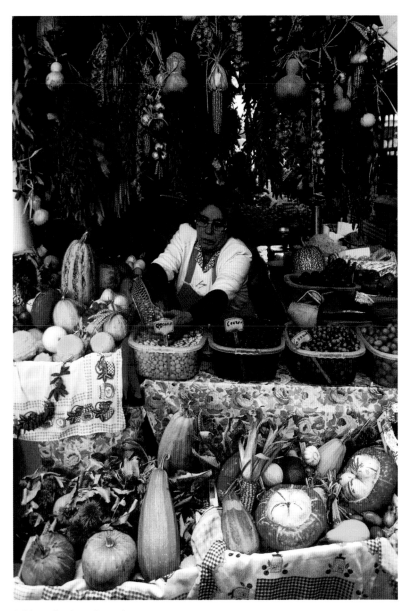

Bolhão market, Porto, Portugal

On a very bad weather day I was grateful that one of Porto's markets was covered. This stall was on a corner with its main counter facing a narrow, dark passageway, quite unsuitable for decent pictures. I waited at the end for the owner to come into the light as she filled an order.

▲ 35mm SLR, 24mm lens, 1/30 f2, Ektachrome E100SW rated at 400 ISO (two-stop push)

FOOD

Food is high on the priority list of many a traveller. Where, what and when to eat are important decisions that can consume hours of each day. While you're thinking about it, why not photograph it? The way food is cooked and displayed in many markets is close to being an art form. Catch a cook dishing up a meal or fill the frame with fruit to emphasise its colour and texture. Try including several different fruits or vegetables to highlight the colour and design of the display.

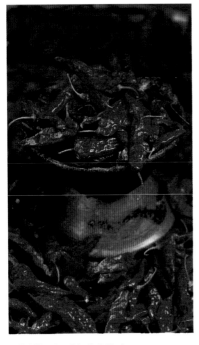

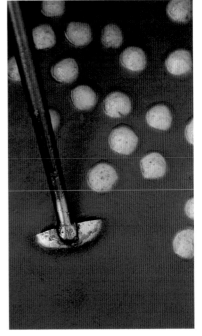

Red chillies, San Cristóbal, Mexico
▲ 35mm SLR, 100mm, 1/125 f2.8, Ektachrome E100VS

Soup, Bangkok, Thailand
▲ 35mm SLR, 100mm, 1/125 f4, Ektachrome E100VS

Photograph food up close to emphasise the presentation, textures and colours. When the display is horizontal (ie not stacked high), try to keep the camera parallel with the produce to ensure sharp focus across the entire frame. You'll often have to lean right over the display, so watch for your own shadow. For close-ups the light must be even. Ensure you don't block the light yourself.

Photographing vegetables close up probably confirms the local people's suspicion that tourists are mad, but that's a small price to pay for the colour and interest food pictures add to the overall coverage of a destination.

Lemon water, Yangon, Myanmar
35mm SLR, 50mm lens, 1/60 f4, Ektachrome E100VS ▶

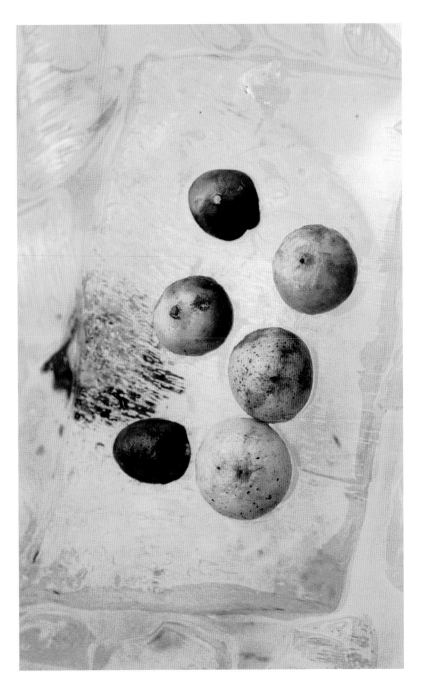

ART & CRAFT

Art and craft for local and tourist consumption is usually available at the general market, but products aimed at tourists are hard to miss in popular destinations. Artisan markets have the added bonus that often you can photograph the craftspeople at work. Although pictures of the products themselves are relatively easy to take (they're stationary, in the same place every day and there's lots of choice), careful composition making the most of the graphic elements in the displays, and good lighting, will always set pictures, even simple ones, apart.

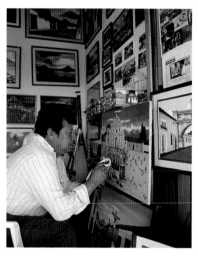

Artist, Antigua, Guatemala

At the handicraft market in Antigua, artist Oscar Perén works on another painting for his collection. Unless you want to photograph a particular art or craft, a quick walk around the market is all it takes to locate people working in conditions favourable to photography. Spend your time in these locations rather than using time and film in difficult and unsatisfactory situations.

▲ 35mm SLR, 24mm lens, 1/125 f8, Ektachrome E100VS

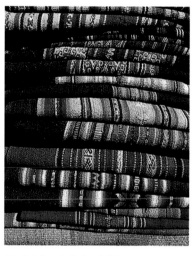

Blankets for sale, La Paz, Bolivia

A common sight at markets is a load of the same product stacked high, hung on walls or laid out on tables. Use the repetition of shape, texture and colour to create graphic images. Even an isolated detail like this gives a sense of place.

▲ 35mm SLR, 100mm lens, 1/125 f8, Kodachrome 64

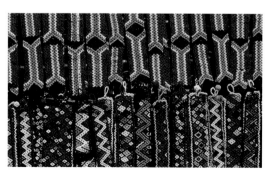

Beadwork at street market, Durban, South Africa

Markets provide an endless supply of items to photograph up close. Most compact cameras have a minimum focussing range of around 0.6m to 1m. Although this limits close-up possibilities, set your camera on its minimum focussing distance and look for subjects that fill the frame. This will extend your vision and range of photos.

◄ 35mm SLR, 100mm lens, 1/125 f8, Ektachrome E100VS

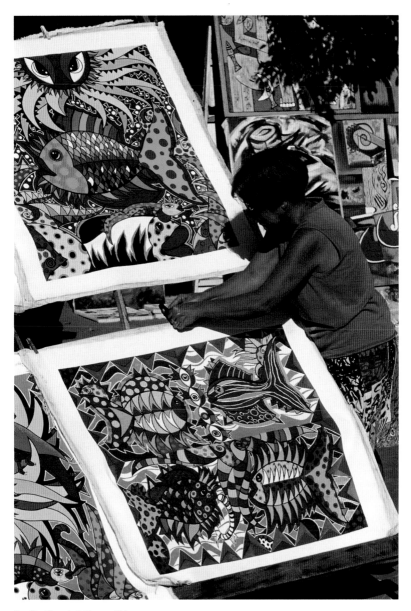

Handicraft market, Havana, Cuba

Large colourful paintings are a feature of the handicraft market on Tacón between the cathedral and the harbour.

▲ 35mm SLR, 100mm lens, 1/250 f8, Ektachrome E100VS

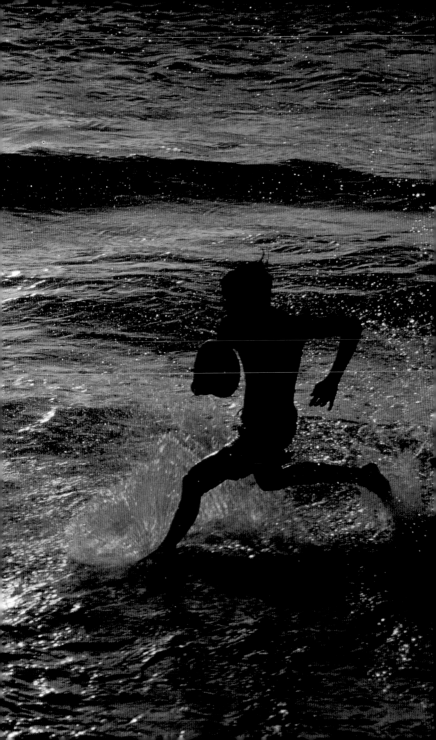

SUNRISE & SUNSET

A coloured sky, swaying palm trees and a couple of boats silhouetted by a golden sun low on the horizon…it's the stuff of holiday dreams and a staple image for travel brochures. Sure it's clichéd, but like famous places, that adds to the challenge. Just because the sky is a nice colour doesn't automatically mean you've got a good picture. Preplanning the place and subject you want to photograph before the sun sets or rises is always a good idea. The sun sets much quicker when you're frantically trying to find a vantage point for photography than when you're sitting on a beach drinking piña coladas.

When there are clouds in the sky the changing colours make a very attractive subject in their own right. Look for a subject that can be silhouetted against the light background. Turn your back to the sun just after it peeps over the horizon or is about to disappear for the night and the world will be washed in a deep, warm, golden light.

When the sun is below the horizon, behind cloud, or isn't in the frame, meter readings are usually accurate. If the sun is in the frame, override the recommended meter settings or the image will be underexposed (leaving you with a well-exposed sun in the middle of a dark background). This effect is exaggerated with telephoto lenses. To retain colour and

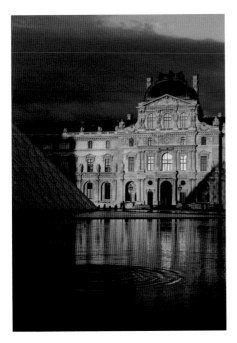

Louvre, Paris, France

A couple of minutes before sunset the Louvre was bathed in a golden light. When there are lots of clouds it's hard to predict if the sun will break through for spectacular effect or just fade away into the night. At these times it pays to be alone. Very few people are willing to stand around in the cold just in case a great photo opportunity arises and it's easy to be talked into leaving.

◀ 35mm SLR, 24mm lens, 1/15 f11, Ektachrome E100SW, tripod

Playing ball on the beach, Colombo, Sri Lanka

A group of boys was playing on the beach and I decided to dedicate the sunset session to getting this shot. I knew what I wanted, but it was an anxious wait for the elements to come together before the setting sun slipped away.

◀ 35mm SLR, 70-200mm lens, 1/400 f7.1, Ektachrome E100VS

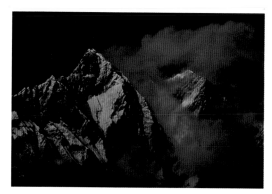

Lhotse and Nuptse, Dingboche, Khumbu Himal, Nepal

For most of the day the Himalayan peaks gleam pure white, but at the very beginning and end of the day there's always the chance that they'll turn orange, red or yellow. Even if the mountain is in cloud, set up and wait – sudden changes in the weather are common.

◀ 35mm SLR, 180mm lens, 1/60 f11, Ektachrome 50STX, tripod

detail in the scene take a meter reading from an area of sky adjacent to the sun and then recompose. With slide film in older cameras, overexpose by one and two stops. With print film underexpose by one and two stops. Modern cameras with advanced metering systems handle these situation pretty well, but it's still worth using a couple of extra frames and overexposing slide film by a half-stop and one stop to be sure.

Bracketing sunrises and sunsets is recommended, particularly if the sun is in the frame. If you have a compact camera avoid including the sun in your composition, or at least take a couple of shots: one with and one without the sun.

FLARE

When shooting directly into the sun, watch for lens flare caused by stray light entering the lens. This reduces contrast, and records as patches of light on the film. With SLRs you can usually see lens flare (if you're looking for it) and it can be highlighted by stopping down the lens with the depth-of-field button. A slight change in camera angle or viewpoint will usually solve the problem. Lens hoods help prevent flare but shading the lens with your hand may also be required (don't let it enter the field of view), or try placing the sun directly behind an element in the scene.

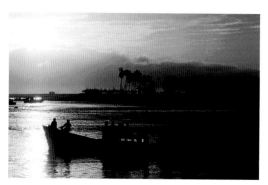

Fishing boat, Marang, Malaysia

As the sun sets, fishing boats head out for the night from the small town of Marang on Malaysia's east coast. With the sun in the frame I took a reading from the sky and then recomposed. Shooting this scene on automatic would have caused underexposure by around two stops. It takes a while to get used to overriding the meter by this much, but even when you're confident, bracketing is recommended when shooting into the sun.

◀ 35mm SLR, 100mm lens, 1/250 f8 (+ one stop), Ektachrome 100STZ

SILHOUETTES

When you expose for the colours of sunrise and sunset, objects in the foreground are back lit and recorded without detail (ie, silhouettes). An interesting or familiar shape silhouetted against a bright and colourful background gives a point of interest and adds depth to an image. Ensure that the subject to be silhouetted is surrounded by a bright background and doesn't disappear into dark areas. Look for separation between elements or their shape and impact will be lost.

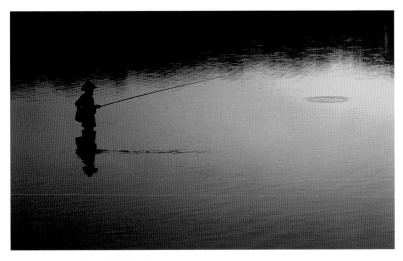

Fishing at sunrise, Sanur, Bali, Indonesia

Isolating the fisherman with a telephoto lens has created a very simple composition. With the light behind the fisherman and exposure set for the highlights in the water he has recorded in silhouette. By placing him on the left side of the frame he's looking into the composition, keeping the viewer's eye within the frame and leading it to the circles on the water.

▲ 35mm SLR, 180mm lens, 1/250 f5.6, Ektachrome 100STZ

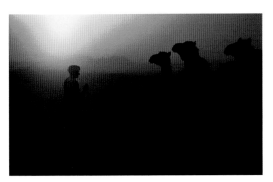

Camel trader, Pushkar, India

A camel trader keeps a close eye on his animals as the sun sets over the Thar Desert. Many of the people were down in the valley, but I searched for an area where I would have a better chance of finding people and camels that could be silhouetted.

◀ 35mm SLR, 100mm lens, 1/125 f5.6, Kodachrome 64

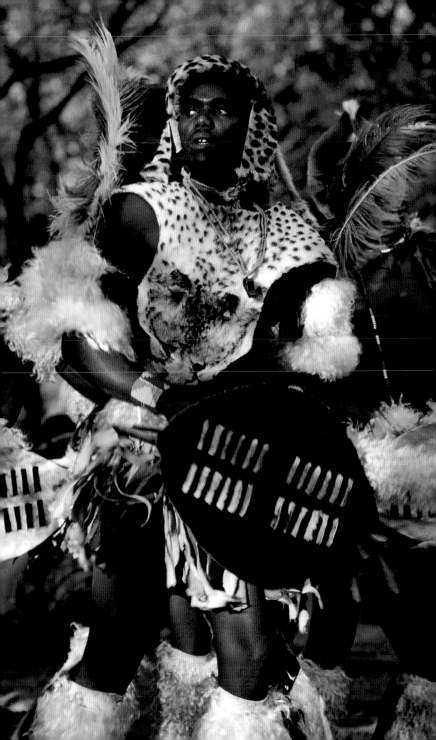

MOVING SUBJECTS

Dancers in Mexico, speeding *becaks* in Yogjakarta, windsurfers in Port Elizabeth, fireworks, moving cars…there are lots of subjects that just won't keep still.

▶ **You'll be more successful if you adopt a 'shoot first and think later' policy with subjects that are on the move.**

Fast shutter speeds will freeze the action at an interesting moment; slower speeds can be used to express movement. If you're the one moving – on a camel, in a train, bus or cable car – success rates are going to be low. If you must shoot under these circumstances:

▸ set the fastest shutter speed possible (aim for 1/1000)
▸ select a standard to short telephoto lens (50mm–70mm) to frame out the foreground
▸ focus on infinity
▸ turn off the flash and switch auto-focus to manual focus if you're shooting through a window
▸ look ahead for a potentially clear viewing spot
▸ don't hesitate.

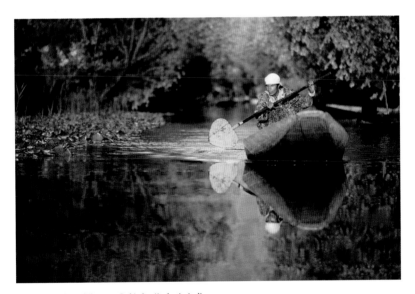

Woman paddling shikara on Dal Lake, Kashmir, India
When you're moving and your subject is moving select the highest shutter speed possible to prevent camera shake and subject blur, unless desired. A subject moving straight towards the camera can be 'frozen' with a shutter speed of 1/125, but a subject going past you will require 1/500 or 1/1000 to freeze its movement.
▲ 35mm SLR, 100mm lens, 1/125 f4, Kodachrome 64

Zulu dancers, Dumazulu, South Africa
The dancers were moving in and out of shadow as the last rays of sun fell on the performance area. There wasn't enough light to use the recommended shutter speed of 1/500 to stop this type of movement. By waiting for the lead dancer to step into the sun I was able to at least shoot at 1/125. To compensate for the slower than preferred shutter speed I timed the exposure with a slight pause in the dancer's movement.
◀ 35mm SLR, 100mm lens, 1/125 f4, Ektachrome E100VS

FREEZING THE ACTION

Where the activity is fast and furious, shutter speeds faster than 1/500 will freeze the action and capture the moment with great detail. Outdoors this should not be a problem with 100 ISO film, or equivalent sensor setting, but indoors use 400 or 800 ISO. Fast shutter speeds will result in wider apertures and less depth of field, so focussing is critical, especially with telephoto lenses.

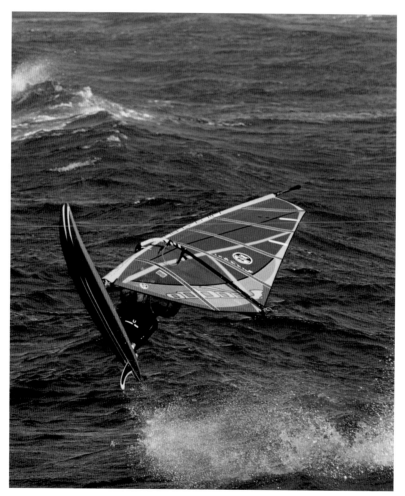

Windsurfer, Port Elizabeth, South Africa

Port Elizabeth is a famous windsurfing centre. I used the fastest shutter speed possible to freeze the movement of the windsurfer and to guard against camera shake – I was having trouble staying on my feet in the windy conditions.

▲ 35mm SLR, 350mm lens, 1/1000 f5.6, Ektachrome E100VS

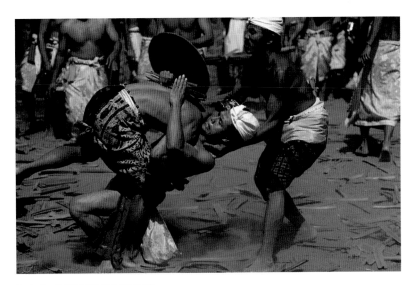

Usuba Sambah festival, Bali, Indonesia

The Usuba Sambah festival is a most unusual event. Amid the beautiful clothing and traditional dancing the men gather in two teams and vigorously rub each other's backs with spiny cactus shards until they bleed. A 180mm lens kept me clear of the blood but let me capture the expression that clearly shows what it's like to have a cactus shard run down your back.

▲ 35mm SLR, 180mm lens, 1/500 f5.6, Ektachrome 100STZ

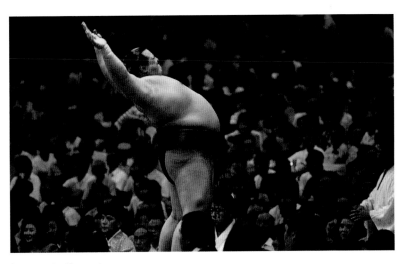

Sumo wrestler, Nagoya, Japan

A sumo wrestler warms up for his next bout. Indoor events will rarely be lit well enough to use 100 ISO film. Often in these situations longer lenses and higher shutter speeds are required to fill the frame with the subject and stop the action.

▲ 35mm SLR, 180mm lens, 1/125 f2.8, Kodachrome 200 rated at 400 ISO (one-stop push)

PANNING & BLUR

Panning and blurring are techniques that allow you to suggest movement in a still photograph. Rather than freezing the subject for maximum detail, part of the image is blurred: either the background or the subject; sometimes both.

Panning

Generally, panning is used to keep a moving subject sharp while blurring the background, giving the impression of movement and speed. The speed the subject is moving at will determine the shutter speed. Start with a 1/30 and 1/15. Train your camera on your subject and follow it as it moves. As it draws level with you press the shutter release and keep following the subject. The shutter must be fired while the camera is moving. Don't expect a high success rate, but, with the right subject, panning produces very effective pictures.

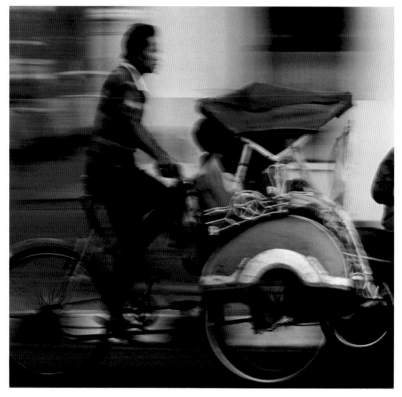

Speeding *becak*, Yogjakarta, Java, Indonesia

The streets of Yogjakarta are filled with three-wheeled *becaks* and two-wheeled scooters. I found a spot where there was a regular stream of traffic and the background wasn't too messy. The results of panning are unpredictable, so allow plenty of film for experimentation.

▲ 35mm SLR, 180mm lens, 1/15 f11, Ektachrome E100SW

Blur

Action and activity can also be suggested by using a shutter speed that is slow enough to blur a moving element in your photograph but still retain sharpness elsewhere. It can be as subtle or as obvious as you like. The key is not to shake the camera or record movement in the wrong part of the image. When a potter is at work a slow shutter speed will blur the spinning wheel with great effect, but if the potter also moves the image won't work.

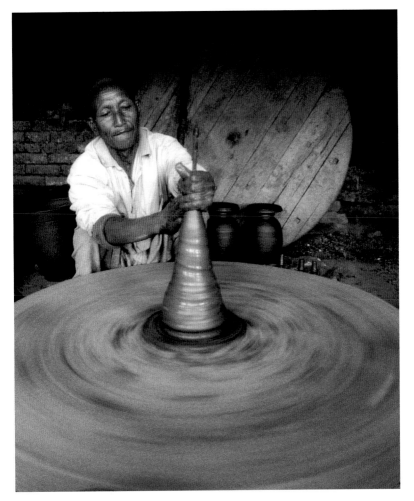

Potter, Bhaktapur, Nepal

A 1/30 shutter speed allowed the movement of the potters wheel to be recorded but was fast enough to prevent subject and camera shake. The minimum shutter speed required to avoid camera shake can be reduced by selecting wide-angle lenses. Don't go too slow, though, or you increase the risk that the subject will move.

▲ 35mm SLR, 24mm lens, 1/30 f2, Kodachrome 200

FIREWORKS & LIGHTS

Fireworks

Fireworks are best photographed using a tripod and cable release. Mount the camera on a tripod and use 100 ISO film, or equivalent sensor setting; much more interesting and colourful pictures can be made if several bursts of light are recorded on the one frame.

- Set the shutter speed on the B setting (which leaves the shutter open for as long as you wish).
- Set the aperture to f8.
- Set the focus on infinity. Switch auto-focus to manual.
- Turn off the built-in flash.
- Frame a part of the sky where you anticipate the fireworks to burst.
- Release the shutter with a cable release and allow several sets of fireworks to trace their paths on the film.
- Between each burst, cover the lens with a dark cloth, ensuring that you don't disturb the camera.

Avoid setting up in a brightly lit place where extraneous light can enter the lens and overexpose the film or sensor. Trial and error is required, so ensure that all your exposures are not the same length.

The same technique can be used for photographing lightning.

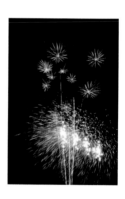

Fireworks, Melbourne, Australia

Fireworks can be photographed hand-held, but you'll get more colourful and interesting pictures with long exposures that record several bursts on one frame. Given you can never be sure exactly where the fireworks will be in the sky, use a lens with a wide field of view to take in the general area. You can always crop later.

◀ 6 x 7cm SLR, 90mm lens, 15 sec f8, Ektachrome 50STX, tripod

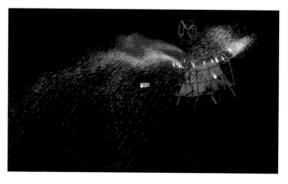

Fireworkman, Antigua, Guatemala

Beware of men wearing wooden frames loaded with fireworks over their heads. When they go off the hiss of eye level rockets will have you ducking for cover. These guys are one of the highlights of New Year's Eve festivities and photographing them requires a fair bit of luck. A telephoto lens is good so you don't have to get too close.

◀ 35mm SLR, 100mm lens, 1/60 f8, Ektachrome E100VS

Lights

Tracing the patterns left by moving lights can add interest and colour to areas that would otherwise record as solid black. Use the technique described for fireworks, but set the aperture at f11 for good depth of field and expose the film at 10, 20 and 30 seconds or longer. There are no guarantees with this subject because the intensity of the lights can vary from frame to frame, so bracket away. Many built-in meters have automatic shutter speeds to 30 seconds. As a starting point, fire the camera on automatic and time how long the shutter is open. Then switch to manual and the B setting and bracket around what the camera recommended.

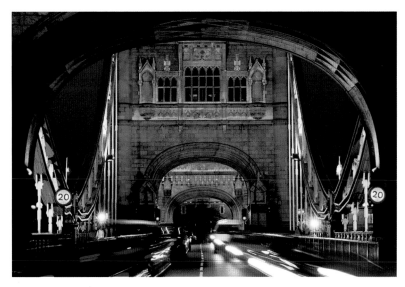

Traffic on Tower Bridge, London, England

There was enough light for a short exposure, which suited me. My camera and tripod were balanced on a road-dividing sign (in the middle of the road) and there was a good chance of it moving as the cars and buses rushed by. I took a reading off the bridge stonework because the headlights would have caused the meter to underexpose.
▲ 35mm SLR, 100mm lens, 1 sec f8, Ektachrome E100SW, tripod

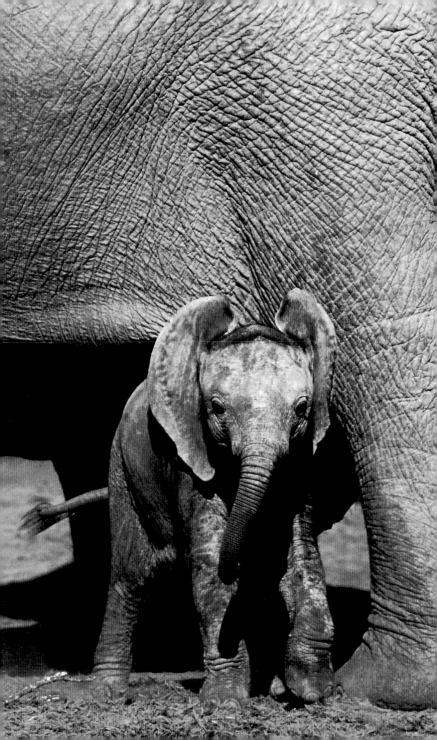

WILDLIFE

Photographing animals requires an abundance of patience, time and luck. Animals aren't renowned for their cooperation and you'll have to work hard to build a collection of recognisable, interesting and varied photos. Seeing animals in the wild is pretty special, but it's no excuse for forgetting everything you've learned about good photography. The first challenge is to get close enough. You might know it's an elephant, but if you have to tell the person looking at the photo what it is, consider the image a failure. It's also important to select a viewpoint that considers the direction of the light and the background, just as with any subject. Always focus on the eyes; everything else can be out of focus but if the eyes are not sharp the photograph will fail. Because the focussing screen is in the centre of the frame, consider recomposing after focussing on the eyes to avoid the central, and often static, placement of the subject in all your pictures.

Some wildlife photography is possible with compact cameras with zoom lenses (38mm–90mm) or SLRs with standard zooms (28mm–105mm). In many national parks, particularly around camp grounds, some animals are quite used to human presence and will allow you to get close enough. In the wild the limitations of the equipment can make for a frustrating experience. The eye will zoom in on distant animals and exaggerate their size, but they will be insignificant on film. To avoid disappointment concentrate your efforts on animals that you can get close to and compositions that show the animal in its habitat.

For wild animals a focal length of 300mm is generally considered essential. The magnification is strong enough to satisfactorily photograph the majority of animals and will allow frame-filling portraits of those you can get close to. If wildlife photography is a part of your travel plans and your longest lens (fixed or zoom) is less than 300mm, consider purchasing a teleconverter, which will give you many more opportunities without the expense and weight of another lens. If you have a 300mm already, a teleconverter will open up a whole new range of opportunities (see p27).

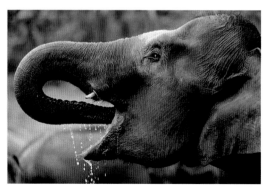

Elephant drinking, Pinnewala, Sri Lanka

When the herd of elephants from the Pinnewala Orphanage are bathing there is plenty of action, especially in the first 30 minutes after they arrive at the river. Look for action that is repeated by individuals and the herd generally, like filling the trunk and drinking, which gives you the opportunity to fine tune your composition and predict the perfect moment to hit the shutter.

◄ 35mm SLR, 70-200mm lens, 1/350 f4, Ektachrome E100VS

Baby elephant, Addo National Park, South Africa

Elephants are great because they're so big and allow you to get so close. Even standard lenses will let you fill the frame. Then again, you may not want to get quite so close. Baby elephants are little, so its back to the big lens. This one was learning to walk and flap its ears. The rangers can give you a good idea of when and where you'll see the herds of elephants in national parks.

◄ 35mm SLR, 350mm lens with 1.4x teleconverter, 1/500 f4, Ektachrome E100VS

ON SAFARI

The wildlife parks of Africa are the most famous destinations for animal encounters. If an African safari is on your itinerary take extra film: most people use a lot more than they expect. Most wildlife viewing is experienced in national parks from vehicles, which you're prohibited to leave. Be constantly aware of the direction of the light so that you can position the vehicle quickly or give directions as to where you want to shoot from. You'll soon learn how close you can get to a particular animal before it moves off and this will allow you to select the right lens, or set your zoom at the appropriate focal length, before you approach the animal. With long lenses fast shutter speeds are required to prevent camera shake, and they also stop blurring if the animal moves.

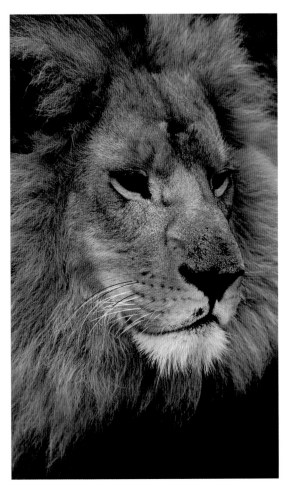

Lion, Moremi Wildlife Reserve, Botswana

After six weeks and sixteen wildlife parks in Southern Africa, it became clear that just seeing the animals could be a challenge. It wasn't until the twelfth park that I finally got to photograph lions, and then they were everywhere – well, all within 500m of where I had to get out of my vehicle to dig it out of the deep sand it had got stuck in.

◄ 35mm SLR, 350mm lens, 1/1000 f5.6, Ektachrome E100VS

You'll find yourself holding the camera to your eye for much longer periods than normal as you observe the animals and wait for the perfect moment. This can be very tiring. The vehicle window makes an excellent support and can be moved up and down to suit your height. In vehicles with pop-up tops, rest your camera on the roof while following the action. Use a piece of clothing or a camera bag to rest the camera on and turn the engine off to stop unnecessary vibrations.

Animals are at their most active early in the morning and late in the day. If you're using zoom lenses at their maximum focal length (210mm, 300mm) you'll need to use the appropriate fast shutter speeds (1/250, 1/500) and your maximum aperture will be around f5.6 to f8. Be prepared to use 400 ISO film at these times and switch to your standard film as soon as it's bright enough.

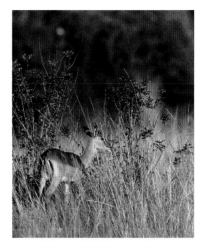

Impala, Mlilwane Wildlife Sanctuary, Swaziland

Impala are everywhere and if you go to enough parks you'll find some you can get close to. If you don't have long lenses look for situations that show the animals in their habitat. These pictures will be particularly pleasing when the animal hasn't been alerted to your presence.

▲ 35mm SLR, 180mm lens, 1/250 f8, Ektachrome E100VS

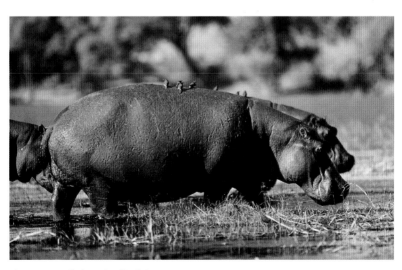

Hippopotamus, Chobe National Park, Botswana

Hippos don't generally do much during the day, so it was good to see this group heading for the water. Make sure that your settings are appropriate for the situation and lens you are using. If you're in a moving boat use the fastest shutter speed you can.

▲ 35mm SLR, 350mm lens with 1.4x teleconverter, 1/1000 f4, Ektachrome E100VS

IN THE GALÁPAGOS

The Galápagos Islands, straddling the equator, 1000km off the coast of Ecuador, offer unique wildlife photography opportunities. It's true that in some places you have to be careful not to step on the animals.

There are sixteen islands in the Galápagos archipelago and only three have human settlements. To see the wildlife you must join a tour group and sail from island to island. You sleep and eat on the boat and use small boats or rubber Zodiacs to access the visitor sites on each island. Typically, you'll go ashore at two different visitor sites a day (one in the morning and one in the afternoon). Snorkelling is also a daily activity. The ship sails between sites and islands in the middle of the day and during the night. This program means a lot of visitor sites are covered in a week and you see a great variety of wildlife. There is also plenty to challenge the photographer.

The Galápagos is a harsh environment for camera equipment. It's always hot, often humid and the heat from the sun can be intense when on land. You'll be on or near the sea all the time and spend a lot of time on beaches. There is little or no shelter at most visitor sites. Keeping your gear and film cool, dry and sand free is a real challenge. Once you leave the ship for a visitor site you can't go back and forth, so everything you anticipate needing has to be carried. A large, strong rubbish bag is useful for placing your entire camera bag in while you're swimming and snorkelling from the beach. For compact camera users this is the perfect environment to take a weatherproof camera. Flash isn't allowed, so make sure you can turn yours off.

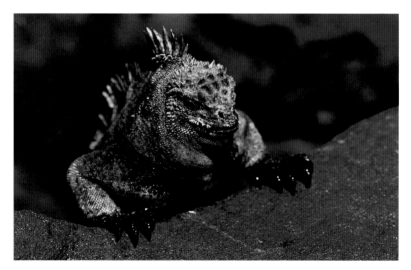

Marine iguana, San Salvador Island, Galápagos, Ecuador

After the thrill of first encounters don't forget that good composition and lighting are as important for wildlife as for other subjects. Iguanas are just about everywhere, but it took a concerted effort to find one as well situated as this, with the light coming from the right direction and a non-distractive background.

▲ 35mm SLR, 180mm lens, 1/250 f8, Ektachrome E100VS

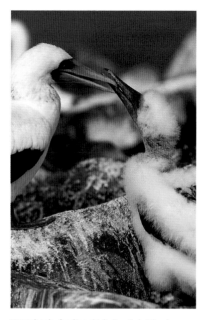

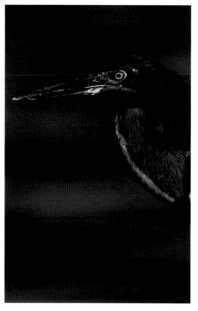

Nazca booby feeding chick, Española Island, Galápagos, Ecuador

The Galápagos really is an exception to the rule that states long lenses are needed to photograph birds. You won't capture close-ups like this of all the birds if you don't have a 400mm or 500mm lens, but you'll still find plenty to photograph within the range of a 200mm lens.

▲ 35mm SLR, 70-200mm lens, 1/500 f8, Ektachrome E100VS

Lava heron, Santa Cruz Island, Galápagos, Ecuador

Animals in the Galápagos will allow close human presence, so take the opportunity to try different compositions that complement the more traditional choice of showing the whole animal. By eliminating the wooden jetty the standing heron becomes a much stronger graphic portrait.

▲ 35mm SLR, 70-200mm lens, 1/200 f6.3, Ektachrome E100VS

Most wildlife viewing is on foot (as opposed to vehicle-based viewing in Africa's wildlife parks), which is great for finding the perfect viewpoint. But also be prepared for viewing wildlife from the small landing boats (on sometimes rocky seas), which is a real test of technical and creative techniques. Either way, you'll find you have to work quite fast. One to two hours is allowed at each site but the tour leaders keep the groups moving to stay on schedule for meals or sailing times and you're not allowed to wander off on your own. Consequently, you'll rarely have more than a few minutes to spend on any one subject. A dedicated photo tour may be worth investigating if photography is the reason you're going to the Galápagos .

Because you can get close to a lot of wildlife, lenses that cover the 100mm to 200mm focal-length range will allow you to capture good close-ups of many of the animals. However, you'll still find plenty of situations where the animals are too far off the track (and you can't leave the track), too high in a tree, too small, or all of the above, to take satisfactory images. The 300mm-plus lenses recommended for wildlife and the 500mm-plus lenses recommended for birds are just as necessary in the Galápagos. Additionally, because snorkelling is a daily activity, an underwater camera or housing is worth considering.

AT THE ZOO

Zoos and wildlife sanctuaries are interesting subjects in their own right but are also great places to practice and prepare for photographing animals in the wild. Spend a day at your local zoo or wildlife park before heading off on safari and you'll discover the limitations of your equipment and how close you need to get to animals large and small to make strong pictures.

Eliminating cage wire is possible by placing your lens against the cage (after you've checked that you're allowed), and selecting the widest aperture available (f2.8 or f4). This technique works best with a telephoto lens and if the animal is at least 2m from the cage. With compact cameras remember that what you see through the viewfinder is not what the lens sees. Place the lens through an opening in the cage wire, and then look through the viewfinder; even if you see wire it won't be recorded on film.

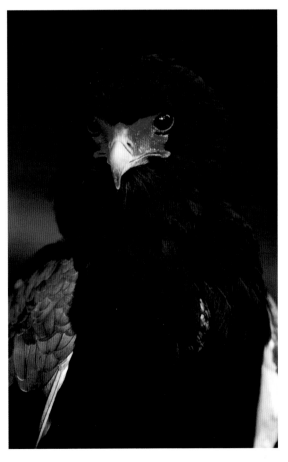

Bateleur eagle, Zimbabwe

This beautiful Bateleur eagle was photographed through the wire of a sanctuary enclosure using a telephoto lens and wide aperture. I'm not a big fan of caging large birds but the opportunity to take a 'portrait' was hard to refuse.

◄ 35mm SLR, 100mm lens, 1/125 f2, Ektachrome E100VS

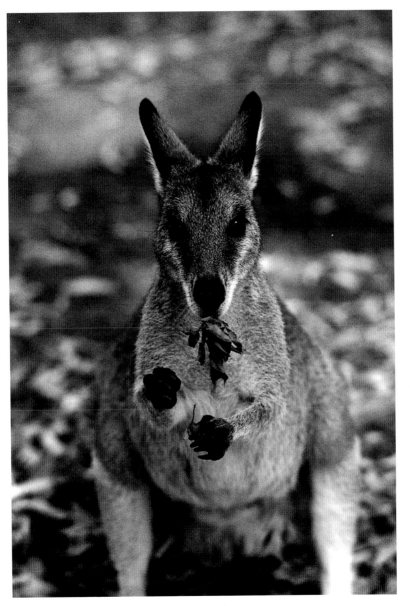

Whiptail wallaby, Cape Hillsborough National Park, Australia

Many national parks have wildlife that's used to the presence of people. These animals provide the perfect subject for practicing wildlife photography. Even when you can get close to animals in the wild, quick and accurate focussing, metering and composition is required.

▲ 35mm SLR, 180mm lens, 1/250 f4, Kodachrome 200

BIRDS

Birds are even harder to photograph than other animals. They're mostly small, rest high up in trees, fly off at the slightest disturbance and rarely sit still for very long. A 300mm lens is adequate for larger birds, but to have any hope of filling the frame you really need a focal length of 500mm or 600mm.

A quick introduction to the trials and tribulations of bird photography is available in your own garden or at local parks.

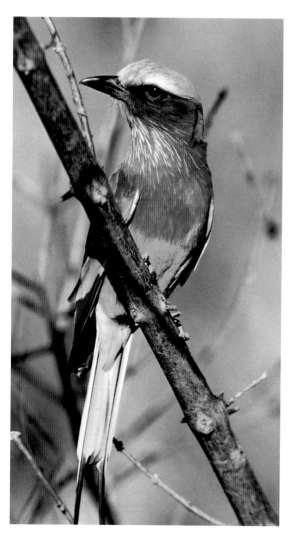

Lilac breasted roller, Hwange National Park, Zimbabwe

Unless you're very well equipped and dedicated, photographing birds can be very frustrating. At least the lilac breasted roller gives you a chance to get close...but that's with a super telephoto lens.

◄ 35mm SLR, 350mm lens with 1.4xteleconverter, 1/1000 f4, Ektachrome E100VS

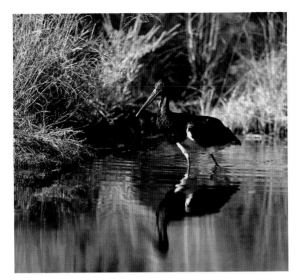

Stork, Kruger National Park, South Africa

Without very long lenses the large waterbirds are a subject that may reward some patience at water holes or rivers. If you arrive first and wait for them to come to the water you may be close enough to take recognisable pictures.

◄ 35mm SLR, 350mm lens, 1/500 f4, Ektachrome E100VS

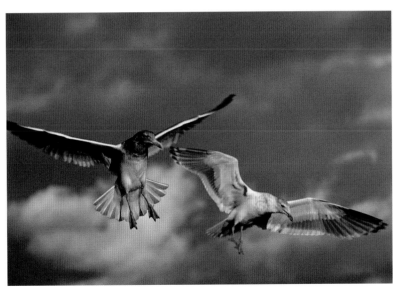

Seabirds above ferry, Seattle, USA

Birds in flight are another challenge altogether. Travelling on the Bainbridge Island ferry across Puget Sound in the late afternoon gave me a chance to practice my fast focus techniques as the birds hovered above the ferry for a few minutes. A zoom lens would have provided more opportunities as the birds moved closer and further from the camera. With a fixed lens I had to wait for them to move into the limited range that suited the lens's angle of view.

▲ 35mm SLR, 180mm lens, 1/500 f4, Ektachrome E100VS

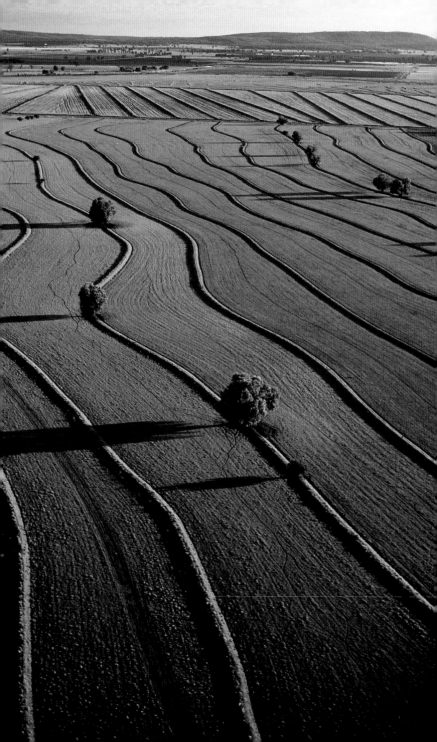

FROM THE AIR

The world certainly looks different from the air and can inspire even the most reluctant camera user to blow the film budget. Opportunities from commercial aircraft are limited, but joy flights in light planes, helicopters and hot-air balloons are offered at many places.

COMMERCIAL FLIGHTS

Good pictures are difficult to get from commercial planes. Often the windows are marked or dirty and the curve in the plastic windows causes the image to go out of focus. If you're behind the wing, vapour from the engines may interfere with the view. To increase the possibility of good aerials from a commercial aircraft:

- Find a seat forward of the wing and on the opposite side to the sun.
- Wipe marks and fingerprints off the window.
- Place the lens close to the centre of the window to minimise reflections from the cabin and blurring from the curved Perspex. Don't rest it against the window.
- Don't use a polarising filter because it doesn't work with Perspex.
- Use standard focal lengths (35mm-70mm).
- Keep shutter speeds high to minimise camera shake and vibration.
- Look for photo opportunities just after takeoff and during the longer descent.

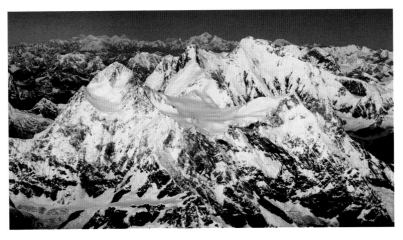

The Himalaya, Nepal
The low-altitude flight between Lhasa and Kathmandu has to be one of the most spectacular commercial flights in the world – and the view is great from both sides of the plane. Cruising at 10,500m you're only 1700m higher than Mt Everest.
▲ 35mm SLR, 50mm lens, 1/250 f8, Kodachrome 64

Rice bays, Leeton, Australia
As with all landscapes, aerials benefit from shooting early in the day. The low angle of the sun casts shadows that emphasise the texture and form of the land. The lower light levels can mean having to use slower than preferred shutter speeds, but light plane flights are often smoother early, before the wind picks up.
◀ 35mm SLR, 35mm lens, 1/125 f8, Ektachrome E100VS

LIGHT PLANES & HELICOPTERS

Flying at low altitudes over natural attractions is a wonderful experience. To capture it on film is a challenge, but a little planning will help. Helicopters provide clear views, but make sure you request a window seat. High-winged planes offer a clearer view than low-winged planes. Talk to the pilot about the best place to sit to take photos and ask if a window can be opened. If you're with family or friends and are taking every seat, you could inquire about having the door of the plane or helicopter removed. It's not as radical as it sounds. Most companies work with photographers and will treat this as a standard request. When photographing from planes and helicopters:

- Set the shutter speed at 1/1000, or as high as possible.
- Don't rest any part of your body against the aircraft. Vibrations will cause camera shake.
- Don't hesitate – shoot quickly and often.
- Keep horizons straight. This requires constant adjustment.
- Use a polarising filter over water.
- Keep the camera within the cabin. Don't let it protrude through the window or open door as it's impossible to keep it still.
- Wear camera straps around your neck if the door is off (and keep your seatbelt on!).
- Start the flight with a fresh roll of 36-exposure film or enough space on the memory card to take 50 or 60 photos.
- Have spare film or memory cards handy and out of all packaging.

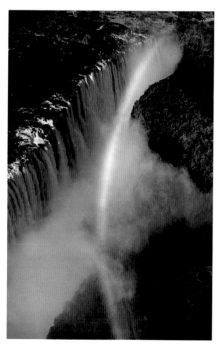

Victoria Falls, Zimbabwe

I booked the helicopter flight over the falls to coincide with the time of day when the sun was lighting up the narrow gorge and rainbows were appearing in the spray. It's hard to beat the unimpeded view from a helicopter with the door off. The main thing to watch for is to not photograph the blades when framing vertically or when the pilot is turning to your side.

◄ 35mm SLR, 35mm lens, 1/1000 f5.6, polarising filter, Ektachrome E100VS

HOT-AIR BALLOONS

Balloons are an ideal camera platform. They're steady and provide an unhindered view down to earth (if you lean out a bit) and out to the horizon. They can't be manipulated with the speed of a helicopter or plane but they provide a much more peaceful and relaxed environment for taking pictures. Shutter speeds of 1/125 and 1/250 are sufficient and once at cruising height there's time to consider compositions, change lenses and films…and enjoy the view.

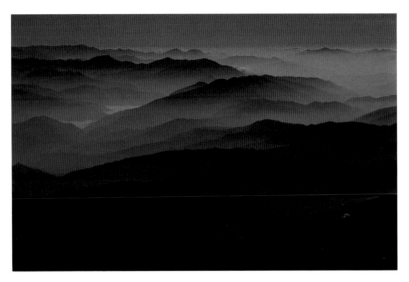

Kathmandu Valley, Nepal

It took a couple of hours of standing around in the cold, waiting for the fog to lift before our balloon could take off, but it was worth it. There is no other viewpoint in the Kathmandu Valley where you can see the layering of the middle hills like this.

▲ 35mm SLR, 100mm lens, 1/250 f4, Ektachrome E100SW

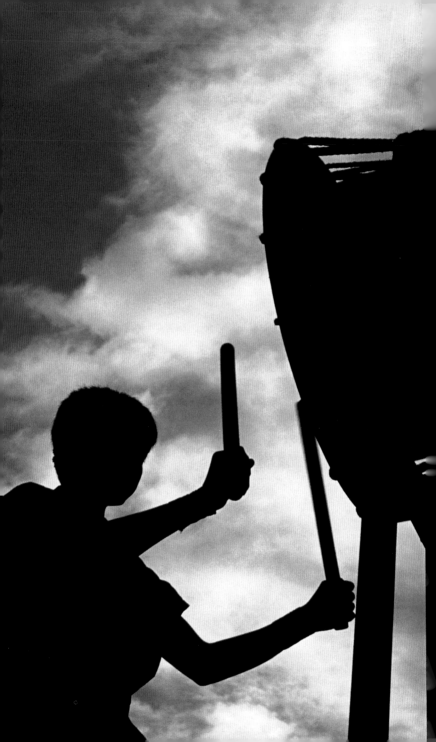

PART FIVE:

Arriving home and going through the photographs from a trip is pretty exciting. This part of the book covers how to make the most of all those travel photos once you arrive back home – from assessing, storing and displaying the photographs to maybe even making some money from them.

BACK AT HOME

Silhouetted drummer, Angkor Thom, Cambodia
◄ 35mm SLR, 35mm lens, 1/250 f11, Ektachrome E100VS

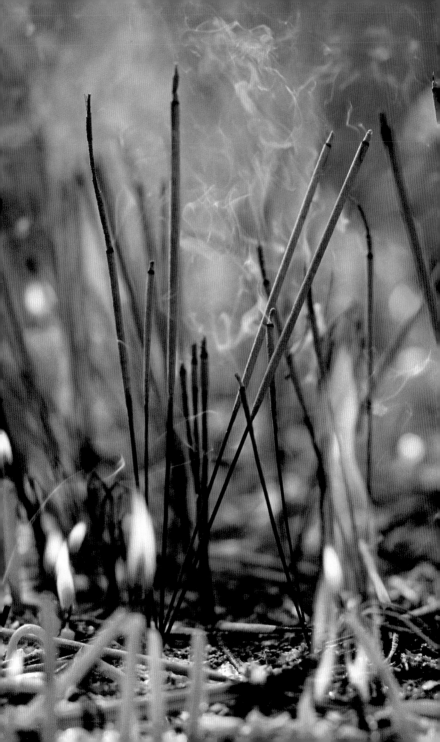

ASSESSING YOUR PHOTOGRAPHS

Once you've got your prints or slides back from the lab, or have transferred your digital images to a computer, sorting them out and getting them ready to show others can be achieved in a variety of ways. If you've taken prints you can show them without any further effort by handing out the packets from the minilab. If you've taken colour slides you have to prepare them for projection. If you've shot digitally you can make prints, show the pictures on a TV or computer monitor like a slide show or use software programs to make a sophisticated presentation. Given that you've gone to a lot of trouble to take the photos, why not go to a little extra trouble and present them well? The process of assessing and editing your photos is a great way to improve your photography. And while you're at it you may as well get really organised and store your negatives, prints, slides and digital images in a way that protects them and makes them easy to find. If you've done really well you might even start to contemplate the possibility of selling your images.

ASSESSING SLIDES

Assessing colour slides requires additional equipment, unless you want to hold them up to the sky or room lamp. You need a light source to shine through the slide and a magnifier to enlarge it. The cheapest and simplest option is a slide viewer. Slides are viewed one at a time by placing them into the unit between a small light globe and a magnifying lens. Apply slight pressure to the slide mount and the light comes on. The unit is handy because it enlarges the image slightly, but it makes comparing slides difficult and involves a lot of handling of the slides. You could also use a slide projector to view your slides, but that's time consuming and impractical if you have anything more than a few rolls.

The only way to assess slides properly is on a colour-corrected light box (or light table). The fluorescent tubes provided produce the same colour as daylight, so that the colours in your slides are faithful to the film. Slide viewing will be much more enjoyable and practical if your light box is large enough to see at least an entire slide-filing sheet of 24 mounted slides (see p246). If you're going to prepare slide shows you'll appreciate a light box that is large enough to lay out a hundred slides at once. Slides on a light box are viewed with a loupe, an optical accessory that magnifies the slide. Loupe prices range from US$15 to US$280. Buy the best you can afford. A good-quality loupe is an essential piece of equipment for anyone using slide film. Viewing slides with the naked eye, or a cheap loupe, is not practical or fun. If you don't use a loupe you will not only miss much of the detail and colour saturation in the slides, you'll mislead yourself as to their sharpness: slides nearly always look deceptively sharp when viewed with the naked eye.

**Burning incense at Songkran festival,
Bangkok, Thailand**
◀ 35mm SLR, 100mm lens, 1/125 f8,
Ektachrome E100VS

ASSESSING PRINTS

Colour prints are easy to assess because they're returned from the minilab in a print size that's easy to see. Many people choose to have their colour prints processed as they're travelling, but it isn't until you get home that you'll have the final set. If you do bring all your films home you may be able to negotiate a cheaper rate with a local minilab if you have more than 20 films.

Unfortunately, the standard of prints that minilabs produce varies wildly. If you get a set of prints that are really disappointing it's well worth explaining the problem to your photo-finisher and requesting a reprint. If they refuse or suggest that they've supplied the best prints possible, get a second opinion from another minilab.

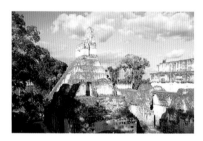 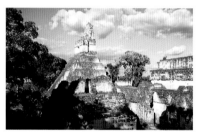

Temple of the Grand Jaguar, Tikal, Guatemala
Same print, different minilab. If you're unhappy with the prints you're given it's well worth asking for a reprint.
▲ 35mm compact, Ektapress 100

ASSESSING DIGITAL IMAGES

If you're shooting digital images seriously, investment in a good-quality, decent size (at least 48cm) monitor is money well spent, especially if you intend to use image-editing software to work creatively with your photographs. The monitor should be positioned so that stray light and reflections don't degrade the colour and brightness of the image. Delve into the equipment manuals to ensure that it's displaying the right number of colours, that the screen resolution setting is correct and that the monitor is accurately colour calibrated. Displaying an image so that it fills the screen of a large monitor will soon reveal how good it is, or if it has to be sent to the recycle bin.

EDITING PHOTOGRAPHS

It doesn't matter who you're showing your photos to (except perhaps people who were there), you should edit your photos tightly. Heavy sighs and excuses are not what you want to hear when you invite friends and family around to see your latest travel pictures. That's what you'll get if you bore everyone with several images of the same thing and a long-winded story about every photograph.

We all take bad pictures – the trick is not to show them to anyone. Edit the technically poor and creatively weak pictures out and you'll be left with a much stronger and more interesting set of photos. It takes a fair bit of discipline to discard pictures. Consider the place of each picture in the overall presentation and think of the whole rather than each picture.

The assessing and editing process is also an excellent time for reflection and self-teaching. Your best pictures and worst failures will stand out clearly. Study them to see what you did wrong and what you did right. Look for patterns. Are all you best pictures taken on a tripod? Are all the out-of-focus frames taken with the zoom at its maximum focal length? Next time you can eliminate the cause of your failures and concentrate on the things that worked. Your percentage of acceptable pictures will start to rise. Self-critique is an important and never-ending process in the life of a photographer.

CAPTIONING & FILING

Captioning pictures is hard work. If you've kept notes during your travels your life will be a lot easier. If you do nothing else, number and title the negative and slide sheets by destination and file them by country. Do the same if your digital images are on compact disks. You'll probably always remember which country a picture was taken in.

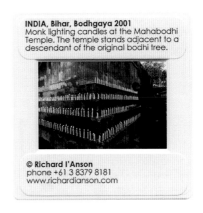

INDIA, Bihar, Bodhgaya 2001
Monk lighting candles at the Mahabodhi Temple. The temple stands adjacent to a descendant of the original bodhi tree.

© Richard I'Anson
phone +61 3 8379 8181
www.richardianson.com

Mounted 35mm slide showing appropriate captioning and photographer identification

STORING NEGATIVES, SLIDES, PRINTS & DIGITAL IMAGES

Prints, slides and negatives should be stored in a cool, dry, dark place for protection and easy access. Digital storage media such as CDs and DVDs should also be stored in a cool, dry place away from direct sunlight. The most popular way to store negatives, slides and prints is to leave them in the packets and boxes they're returned from the lab in…and then every year promise yourself you'll organise them. But there are better ways. Photographic materials fade over time, and that can be a very long time, if they're stored properly. The things to avoid are heat, humidity and storage materials such as vinyls and wood that can emit harmful chemicals that react with photographic materials. Use archival-quality products that are chemical and acid free.

Negatives

Negatives generally come back from photo-finishers in clear negative holders cut into strips of four, which satisfy most people. If you're taking lots of film and would like to get really organised you can buy negative filing sheets. (Archival sheets are made from polyethylene or polypropylene.) Generally, they take seven strips of six exposures and are made for ring binders and hanging in filing cabinets. They have room for writing relevant information at the top. Ask your lab not to cut the film so you can cut it yourself into strips of six exposures for most efficient use of the negative files.

Slides

Slides are generally stored in boxes or slide-filing sheets. Boxes are not recommended if you intend to access your slides regularly. They require excessive handling and don't allow easy viewing. The recommended option is to use archival slide-filing sheets that hold 20 or 24 mounted slides. These are then stored in ring binders or in filing cabinets. They allow easy viewing on a light box or can be held up to any light source. There's a wide range to choose from and some are better than others. Ensure that the slides fit snugly into the pockets so that they're easy to put in and remove but don't fall out if the sheet is held upside down. Also, make sure that they are truly clear. There are some on the market that make it almost impossible to see what the slide is of, let alone judge exposure and sharpness. If you're handling a lot of slides you'll also find the top-loading sheets are best for quick access.

Prints

Prints are traditionally stored in photo albums. The main album styles have self-adhesive pages, plain pages or slip-in pockets. Many of the self-adhesive pages are cheap, but over time the contact can wear off and the prints fall out. Even if they don't fall out they're probably in contact with harmful chemicals. Albums of plain paper allow you to write directly below the photographs but require you to supply adhesive or photo corners. Most of us don't expect to remove pictures once they're in an album, but, if you do, photo corners might suit you, although they're very fiddly. If you're sticking the pictures in, ask your photo retailer what they recommend rather than using normal glue. The slip-in, clear-pocket albums don't allow for various size pictures and you can't be creative with how you lay the pictures out. Captions are important, not just so that you can remember where you've been; also they allow the photos to be enjoyed by people who weren't there.

Before you quickly put every photo in the album why not pick out your favourites for enlarging? This will highlight your best photos and make sure they get the extra attention they deserve. You could also use enlargements to introduce each new country or theme. One big advantage of prints is that you can crop them. Cropping allows you to enlarge the main subject or eliminate unwanted elements around the edges of the print.

Digital Images

Most digital cameras come with basic software that lets you file images in folders or albums that can be named to indicate their contents. At the very least you should organise your digital images this way. It's the equivalent of writing the destination or country on a slide sheet. However, as your collection grows you'll notice it takes longer and longer to find the exact image you're looking for. Dedicated cataloguing software programs allow you to caption and keyword images that can then be quickly located through a search function.

Unless you keep buying computer hard-disk space to keep up with your growing collection you'll also need to transfer the high-resolution files from your computer to other storage media such as CDs or DVDs (see p81). Label the media promptly for easy retrieval. Transferring images from the computer is also advisable for security reasons (see p83).

WALL PRINTS

Framing your favourite prints for wall display is very satisfying. If you've used colour negative film or shot digitally most minilabs can print or organise enlargements up to poster size (50cm x 76cm; 20in x 30in). If you've used colour slide film, or want the best possible print from a negative or digital file, seek out a professional lab to handle the enlargements. A good lab will advise which slides, negatives and files will and won't print well, rather than just taking your order. If you decide to frame your print behind glass, use plain glass, not non-reflective glass. Non-reflective glass takes the edge off the sharpness and dulls the colours. Careful positioning of the print on the wall helps minimise reflections…as does a little step to the left or right by the viewer.

Prints should not be placed in direct contact with the glass. Traditionally, a border called a window mount goes around the print and separates the print from the glass. If that look doesn't suit you, a good picture framer will advise on the options. You'll also have choice of mount board and mounting adhesives. Ask for the archival products. Place the framed print in an area that doesn't receive direct sunlight.

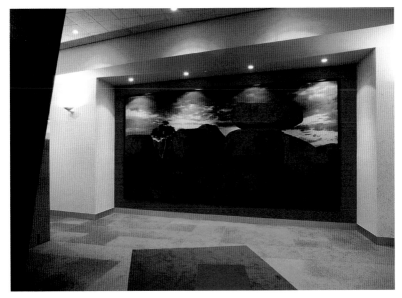

Devil's Marbles, Australia
Get everything right when you take the photo and you'll be able to fill whole walls with your images. This photograph makes a dramatic focal point in an office reception. The print is a large 315cm x 183cm (124in x 72in) and was captured on 6 x 7cm transparency film.

SLIDE SHOWS

The only way to show any quantity of slides to others is to project them. Original slides shouldn't be projected; instead, have a set of duplicate slides made. The intense light from projection globes will fade slides over time. There's also the possibility of damage from a projector malfunction. Slides should be glass mounted as this stops them popping out of focus, which is a very annoying feature of many presentations.

Slide shows are a great way to present a lot of photos in a short time and the images themselves will never look better. But it's easy to turn a set of great pictures into a dry slide show instead of the entertaining and informative experience it should be. You have a captive audience and it's your duty not to bore them. Below are a few suggestions that will have your family and friends calling out for more.

▸ Always view the show yourself first to ensure the slides are the right way up and there are no large dust spots or hairs.
▸ Don't leave slides on the screen for more than six seconds, and four seconds is fine. At four seconds each you can show 225 slides in 15 minutes.
▸ Don't show similar pictures of the same subject. Just select the best one.
▸ Edit hard and only show your best images.
▸ Grouping destinations or themes reduces the commentary because you can introduce a sequence of slides with the first image.
▸ Have some order to the slides. The chronological order of the trip is most logical. If you're coming and going from a home base or a country more than once, group the slides into countries rather than jumping back and forth.
▸ Keep the length of the show to around fifteen minutes.
▸ Play appropriate music to cover the sound of the projector, to set the atmosphere and to help prevent you feeling the need to talk about every slide. Let some of the slides speak for themselves.
▸ Project slides in the darkest room possible. Too much stray light will reduce the impact of your images.
▸ Show the slides earlier in the evening rather than later. After dinner and a couple of drinks it's easy for people to fall asleep in a dark room with music playing.

STOCK PHOTOGRAPHY

If you feel your photographs are good enough and might be of interest to others, you may want to investigate ways of selling your work. You can contact potential users directly to find out what their needs are and how they go about buying pictures. Before you do that, study their products carefully to see the kind of pictures they use; this will let you concentrate on contacting relevant publications. Most magazines have a submission-guideline document available on request or on their website. Careful study of these will save you a lot of time.

The largest market for travel photographs is book and magazine publishers who buy stock photographs. 'Stock' refers to images that are shot speculatively at the photographer's expense and then placed in an image library ready to meet the needs of picture buyers who require existing images, instead of commissioning new ones. There are specialist libraries that hold extensive collections of one subject, such as wildlife or sport, but the majority of stock libraries cover all subjects, including travel. Libraries represent the work of many photographers with the aim of always having an appropriate image on file to meet their clients' requests.

Travel stock is very competitive. To even get pictures into a library can be tough and the terms and conditions may not suit you. Libraries are businesses and they're there to represent the work of photographers, many of whom rely on stock sales for their living. Your pictures will not only be judged on their own merits, but against the images that are already in the library. Then, when they go before a customer, they'll have to compete against the best pictures from other libraries for the buyer's attention. The more common subjects and the most popular destinations face the greatest competition. You only get paid for a stock image when it's used.

Once you're represented by a library, you'll be expected to make regular submissions. The way to make money from stock is to be continually adding to your own collection and to have as wide a coverage as possible. The more pictures and the wider their coverage, the more times they'll go in front of picture buyers. The key is variety. If you can provide a range of views of a particular subject under different lighting conditions you greatly increase your chances of filling the requirements of a picture buyer.

Professional stock photographers plan their travels carefully and shoot stock in a very organised way. While researching a destination a shot list is developed of subjects that need to be covered, based on what's already in the library, requests already received from the library, and on anticipated requests.

If you want to sell pictures you've got to take the kinds of pictures that people are going to want to buy. You can start educating yourself by checking the picture credits in books and magazines. Often the photographer and library are both named. After a while you'll start to know the kind of pictures that sell and the sort of publications that buy them.

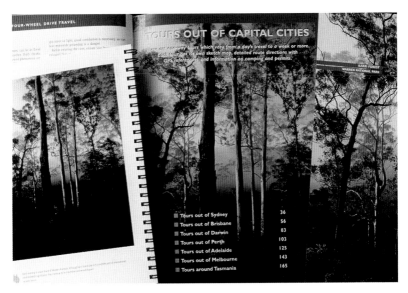

Tall trees, Warren National Park, Australia
Good stock images sell again and again. This shot has been licensed many times and is shown here appearing in a diary, airline holiday brochure and a road atlas.

Submitting to Stock Libraries

Stock libraries all have their own requirements and guidelines on how they prefer to receive submissions. Generally, to establish whether or not your images are of suitable quality and content, a library will want to see an initial submission of around 200 images, either original colour slides or digital files presented on CD. When preparing your submission remember that the people assessing your work will not have the same emotional attachment to the pictures you have. In my role at Lonely Planet Images I've looked at over 300,000 slides in the last six years from all over the world. I suggest the following to ensure that you make the best impression with your first submission.

▸ If the library you're interested in has a website, study it carefully with particular attention to the coverage of the places and subjects you intend to submit.
▸ Read the submission guidelines and follow them exactly.
▸ Edit your submission tightly. Don't send in technically poor images. Out of focus, over- or underexposed pictures will detract from your overall submission.
▸ Caption your slides with typed labels. Put the image caption on the top half of the slide mount and your details on the bottom half. Typed captions look professional and are easy to read.
▸ Use slide sheets that are clean and clear, and make sure the slides can be easily removed and replaced.
▸ Don't use tape to secure slides in the sheets.
▸ Make sure all slides are up the right way.

RELEASE FORMS

If you intend to make commercial use (submit to an image library, or otherwise license or sell) of photographs of people, private property, artworks or trademarks, you need to know about releases. Model and property releases are used by photographers to obtain permission from a person or rights holder to use their image or property in a photograph. Getting written permission makes it difficult for a person to later claim that the use of the photograph has breached their rights.

Practically it's difficult and time consuming to ask everyone you photograph to sign a form (and that's if you speak their language). Generally, editorial uses, such as books, magazines and newspapers, don't require releases, unless the use of the image might be defamatory. But in the advertising world, which pays the highest fees for licensing stock images, images will usually not be accepted without signed releases.

These sample releases can be copied onto your own letterhead and adapted for your use. As every situation is different you may want to get some more information and advice about what you need for your particular subject and use. For example, if you're going to use images for non-editorial purposes, bear in mind you may need to provide some compensation (even nominal) for the release to be enforceable.

MODEL RELEASE

By signing this document:

I irrevocably consent to the Photographer (and its licensees and assigns) incorporating my image or likeness in photographs or illustrations in any form or media (images) and reproducing, publishing and communicating the Images in any form and media for any purpose, whether commercial or otherwise (including advertising), and to the use of my name and any other text or works in connection with the Images. I waive any right to inspect or approve the Images or any publication incorporating the Images and any right to compensation for the use of the Images by the Photographer, its licensees and assigns. I release the Photographer, its licensees and assigns from any or all claims, actions, proceedings, demands and expenses and other liability that may arise in connection with the use of the Images by any person. 4. I confirm that I am either over 18 years of age or that my parent or guardian has also agreed to these terms by signing in the space provided below.

I understand and agree to the above.

Signed: _____ Signed by parent/guardian: _____

Print Name: _____ Print name: _____

Address/email/phone number: _____

Date: _____

Description of image: _____

_____

PROPERTY RELEASE

By signing this document:

I irrevocably consent to the Photographer (and its licensees and assigns) incorporating an image or likeness of the property described below in photographs or illustrations in any form or media (images) and reproducing, publishing and communicating the Images in any form and media for any purpose, whether commercial or otherwise (including advertising). I waive any right to inspect or approve the Images or any publication incorporating the Images and any right to compensation for the use of the Images by the Photographer, its licensees and assigns. I release the Photographer, its licensees and assigns from any or all claims, actions, proceedings, demands and expenses and other liability that may arise in connection with the use of the Images by any person.

I warrant that I am the owner of the property and/or am fully authorised to enter this property release.

Signed: _____ Print Name: _____

Address/email/phone number: _____

Date: _____

Property description: _____

Property address: _____

_____

Description of image: _____

_____

GLOSSARY OF PHOTOGRAPHIC TERMS

A

angle of view – image area that the lens cover measured in degrees and determined by the focal length; the shorter the focal length, the greater the coverage

aperture – hole in the lens that allows light into the camera body; variable in size and expressed in f-numbers

auto-exposure lock – control that locks and holds exposure on the subject while recomposing (also known as AE Lock)

auto-focus – system that allows focus to be set automatically (also known as AF)

auto-focus lock – control that locks and holds focus on the subject while recomposing (also known as AF Lock)

B

bounce flash – technique of reflecting the flashgun light from a ceiling, wall or other reflective surfaces to diffuse and soften the light

bracketing – technique used to ensure that the best possible exposure is achieved by adjusting the exposure for each frame; particularly useful when using slide films

C

C-41 – common term for the chemistry used to process colour negative films

cable release – an accessory that allows the shutter to be released without the photographer touching the camera, thereby preventing camera shake

camera dock – digital camera accessory for transferring images to a computer and recharging battery (also known as a cradle or power base)

card reader – device that accepts memory card(s) for transferring images to a computer via a USB port

card slot – opening in a digital camera to insert memory card

centre-weighted metering – reads the light reflected from the entire scene and provides an average exposure reading biased towards the centre section of the viewfinder

charge coupled device (CCD) – common light-sensitive sensor used in digital cameras that converts light into data

colour space – spectrum of colours available from which a digital image can be created

compact disk (CD) – common storage medium that can hold up to 650 MB of data; disks can be read-only memory (CR-ROM), recordable (CD-R) or rewritable (CD-RW)

complementary metal oxide semiconductor (CMOS) – common light-sensitive sensor used in digital cameras that converts light into data

compression – mathematical process for reducing digital image file size by discarding some of the data

contrast – the difference between the lightest and darkest parts of a scene

conversion lenses – accessories that clip or screw onto the front of the prime lens of a compact digital camera to alter the angle of view (also called auxiliary lenses)

D

dedicated flash – flashgun that connects to the camera's metering system and controls the power of the flash to produce a correct exposure

depth of field – the area of a photograph that is considered acceptably sharp

depth-of-field preview – control that allows the aperture to be stopped down manually and provides a visual check of the depth of field at any given aperture

digital versatile disk (DVD) – common storage medium that can hold up to 17 GB of data

digital zoom – digital camera feature that uses the camera's computer and software to enlarge a portion of the image by creating and adding pixels through interpolation software to give the appearance of varying the lens's focal length

diopter correction lens – optical accessory mounted on camera viewfinder to enable photographers who wear glasses to compose and focus without glasses

DX coding – system that automatically sets the ISO by reading the film speed from a barcode printed on the cassette

E

E-6 – common term for the chemistry used to process slide film (except Kodachrome)

effective pixels – the pixels on a sensor that are used to create an image

electronic viewfinder – advanced compact digital camera feature that displays what the lens sees

emulsion – light-sensitive material

EXIF (Exchangeable Image Format) – file format that embeds image-capture information within a file

exposure compensation dial – allows over or underexposure of the film by a third, or half stops up to two or three stops, when using automatic exposure modes

F

fast film – very light sensitive film

fast lens – lens with a very wide maximum aperture

file format – allows digital images to be stored so they can be retrieved and processed using photo-editing software

fill-flash – technique used to add light to shadow areas containing important detail

filter – optical accessory that is attached to the front of the lens, altering the light reaching the film; used for a wide range of technical and creative applications

firewire (IEEE 1394) – connector or port designed for high-speed data transfer between peripherals such as digital cameras

flare – stray light that degrades picture quality by reducing contrast and recording as patches of light on the film

focal length – the distance from the centre of the lens when it is focussed at infinity to the focal plane

focal length conversion factor – the number the focal length of a lens is multiplied by to determine new focal length when used with a digital camera; the conversion factor is determined by the sensor's size relative to a 35mm film frame

focal plane – the flat surface on which a sharp image of the subject is formed; film is stretched across the focal plane

f-stop – numbers that indicate the size of the lens aperture

full frame sensor – digital camera sensor equal in size to a 35mm film frame (24mm x 36mm)

G

gigabyte (GB) – 1024 megabytes (MB) of digital data

grain – silver halide crystals of a film emulsion visible in a photographic image; the faster the film, the coarser the grain

guide number (GN) – indicates the power output of a flash unit with 100 ISO film

H

highlight – the brightest area of the subject

histogram – graphic representation of the distribution of pixels in a digital image

hot-shoe – place on camera body for mounting an accessory flash unit

I

image-editing software – computer application for enhancing and manipulating images

incandescent lighting – artificial light source

interpolation – creation of new pixels to fill in data gaps between existing pixels, typically used when images are enlarged

ISO – abbreviation for International Standards Organisation, which sets the standards for film-speed rating

ISO equivalent – the sensitivity of digital camera sensors to light, based on the sensitivity of film to light

ISO rating – the sensitivity of the film to light; the higher the ISO, the more light sensitive the film

J

JPEG (Joint Photographic Experts Group) – industry-standard file format and compression routine that uses lossy process

L

liquid crystal display (LCD) – screen built into digital camera body for image review and access to control menus and camera settings; can be used as an alternative to the viewfinder to compose images

lossless compression – compression process that results in smaller digital file size without compromising image quality

lossy compression – compression process used to reduce image files to varying degrees, discarding more and more data as compression is increased

M

macro lens – lens designed to give a life-size image of a subject

megabyte (MB) – 1024 kilobytes (KB) of digital data

megapixel (MP) – one million pixels

memory card – removable and reusable storage medium used by digital cameras

memory-card format – type of memory card accepted by digital cameras

metadata – information about the image, attached to a digital file

multi-zone metering – measures the light from several areas of the scene and gives a reading based on what it evaluates as the most important parts of the scene (also called matrix, evaluative, multi-segment, multi-pattern and honeycomb-pattern metering)

N

noise – error or stuck pixels in digital image file generated during the conversion of data to pixels

O

optical zoom – lens with variable focal lengths; zoom effect is achieved by physically moving the lens in and out of the camera body

P

perspective control – allows control of the angle of the plane of focus through tilt and shift movements on special lenses to prevent distortion of perspective

photodiode – light-sensitive cell on surface of sensor that converts light into numerical data

Photoshop – professional image-editing software product by Adobe

PictBridge – industry-standard technology that allows devices made by different manufacturers to be connected

pixel – abbreviation for picture (pix) elements (el); the smallest bits of information that combine to form a digital image

pixel count – total number of pixels on a sensor; calculated by multiplying the number of pixels on the vertical and horizontal axes

predictive auto-focus – sophisticated focussing system that continuously tracks a moving subject (also known as tracking focus)

programmed exposure – fully automatic exposure setting in which the camera's metering system sets both aperture and shutter speed

push processing – increased development time to compensate for underexposure when film is pushed

pushing film – intentional underexposure of colour slide or B&W film by exposing it at a higher ISO setting than its actual film speed

R

random access memory (RAM) – computer memory that holds data while it is being worked with

rangefinder – focussing system that measures the distance from camera to subject by viewing it from two positions

RAW – file format not processed by the camera's software

resolution – degree to which digitally captured information displays detail, sharpness and colour accuracy

S

sensor – semiconductor chip made up of light-sensitive cells called photodiodes that convert light into numerical data so that it can be processed, stored and retrieved using computer language

short lens – wide-angle lens

shutter – mechanism built into the lens or camera that controls the time that light is allowed to reach the film

shutter speed – the amount of time that the camera's shutter remains open to allow light onto the film

SLR (Single Lens Reflex) – a camera design that allows lenses to be interchanged and

for the user to view subjects through the lens being used to take the picture

spot-metering – light meter reading from a very small area of the total scene

sync speed – fastest shutter speed that can be used to synchronise the firing of the flash with the time the shutter is open

T

teleconverter – optical accessory that fits between the camera body and the lens to increase the focal length of the lens

telephoto lens – lens with a focal length longer than a standard 50mm lens

TIFF (Tagged Image File Format) – industry-standard file format commonly used for storing images intended for print publishing

TTL – abbreviation for Through the Lens metering; light-sensitive cells in the camera body measure light passing through the lens

tungsten lighting – artificial light source

U

USB (universal serial bus) – connector or port for connecting a computer to peripheral devices such as digital cameras, camera docks or card readers

V

viewfinder – camera's optical system used to view a subject

W

white balance – digital camera function that adjusts colour to ensure that white is recorded as white under all light conditions

wide-angle lens – lens with a focal length shorter than a standard 50mm lens

Z

zoom lens – lens with variable focal lengths

FURTHER READING

Andrews, Philip. *The Digital Photography Manual*. 2nd ed. Carlton Books, 2002.

Brown, Margaret. *Digital Camera Pocket Guide*. Media Publishing, 2003.

Brown, Margaret. *Digital Photo Beginners' Guide*. Media Publishing, 2003.

Burian, Peter K, and Robert Caputo. *National Geographic Photography Field Guide: Secrets to Making Great Pictures*. 2nd ed. National Geographic, 2003.

Busselle, Michael. *Better Picture Guide to Travel Photography*. Rotovision, 1998.

Busselle, Michael. *Guide to Travel & Vacation Photography*. Rotovision, 2003.

Calder, Julian, and John Garrett. *The New 35mm Photographer's Handbook: Everything You Need to Get the Most Out of Your Camera*. 3rd ed. Crown, 1999.

Cope, Peter. *The Digital Photographer's Pocket Encyclopedia*. Silver Pixel Press, 2002.

Daly, Tim. *Encyclopedia of Digital Photography: The Complete Guide to Digital Imaging and Artistry*. New Burlington Books, 2003.

Evening, Martin. *Adobe Photoshop 7.0 for Photographers*. Focal Press, 2002.

Galer, Mark, and Les Horvat. *Essential Skills: Digital Imaging*. 2nd ed. Focal Press, 2002.

Hedgecoe, John. *The Photographer's Handbook*. 3rd ed. Knopf, 1992.

Heeb, Christian and Detley Motz. *Travel Photography*. David & Charles, 2003.

Hicks, Roger, and Frances Schultz. *Travel Photography: How to Research, Produce and Sell Great Travel Pictures*. Focal Press, 1998.

Joinson, Simon. *Travel: The Digital Photographer's Handbook*. Rotovision, 2003.

Krist, Bob. *Spirit of Place: The Art of the Traveling Photographer*. Amphoto Books, 2000.

Langford, Michael. *35mm Handbook*. Knopf, 1993.

McCartney, Susan. *Travel Photography: A Complete Guide to How to Shoot and Sell*. 2nd Ed. Allworth Press, 1999.

McDonald, Joe. *The New Complete Guide to Wildlife Photography*. Watson-Guptill, 1998.

Millman, Anne, and Allen Rokach. *Focus on Travel: Creating Memorable Photographs of Journeys to New Places*. Abbeville Press, 1993.

Norton, Boyd. *The Art of Outdoor Photography: Techniques for the Advanced Amateur and Professional*. 2nd ed. Voyageur Press, 2002.

Peterson, B Moose. *Guide to Wildlife Photography: Conventional and Digital Techniques*. 2nd ed. Lark Books, 2003.

Rowell, Galen. *Mountain Light*. 10th ed. Sierra Club Books, 1995.

Waite, Charlie. *The Making of Landscape Photographs*. Collins & Brown, 1992.

Wignall, Jeff. *Kodak Guide to Shooting Great Travel Pictures: The Most Authoritative Guide to Travel Photography for Vacationers*. 2nd ed. Fodor's, 2000.

USEFUL WEBSITES

EQUIPMENT, FILM & SOFTWARE

Adobe Software Products	www.adobe.com
Agfa	www.agfanet.com/en
Canon	www.canon.com
Data Rescue Software	www.datarescue.com
Kodak	www.kodak.com
Epson	www.epson.com
Fuji	www.fujifilm.com
Hewlet Packard	www.hp.com
Minolta & Konica	www.konicaminolta.com
Nikon	www.nikon.com
Olympus	www.olympus.com
Pentax	www.pentax.com
Sigma	www.sigmaphoto.com
Sony	www.sony.com

PHOTOGRAPHY: REVIEWS & RESOURCES

eBook	www.123di.com
Digital Image Submission Criteria	www.disc-info.org
Digital Photography	www.betterdigitalonline.com
	www.camerastore.com.au
	www.dcviews.com
	www.dpreview.com
	www.imaging-resource.com
	www.steves-digicams.com
Photography and Travel Magazines	www.photosecrets.com
	www.betterphotography.com
	www.megapixel.net
	www.nationalgeographic.com
	www.outdoorphotographer.com
	www.photoreview.com.au
	www.photo.net
	www.shutterbug.net
Photo Sharing	www.fotki.com
Photo Travel Guides	www.phototravel.com
Photography Courses	www.shortcourses.com

TRAVEL

Health	www.tripprep.com
Internet Café Guide	www.cybercaptive.com
Lonely Planet	www.lonelyplanet.com
Weather	www.accuweather.com

INDEX

bold refers to image captions

35mm cameras   19, **21**
   compact   22-3
   rangefinders   23
   SLR   23

A

aerial photography   237-9
animals, *see* wildlife, photographing
aperture   89, 94, 95
APS cameras   19, **21**
autowinders   34

B

B&W prints   44
bags   39, 52
batteries
   cold weather   136
   for digital cameras   71
   for film cameras   40
birds, photographing   234
blur   223
bracketing   97
burst mode   70
buying
   digital cameras   75-9
   film cameras   36-7
   memory cards   66

C

cable releases   40
camera
   autowinders   34
   bags   39, 52
   batteries   40, 71
   care   40, 126, 133-8
   exposure meters   34, 89-90
   filters   28-31, 174, 176

flash units   34-5
formats   19-21
lenses   24-7, 106-7
tripods   32-3
cameras
   35mm   19, **21**
   APS   19, **21**
   buying   36, 75-9
   compact   22-3, 98-9
   digital   55-85
   film cameras   19-21
   panoramic   19, **21**
   rangefinders   23
   SLR   23
camera shake   96, *see also* cable re-
      leases, image stabilisation
captions   245
care   40, 126, 133-8
carrying equipment   39, 52
cityscapes, photographing   183-96
cleaning   126
   cleaning kit   40
   salt water   136
   sand   138
compact cameras   22-3, 98-9
composition   101-7
   framing   102
   portraits   143, 146-9
   rule of thirds   101
contrast   72-4

D

depth of field   95, 107
digital cameras   55-85
   batteries   71
   buying   75-9
   compact   76-8
   DSLR   78-9
   lenses   80-1
digital capture
   burst mode   70
   computers   57, 82-3